Studies in Comparative Politics

ANARCHISM TODAY

ANARCHISM TODAY

edited by

DAVID E. APTER

Professor of Political Science
Yale University

and

JAMES JOLL

Stevenson Professor of International History
London School of Economics and Political Science

MACMILLAN

Published 1971 by
THE MACMILLAN PRESS LTD
London and Basingstoke
Associated companies in New York Toronto
Dublin Melbourne Johannesburg and Madras

SBN 333 12039 6 (hard cover)

Printed in Great Britain by
RICHARD CLAY (THE CHAUCER PRESS), LTD
Bungay, Suffolk

Contents

David E. Apter

The Old Anarchism and the New – Some Comments

ANARCHISM AS A DOCTRINE HAS A PECULIAR FASCINATION FOR scholars. It both repels and attracts. It attracts because it embodies rage – the particular rage people have when they see man as an obstacle to his own humaneness. It is the ultimate statement of how outrageous the human condition can be. But it is precisely because man does not live by rage alone, but must master it by discovering proximate means to solving the ordinary problems of daily life, that anarchism repels. It seem a romantic luxury at best – a cry of pain for the future, just as nostalgia is for the past and, like nostalgia, this cannot fail to be attractive.

Perhaps because of this anarchism is not a mere reflection of anger but also a contributing source. It is thus more than a lightning rod for the anger that exists. Anarchism is associated with unreason and bombs, violence and irresponsibility. The ancestral cry of the anarchist in the 19th century is that 'the only good bourgeois is a dead one'. On this score the doctrine remains unregenerate. But its attack is not limited to capitalism. The anarchist rejection of socialism and Marx because of their centralist contradictions is equally complete. Hence anarchism assigns itself a position of extreme vulnerability. Moreover none of the major social doctrines can absorb anarchism because, where it is most fundamental, it is anti-political – that is, it does not really offer political solutions. Although the language of today's anarchism is more psychologically sophisticated it remains a primitive doctrine which wants to convert a structural condition of hate into a sentiment of love, and by the same token transform rage into peace.

Some theorists of anarchism such as Kropotkin stressed the need for rationality and theory. Others perhaps more persuasive because of their own personal vitalism urged the importance of violence, as did Bakunin. The virtue of anarchism as a doctrine is that it employs

1

a socialist critique of capitalism and a liberal critique of socialism. Because of this its doctrines remain important even when they lead it in the direction of terrorism and agitation, much of it of the hit-and-run variety. This critique is one cause for its revival which comes as a surprise because anarchism had appeared to have run its course in the early part of the 20th century. It was quaint, its leaders slightly comical, and relegated to a shelf of antique doctrine which included Annie Besant and the Theosophist movement and the burned out engineers of Technocracy, Inc.

Clearly, anarchism has turned out to be like other antiques, capable of renewed significance in the social and aesthetic lives of many people. It has darkened with time. Some of its power is black. The black flag belongs now to black people as well as others. (In this respect anarchism is reaching out to people other than the bourgeois radicals who were its most ardent followers in the past.) In India the effects of Ruskin's doctrines on Gandhi and in Japan the more direct acquaintance with the writings of early anarchists also helped to give anarchism a more international flavour, and a universality lacking in its earlier period when confined to Western Europe, Russia and the USA. Anarchism today is a form of liberalism which rejects capitalism; as a doctrine of individualism divorced from the classic western form it has relevance despite the flamboyance and gesticulations of some of its practitioners. The latter should not dissuade us from recognizing that the ground covered by anarchism is as a normative antithesis to contemporary capitalism and socialism. Anarchism in this normative sense can be separated from its organizational characteristics and seen to stand on its own. Indeed, in the nature of the case organization could never be a strong point of anarchists. As a moral phenomenon, no matter how much it waxes and wanes it has constant roots in the fundamentally offending character of organization *qua* organization.

In this commentary, and it can be no more than that, I will consider four main aspects of anarchism as a normative force. First, compared with socialism or liberalism it can be seen as a discontinuous phenomenon. There has been no consistent accumulation of ideas and theories. This discontinuous quality of anarchism, however, is as we have suggested, likely to be confusing. Anarchism may appear to be dead when it is dormant and exceptionally fresh when it springs to life. Secondly, as a doctrine it differs from others insofar as it is concerned with meaning more as rejection but projects no specific structural solution. Moreover, because anarchism leaves meaning 'open' its receptivity to violence or to use the contemporary language, of each man 'doing his thing', makes happenings into a substitute solution for programmes. This aspect is particularly important with respect to contemporary youth subcultures where the ambiguity of meaning is greatest to start out with. As part of a subculture which has become both more structurally important and powerful as time has gone on, anarchism has recently been able to enlarge its significance without any increase in organizational power as such. It is a piggy-back normative doctrine able to join on, as it were, to quite diverse groups. Indeed such normative power is almost inverse in significance to its degree of organization. But it is by joining particular subcultures, with all the special conditions these encounter, that contemporary anarchism takes on a peculiarly psychological dimension which in the past it lacked.

Before going on to a discussion of these points, let us try to review some of the main characteristics of anarchism as a doctrine both in its older and newer forms. We seek that common core of belief which forms the substance of its own debate.

RATIONALITY AND CREATIVITY

The primitive core of anarchism is not so very different from Christianity. That is, it rests on the notion that man has a need, not just a preference, to love. Love in its generic sense is the central principle from which two other needs derive. One is rationality. The other is emotionality. Religious and political doctrines tend to come down on one side or the other of these and make one serve the other. Emotionality may use rationality but it restricts its appropriateness. Rationality may recognize the importance of emotionality but it tries to channel it into approved directions, destroying its spontaneousness.

For anarchists the appropriate balance between the two is creativity. Creativity emerges both from rational and emotional processes. The language used must reflect the blend. The pure doctrine may be said to originate in love which in turn is expressed in emotionality and rationality which in turn must be integrated in creativity. Since emotionality derives from action and rationality from reflection, maximizing creativity is a balance of action and reflection which in turn enlarges man's capacity for love.

If contemporary anarchists are less rational they are also more psychological. They combine the radical critique of society by Marx with the insights of Freud. What the early anarchists particularly objected to was Darwinism, preferring mutual aid to mutual struggle.[1] Today's attack on capitalism is not only because of the injustices of capitalism but also includes a strong desire to create a new symbolic aesthetic designed to break through the many layers of human consciousness which organized life restricts and stunts. While it is true that all radicalism tried to deal with these matters, it is particularly the contemporary form of anarchism which gives a high priority to the psychosexual and symbolic aspects. Hence the significance of the work of Erich Fromm, Wilhelm Reich, Herbert Marcuse, Paul Goodman, R. D. Laing and others who have had a sudden (and in many cases belated) prosperity among more radical students in particular.

THE ROLE OF THEORY IN ANARCHISM

Having tried to suggest some differences between the new emphases in anarchism and the old we can now suggest some differences between ideologies and social movements which have had a continuous organized existence for a long time and those which have not. In the first instance we encounter the problems of orthodoxy and of the hardening of the doctrinal arteries. To some extent it becomes a matter of retranslation and language whether or not change is to be welcomed or fought. Debate centres about how much doctrine should each inheriting group absorb and in turn pass on as values or norms. How much that is embedded in the old structural forms of party and organization should be reaffirmed in orthodoxy lest the pristine quality or originating ideology of the movement be destroyed? These concerns are irrelevant with ideologies which come and go like rashes or epidemics. Orthodoxy is not at issue. As a result the ideology when it has subsided becomes difficult to recapture. The singular quality of origin which gave it significance is lost. But such doctrines, when they do appear, capture the quintessence of relevance. They define the hypocrisies of society. Their proponents lance the swollen, more fatuous phrases on which all orthodoxies depend. It is precisely the lack of continuity of movements like anarchism which given them exceptional moral

[1] See P. Kropotkin, *Memoirs of a Revolutionist*, New York, Doubleday, Anchor Books, 1962, p. 299.

4

power. They are released from the burdens of past error. Orthodoxy is not at issue with anarchism but substance, the substantiality of the doctrine. As a matter of sheer continuity the new anarchism can have little in common with the old except in language.

This leads to another point. Anarchism stresses the role of theory far less than socialism for example. It is also less intellectual. The central and institutionalized values of socialist doctrine are theoretically complex and ideologically elaborate. Within the ideology of anarchism there is sufficient attraction to old concepts so that it is possible to discover a fresh interpretation. Not requiring a rejection of the revolutionary past this allows a look towards a radically different future. And that itself is a source of creativity. This is quite different from conflicts between various forms of Marxism which are more a function of theory *qua* theory.

What do we mean then when we say that anarchism has come back, but in a new form? For one thing those who raise the black flag are probably less serious than in the past and much less so than socialists requiring theory and organization. For the latter, party must be everything or there will be nothing. The memory of Marx's attitude towards the classic figures like Bakunin and Kropotkin is perhaps in point. But the latter were concerned with total change. In contrast there has been no call today for an organized anarchistic movement such as a revival of the first international for example. Contemporary radicals read anarchism along with Tarot cards. Thus if it has a resonance of its own it is also difficult to take too seriously. It is instead redolent of experiments in the simple life.

With such emphases anarchism can never have a permanent reputation. Whatever its prosperity at any moment, its origin lies in some important and continuing inadequacy of existing systems, *qua* system and extends as well to the standardized solutions. We say system because it is not the event that causes anarchism but an interpretation of it which says that present arrangements are responsible and not chance or some temporary considerations. The ingredients which make up the system whether real or concrete, whether theory or practice, *need* to produce the inadequacy. This is as true of a system of theory as of a system in practice. Both are irredeemable because their important conditions depend on organizational means.

For this reason, even when a system is generally perceived as bad, anarchism is bound to appeal to a minority. For one thing people are afraid of changes which they cannot predict, which is the reason why theory remains so important for radicals other than anarchists! Theories are a part of revolution. They are a means. By reducing the ambiguity of change the translated and convenient ideological expressions make projective sense about change and point in a desired direction. Anarchist 'theories' do this only slightly at best and in a relatively utopian manner. That is to say few offer detailed empirical analysis. What a contrast between say Bakunin and Marx for whom radicalism was less a matter of disgruntlement than prediction.

If anarchism is not very concerned with theory *per se*, anarchists commonly assume that human affairs constitute a naturalistic order which *needs* to be rendered 'uncontrived'. Spontaneity and even a certain randomness can be seen to go together. Theory in the view of anarchists should not be an intellectual contrivance because this will reduce freedom and clutter the will with tempering injunctions. The contrast is complete. For Lenin or Mao, theory is all important. It represents the basis for a new system, i.e. a different structural order based on particular norms, which endows behaviour with an element of puritanism. Theory for them is important because it enables doctrine and action to go hand in hand.

How can one explain this continuous preference by anarchists for spontaneous association? Behind the appearance of anti-intellectualism there lies a presumptive belief in an ultimate rationality as the common and unifying property of all men if unfettered by an inappropriate system, a rationality which, moreover, will temper relationships of people whose lives are based upon intimate and localized associations.

Such views are, of course, not too different from traditions of evangelical radicalism based on personal vision, the denunciation of injustice and the regeneration of self as a continued approach to social betterment. To convert the group it is necessary to begin with the self. With such views it is not surprising that anarchists tended to be strong and independent characters.

Anarchism contrasts most sharply with socialism in the particular substance of ideas and attitudes about organization. The fear of a political infrastructure asserts above all the primacy of the individual. But if it emphasizes the tyranny of the collectivity, it lacks a clear picture of what kind of social community is necessary to replace what we have. Anarchists may be closest to socialists in their common critique of capitalist society, but they are diametrically opposed in the matter of solutions.

HAPPENINGS NOT PROGRAMMES

We said that anarchism lacks doctrinal continuity. It has no younger generation which arises explicitly out of the older one, as does Marxism, or liberalism. In what sense does it have a new relevance if few are informed by its doctrines and live under its banner? In one sense the answer is metaphorical. Students who proclaim communes, wave the black flag, and strike out against organization are anarchic or have anarchic tendencies. That is, in the contemporary social and moral gesticulation of the youth subcultures of many societies we find the equivalent to earlier anarchism.

Today's anarchists in this respect are different from their earlier counterparts in ideas about the collectivity. They themselves are organized differently. They are younger. If they can join with various militant bodies in the attack on capitalist society they also feel free to collide with them. With their highly individualized styles they conflict with other anarchists. They are Rorschach radicals. One needs conflicts to obtain clues to the next concern. Each conflict in the context of youth is part theatre, most particularly the theatre of the absurd, in which public happenings are staged in order to demonstrate the falseness, the emptiness and the perfunctory quality of the symbols of society, law, school, family, and church, i.e. of the stable institutions of the middle aged.

Since today's anarchism is more a part of a youth culture than in the past, anarchism is a contributing source of normative conflict. Youth, not the whole of it, but the counter-culture, serves as the main carrier of anarchist ideas. Anarchism today depends on the power and position of youth as a counter-culture. In this it is very different from the past when anarchism was more inter-generational.

This is perhaps another reason why anarchism remains so anti-theoretical. The simplicity of anarchism is in part a basis of its generational appeal. Youth today is bored with the doctrinal complexity of alternative and competing ideologies. The early figures associated with anarchist movements in England, France, Switzerland, Russia, Germany, and the United States recognized that the guide to action was a theory. This was as true of Proudhon's mutualist doctrines as it was of Tolstoy's primitive Christianity. Even the pamphlets and memorials of Bakunin and Kropotkin showed a concern to spell out the conditions necessary for an improved and different social condition. Theory was a part of life as an enduring radical pre-occupation. But youth today reads very little such literature.

Anarchism as a youth counter-culture is a genuinely different structural phenomenon than in the past. The more so since although generational time shrinks, the period of youthfulness expands. In the days of the old anarchists, one went from childhood to manhood very quickly – overnight as it were. Today what we call youth refers to an extended period of role search, the trying on of different identities. Anarchism challenges this. It downgrades the roles and the identities offered by society. In a very real way it denies what youth in general is for. That is, if youth can be defined as the period of role search between childhood and working adulthood, then the new anarchism is an attack on youth. The attack takes such an attractive form because more and more members of the youth subculture find themselves repelled by the roles and identities which society provides. The result is that anarchism as a counter-culture provides a double basis for rebellion, first against society as it is, and second, against the youth subculture as a preparatory period. Its relevance depends on how youth feels as a whole about societies' roles, i.e. whether they are reluctant to be recruited to them when society ordains that they should. Whether they basically do not reject such roles. Whether they reject them as a system. Anarchism does not mean mere rebellion, i.e. an unwillingness to make a commitment in the face of pressure to select roles and conform, a kind of rebellion associated with a more generalized irresponsibility and a desire for a longer period of exemption. Anarchism means the rejection of the roles themselves. Youth represents a period of exemption granted to youth by society in order to provide a longer period of role search. Anarchism annihilates the roles. It is a doctrine of role rejection.

ROLELESSNESS

A youth culture is part and parcel of the need for more time before accepting society's roles, of sorting them out, and trying, with many false starts, to adopt an appropriate set. This is essentially a method of socializing individuals into the structure of existing social roles. Anarchism as a counter-culture may reject those roles but can it create new and alternative ones as could be done by making more central those activities which had been peripheral in the past? For example, law students can change the role of lawyers from those of practitioners of the art of mediation into investigators of social abuse. Teachers may be redefined outside the specific institutional setting of schools. Socialism and related doctrines do just this. Their proponents look for a redefinition of roles according to their varied ideas of how the structure of society should be altered.

Here anarchism is not very helpful. Since it seeks not alternative roles but their obliteration, this may, when pushed to extremes, end in the obliteration of self instead of its liberation. Rolelessness is the social equivalent of randomness. A random universe cannot define freedom. When the self is obliterated as a social person, the result is withdrawal from action rather than intensified action, or violence for the sake of violence. One sees the pathological aspect in the use of drugs, the emergence of what perhaps can best be called the cult of solipsism, and the alternation of extreme passivity with extreme violence and anxiety.

True the anti-role is not rolelessness. It is a role, too, and one directly involved with other roles. Perhaps we need to distinguish between the 'anti-role' which produces a fierce and continuous controversy over the terms of group action and sheer rolelessness. Moreover, there are 'advantages' to 'anti-roles' as distinct from 'rolelessness'. The anti-role sets itself against socially validated roles. But it has a place in history. The history may not be very edifying. But that does not matter, even if history in this sense replaces economics as the dismal science with 'system' its contemporary voice.

The anti-roles generate the rebirth of innocence. In order to be innocent (and pure) it is necessary to take an anti-role. Each person then 'does his thing' but dares not have a theory about it. (Theory would be a source of weakness not of strength.) The contemporary anarchists most commonly accused of anti-intellectualism are in this sense being misunderstood. Contemporary critics fail to recognize that innocence is itself the goal, the source of redemption, the means and the end. The search for directness and simplicity is precisely what is wanted as the ultimate answer to complexity and compromise.

This brings us to the key question. The relationship between innocence and violence. If our assumptions are correct, violence, because it becomes a total non-answer (which is no answer) is the key to innocence. Here the modern anarchists can relate the theatre of the absurd to the existential quality of death. To prove innocence and protect it is to smash society and turn against confounding theoretical constructions. Out of the first, the smashing of society, the hope is that something new will emerge since from the violence itself will come a more purified image of man. This is where anarchism is perhaps closest to its traditional form. But today, insofar as such views are primarily the preoccupation of youth subculture and most particularly that part which denies itself roles and identity, then violence has quite a different cause than in the traditional anarchist movement, namely violence is both a function and a cause of identity smashing. If this is true then today's youth culture anarchism acts first on itself. It smashed its own identity. But the resulting innocence is behaviourally not supportable without violence. This contrasts with the old anarchism where violence was a tactic or a weapon. In short, when the property of a youth subculture, violence is a psychological necessity.

IN SEARCH OF LIBERATION

If this is the case then what are we to make of anarchism in its present form? At its best, it has its liberating side. It represents a form of social criticism against capitalism as a system and socialism as a form of bureaucratic tyranny. At the worst extreme, it liberates individuals from society only in order to help them destroy themselves as individuals. But what about the larger intermediate group attracted to the doctrines of anarchism? Here the history of doctrine provides its own answers. Future anarchism like the past will prove to be episodic, providing those engaged in role searching with the chance to create some new roles which are partly inside the system and partly not (particularly in the arts). That at least is for the more gifted.

For others, perhaps, it will mean a search for some patterned irregularity in their lives particularly in the alteration of those roles embodied in the sacred social institutions of family, church, school and court. Anarchists may modify the family through communes or other types of association, create new holy days, chants and festivals, alter the quality and the form of education, and redefine both grievances and their redress. In this respect the most important contribution which the new anarchists can make is indirect. Anarchism if it can be anything is likely to be a social doctrine for more personalized living, a recipe for the homespun, and not a political solution for the world's problems. It is more a matter of lifestyle than explicit revolution. But perhaps there is nothing more revolutionary than that.

From a doctrinal standpoint we have said that anarchism represents the most libertarian of socialist ideologies. It begins in the view that men as individuals are, given half a chance, better than the societies in which they live. But to change society is not enough. Individuals need to see in their own salvation a new way to live together. A kind of rational ecclesiasticism pervades traditional anarchist thought.

If it is necessary to break through the shell of society by means of violence, then anarchism has on the whole accepted the principle of violent means. In some of its earlier varieties, at least, it embodied a devotion to discipline and asceticism which at times took narrow forms. Violence might be necessary to free the human spirit from its containment within an unsatisfactory social environment. But once this freedom has been attained it was up to the individual, indeed his obligation, to direct it into constructive and socially useful channels. Whatever it was, anarchism was not a doctrine for the lazy. Quite the contrary, it made exceptional demands on its adherents.

Too many demands, one might argue. This has perhaps been one of the causes of its unevenness. Anarchism is in perpetual danger, not least because of the hammer blows of Marxism and the new organized left. It remains a doctrine of the absurd. Even today when its resonance is stronger than ever before its proponents, from Kropotkin to Malatesta seem *bouffe*. Witness Malatesta, 'I am an anarchist because it seems to me that anarchy would correspond better than any other way of social life, to my desire for the good of all, to my aspirations towards a society which reconciles the liberty of everyone with co-operation and love among men, and not because anarchism is a scientific truth and a natural law. It is enough for me that it should not contradict any known law of nature to consider it possible and to struggle to win the support needed to achieve it.'[2] One can hear the snorts of derision from the Marxists. For it is a fundamental point, whether or not a revolution is based upon a scientific understanding of certain developmental laws, or the more uncertain reliance on an attitude of mind and a sense of solidarity. For the Marxist it is the first which makes revolution necessary. For the anarchist, it is the second which makes revolution desirable.

[2] See Errico Malatesta, *Life and Ideas*, V. Richards, ed., London, Freedom Press, 1965, p. 25.

For all that, both Marxism and anarchism have been 'right' in the special sense that the weaknesses and ills of each have become the accurate prediction of the other. Marxists see the absurd in anarchism, its lack of a programme, the vagueness of its grand design. Anarchists see the implications of statism in Marxism, and the magnified control granted by the apparatus of industrial power. They find bureaucracy and control under socialism no more appetizing than under capitalism.

Perhaps, however, as issues are raised and morality speaks from impromptu pulpits in the socialist societies as well as in capitalist, anarchism is a language useful for identifying the more grotesque anomalies of these systems. It is a doctrine for the young in their anti-roles instead of being nursed along in dark and obscure places by the immigrant Italian printers in Buenos Aires or New York who carried the faded memories of their anarchist days carefully wrapped in the old newspapers of their minds. They had no hope, only regrets. Old anarchists have a better sense of tragedy than young ones.

Today's anarchism is fresh because its innocence grows out of the degenerate sophistication of the past, like the flower on the dungheap. Indeed that is precisely how it began, with 'flower children' and 'happenings'. It is as if a new entrance to the corridor of the human mind had been suddenly exposed and an important part of a whole generation has dashed down it expecting it to lead to unexpected but exciting outcomes. Today's anarchism randomizing the universe and hoping that by keeping it unpredictable, it will be possible to generate freedom, is a far cry from the rationalistic anarchism of the 19th century. It is no wonder that the elders of society shake their heads in disbelief. What they see and fear are the wonders of indiscipline, the medicines of hallucination, the physicalism which produces an erogenous solidarity, alternating periods of self withdrawal and intense social living, the privacy of total self pre-occupation with the giving and sharing of the commune.

Certainly one message is clear. That is the growing importance of the fringe or the margin of society for the whole. For the first time, the margin of the society has the capacity to define the morality of the whole. What begins in society's moral rejection of some becomes the moral rejection of society itself. Anarchism is an important doctrine for this and it remains on the whole imbued with the moral. It also lacks humour, although it may embody sweetness.

It has already shown great power to define caricature and assault. And it is not an accident that its first contemporary arena of action has been the universities for it is here that human promise seems to be sliced and packaged more systematically than in any other institution, and done with a more incredible piety. The universities are the instruments with the greatest singular significance in highly industrial societies because they create knowledge, define validity, establish priorities, and screen individuals accordingly. They thus represent all the inherited wisdom of the past which can then be used as a form of authority for the present. In this sense the central significance of the university as an arbiter of ideas and roles makes it the natural focus of attack, Moreover, precisely because the university provides the place of congregation, creates the groups and its facilities, much of the contemporary anarchist activity takes place in the university setting. Ex-students and 'non-students' live around the university creating youth subcultures. But the focus is shifting. Groups of anarchists as well as individuals have become wanderers. They may be found in Nepal as well as on the left bank. They ask for little. They are willing to pay with their health. Violence and self-destruction are forms of existentially necessary penance. Every man is his own Christ.

Richard Gombin

The Ideology and Practice of Contestation seen through Recent Events in France

THE NEW FORMS OF SOCIAL CONFLICT IN FRANCE AND THE IDEOLOGIES underlying them pose some formidable questions to the historian and the sociologist of the workers' movement. Those which particularly interest us deal, on the one hand, with the existence of anarchist ideas and concepts within the sum total of ideological utterances in May and June 1968 and, on the other, with the libertarian character of the methods of contestation which have appeared in France during recent years. I have deliberately confined myself to the wide notion of the 'practice of contestation' precisely because it goes beyond the phenomenon of the wildcat strike or the unrest in the universities and corresponds to a more general concept which has not as yet been monopolized by any theory. 'Generalized contestation' does not claim to be a definitive sociological category. On the contrary, it is a provisional portmanteau word which will take a more definite shape once we emerge from the chiaroscuro of impressionistic criticism and philosophical reflection.

To reply to the question: what part do anarchist theory and practices play in the generalized contestation in contemporary France does not mean that we are going to leave the quicksands of conjecture for the solid ground of scientific truths. Only a tentative answer can as yet be put forward and it can do no more than introduce a series of other questions which try to situate in the long term the phenomenon of contemporary revolt. In other words, there is need for continuous research if we are to find out whether the chain of events which have taken place in France marks the end of an epoch of social struggle or, on the contrary, if it has inaugurated and heralded a new era. In the first case, what we have called 'generalized contestation', would prove to have been only the last flare up of a dying ember, the last occasion on which the opposition could permit itself the luxury of a wildcat strike, of disorganizing the universities, of a major political crisis, before the rationality, the planning, in short the effective programming of French society (as of all technologically advanced countries) put an end to the cacophony, 'out of place' in the second half of the 20th century. The second hypothesis sees in the events, not the death-rattle of a dying man, but the wailing of a newborn infant. In this case, what has happened is a definitive milestone in a phase of conflict which was held in a vicious circle. During that phase, attempts to bring about emancipation from bureaucratic capitalism spent themselves in a futile reformist struggle in the name of a socialism just as bureaucratic and totalitarian and which offered the workers simply a choice between private or state capitalism. In this last instance, the extent and the characteristics of the contemporary social struggle marked the breaking of a link in this vicious circle, the opening of a breach through which revolutionary energy could pour out in the future.

It goes without saying that I shall naturally not attempt to decide between these two alternatives. But in attempting to delimit the problem of the libertarian trend in the May 1968 revolt, some preliminary answers will emerge which I do not feel authorized to elaborate in this study. I will try first of all to describe this trend at the level of its ideological expression and then at the level of social, economic and university conflicts.

THE AMALGAM

It is customary to speak of anarchism when describing the events which shook France for almost six weeks in 1968.[1] But one must specify what kind of anarchism one means and what form it took. Every social upheaval, from the good-tempered strike to the revolutionary insurrection brings in its wake an *ensemble* of libertarian actions and attitudes, for every upheaval is felt by the crowd to be an extraordinary moment, a sudden and welcome break in the daily routine: a rigid timetable is replaced by leisure and all becomes play. But generally this collective relaxation, this social catharsis is

[1] Genuine anarchists like Daniel Guérin ('Mai, une continuité, un renouveau' in *Le fait public*, 6, May 1969) or historians of anarchism like Jean Maitron ('Anarchisme' in *Le mouvement social*, 69, October–December 1969) have stressed the libertarian inspiration of the 'events'.

contained within precise limits and is only a secondary aspect of the revolutionary process.

This being said, it must be stressed that during the events of May–June 1968, this particular aspect passed beyond the stage of contingency.

In reality the main factor in the immense psychological drama was *collective decompression*. All facets of daily life were attacked, contested, destructuralized. The political aspect which, in a revolution of the 'classic' type dominates and overshadows all the others, was present only in the background, in the corridors in which moved the habitual actors of the parliamentary opposition.[2] Here probably lay the movement's originality, in regard to what was new when compared to revolutionary orthodoxy. In the absence of a unique revolutionary leadership, of a predominant ideological framework, ideas flowed freely, and everyone joined in the debate. As in all revolutions which have missed the mark, that of 1968 was rich in ideas, in possibilities and in plans.

Nevertheless, among the political themes which had some coherence and impact, three groups can be singled out: on the one hand, the programmes and tactics of the classic bodies of the Left (FGDS, PCF, CGT, PSU, etc.); on the other, the ideologies of small groups descended from Marxism–Leninism (Trotskyists, Maoists, dissident communists); and lastly, the ideas put forward by the anti-authoritarian groups (essentially the Movement of 22 March and the Situationist International).

It is clearly among the anti-authoritarian groups that the greatest libertarian impetus was to be found. But these groups were far from having a monopoly of all the contestarian ideas current at the time; nine-tenths of the ideas expressed were put forward by people who belonged to no organization, by the anonymous crowds who were the true protagonists of the May revolt. But it is also true to say that the ideologies of the anti-authoritarian groups contained, in a concentrated and directly political form, the greater part of the images and clichés, memories and archetypes met with in May–June 1968.

Here one comes to the second question: what kind of anarchism was it, to what ideal-type of libertarian thought must one refer

---

[2] The almost complete absence of the political aspect before the end of May has been noted, but less than one might have expected, seeing how obvious it was. See, for example Harvey G. Simmonds: 'The French Socialist Opposition' in *Government and Opposition*, Vol. 4, No. 3, p. 306.

when speaking of influences or affiliations? At the outset, the problem can be situated by stating that anarchism as an *organized movement* played no part in the development of events[3]; anarchist groups in the true sense played a negligible part in the spreading of their doctrine or in the succession of strikes. One can even go further and say that the doctrine of anarchism slumbered in contemporary France, respected and supported only by a few elderly writers and journalists. In other words, the French anarchist movement supplied very little of the driving force in the events as an organization (unlike the FAI and the CNT in the Spanish Civil War) nor was it a direct source of inspiration (as were the Russian anarchists in relation to the *Makhnovshchina*).

Yet some writers have tried to discern in the historical antecedents of pre-1914 anarchism and anarcho-syndicalism a paternity rendered even more obvious to them in that they see the May revolt as the repetition of an historic archetype, the very model of workers' action, whose avatars have extended throughout the whole history of the French workers' movement.[4] These writers are right to connect contemporary phenomena with the workers' tradition, peculiar to France. One must remember that the French proletariat, even its vanguard, was not influenced by Marxist socialism until fairly late; that Proudhon left an indelible mark on a working class which still stood on the threshold of the industrial age; and finally that the desire for equality and the tradition of direct democracy were already present among the *sans-culottes*.[5]

[3] One of the best-known members of the Anarchist Federation expressed this as follows: 'We had no influence on the events which we had not foreseen'. Maurice Joyeux, in an interview in *Le fait public*, 14, January 1970, p. 40.

[4] Cf. for example, Jacques Julliard 'Syndicalisme révolutionnaire et révolution étudiante', *Esprit*, 6–7, June–July 1968, who believes that the students revived the subterranean current of the workers' movement which seemed to have died in 1914. He also noted the anarchist themes shared by the revolutionary trade unionists and the students in 1968. Similarly, G. Adam asked in 'Mai ou les leçons de l'histoire ouvrière', *France-Forum*, 90–91, October–November 1968, whether the May slogans did not represent the expression of the modern dream of the total emancipation of revolutionary syndicalism.

[5] As M. Rebérioux pointed out ('Tout ça n'empêche pas, Nicholas, que la Commune n'est pas morte') in *Politique aujourd'hui*, No. 5, May 1969. Proudhon's influence on revolutionary trade syndicalism is studied by A. Kriegel: 'Le syndicalisme révolutionnaire et Proudhon' in *L'actualité de Proudhon*, Brussels, published by l'Institut de Sociologie Libre de Bruxelles, 1967. The delayed arrival of Marxism in France has recently been stressed by M. Dommanget, *L'introduction du marxisme en France*, Paris, 1967. The sectional life of the *sans-culotterie* in Paris is analysed by A. Soboul, *Les sans-culottes*, Paris, Seuil, 1968.

But if this ancestry is over-emphasized, if one relies too much on historicism, there is a risk that among the rich crop of the May events one may pick out only those elements which can be linked to the nation's past. There is also a risk that other elements, which are even more interesting in that they are quite new and original will be passed over in silence.[6] It would therefore be methodologically wrong to regard anarchism as a precise historical phenomenon or even as a homogeneous mass of ideas and actions: the whole mutualist and federalist tradition of Proudhon was lacking in May 1968 as was his stress on private property and permanent moral values, not to mention the 're-appropriation' of private property and the individualist tradition of Stirner.

If, on the other hand, we accept that anarchism is such a vast heterogeneous and moving mass, a magma of social ideas and aspirations, above all, a tradition of implacable opposition to partisan authoritarianism, to the omnipotence of the state, then we can discover some of these elements in the present movement, but mediated through a number of stages. For it is the entire lesson of the revolutionary experience of the 20th century which has been learnt; pure anarchism can only claim a part in it, possibly only a minor one. It is thus difficult to extract from this rich and composite seam the pure gold of Anarchy. By studying some of the basic themes put forward by the anti-authoritarian groups we shall discover at what point anarchist ideas are the kernel around which gravitate such contradictory doctrines as Luxemburgism, the socialism of the workers' councils, surrealism, situationism, etc.

Among the most general themes shared by the anti-authoritarian grouplets, we find, in the first place, the same radical criticism of bolshevism, both Leninist and Stalinist.[7] There is criticism of the very nature of the October revolution, a political revolution above all, brought about by a small minority of professional militants who imposed their own tactics and aims on the masses. Here there are of course echoes of the duel between Bakunin and Marx, of the attack by the Jura collectivists on any political taking over of the revolutionary process, on any support of the state, even in the pro-

---

[6] Some of the inscriptions are to be found in *Les murs ont la parole*, Paris, Tchou, 1968.

[7] For a more detailed study of the themes of small groups see my *Le projet révolutionnaire: éléments d'une sociologie des événements de mai–juin 1968*, Paris, The Hague, Mouton, 1969, which also contains references to the original documents which I shall therefore not reproduce here.

visional form of the dictatorship of the proletariat. But the analysis of modern bureaucracy by the May contestarians does not conceal its Trotskyist origin. They adopted the point of view that the revolution had been 'taken over' by the apparat, which had replaced the working class not only in the Soviet Union, but in China and in Cuba.[8]

The end result of this criticism led the 'spontaneists' to some extremely unorthodox conclusions: that the bolshevik revolution was a counter-revolution and that Russian socialism is in reality state capitalism. This enabled them to criticize *en bloc* both the East and the West where the various socio-political regimes are seen as so many varieties of the same species: bureaucratic capitalism. The situationists in particular, sharpened this global and many-sided critique. They pushed to great lengths the theoretical analysis of modern society and their *criticism of daily life* goes much deeper than the *global contestation* of the 22 March Movement which is primarily a tactical concept enabling activist minorities to attack by word and deed the numerous 'forms of repression' of bourgeois society.

For the situationists, the bureaucratic system of industrial society has considerably increased the sum total of the exploitation and repression of man in comparison with competitive capitalism and the liberal 19th-century state. The tremendous development of science and technology has led to the individual being completely taken over by the system; the individual is no more than a commodity, a reified object, placed on show, and manipulated by the specialists in cultural repression: artists, psychiatrists, psychologists, psychoanalysts, sociologists and 'experts' of all kinds.[9] To fight against a 'spectacular' society, in which everything is treated as a commodity and in which creative energy spends itself in the fabrication of pseudo-needs, one must attack on all fronts simultaneously; not only on the economic and social fronts but also (and above all) on the cultural one: the virulent attacks on professors, on the system of education, and on university administration, at Nanterre in 1967–68 sprang from this way of thinking. The groups of *enragés* in Nanterre, Strasbourg, Nantes and Bordeaux were inspired

[8] An analysis which has been perfected and taken to its logical conclusion by I. Deutscher in *The Unfinished Revolution*, London, 1967.

[9] The essence of situationist ideas is to be found in G. Debord, *La société du spectacle*, Paris, Buchet-Chastel, 1967; R. Vaneigem, *Traité de savoir-vivre à l'usage des jeunes générations*, Paris, Gallimard, 1967, and in the twelve numbers of *L'internationale situationniste*, especially in the last five numbers.

by the situationist analysis and were determined 'to organize chaos' on the campus. What must be noticed, however, in the situationist 'system' is the part played by surrealist themes. If it is true that the negation of all authority, of any hierarchy is an old anarchist precept,[10] the sharpening of the criticism of culture and art, the desire to *change life* while at the same time transforming the world is undoubtedly surrealist, if not dadaist.[11] This is not surprising once one realizes that the Situationist International was in its beginning at the confluence of surrealism, *lettrisme*, anarchism and the ideology of the workers' councils.[12] This is a heavy legacy for the situationists to bear; their form of expression suffers from it, a certain hermetism obscures an already very concentrated thought. But from the moment when the International adopted the revolutionary idea in its entirety, that is when it passed beyond cultural criticism alone, all these elements coalesced around criticism of the capitalist system. The fundamental idea remaining from all these influences is that changes in relations of production are not enough in themselves to liberate mankind completely. To be completely emancipated, the individual must be the creator of his own existence and he must shake off the shackles which hinder him. One of these shackles is work. Of course, it is the alienated and alienating work of bureaucratic societies – but it is also every paid, structured and directed activity which is meant. Although one can find in Kropotkin, for example, the exaltation of 'free activity', the idea that work is oppressive in itself is not really an anarchist one. In Proudhon, and also in the anarcho-syndicalists one finds indeed the conception of redemptive work which, rediscovering its true nature in the workshop of the inde-

[10] Cf. especially the prophetic pages of Bakunin on bureaucracy and 'official democracy'.

[11] This is André Breton's expression which he seems to have borrowed from Rimbaud. Maurice Nadeau, *Histoire du surréalisme*, Paris, Seuil, 1964, p. 160. The idea that the cultural revolution is inseparable from the political revolution was very strongly held by the German dadaists, *cf.* the dadaist text: 'What is dadaism and what does it mean for Germany' (which must date from 1919), translated into French by A. Guillerm, *Le luxembourgisme aujourd'hui*, Spartacus, n.d. (1970).

[12] The situationist movement grew out of the Internationale Lettriste and COBRA movement. The first numbers of *L'internationale situationniste* are devoted to art criticism, especially of architecture and modern town-planning. In 1959 a further appeal addressed to intellectuals discounted the possibility of a proletarian revolution, believing solely in a 'cultural' one, brought about by the intellectuals through unitary urbanism. For the origins of the Internationale Situationniste cf. J. L. Brau, *Cours, camarade, le vieux monde est derrière toi!* Paris, A. Michel, 1968.

pendent craftsman, acquires the dimension of a moral value.[13] On the other hand, the inscription which was written up on the walls of Paris, 'Never work' comes in a direct line from the surrealist slogans of the 1920s.[14] Here are to be found affiliations of a different kind which inspire the situationists with the image of a liberated society as a *playful* society in which play replaces compulsory activity. The situationists proclaim, in the writings of Raoul Vaneigem, that only the orientation towards play is a guarantee against alienating work. Vaneigem foretells that the future society, the society founded on the love of free play, will be characterized by the refusal to be led, to make sacrifices, to play a part, and by the freedom of genuine self-expression.[15] Here the situationists move far away from the positivism and scientific rationalism of the 19th century by which the Marxist and the anarchist traditions were equally influenced. An appeal to the primitive-irrational traces its roots a long way back into the past, even to the tradition of feudal chivalry.[16]

The situationists, although in many ways they are the heirs of surrealism, dadaism and some millenarian trends, rejoin the modern currents in post-Marxism and even go further in their quasi-Marcusian analyses of alienation in the capitalist-bureaucratic society, which is the purely political aspect of their ideas. There was at one time in their thinking a meeting and a juxtaposition, rather than a fusion, between the criticism of bourgeois culture, modern culture in general (which they had made since their foundation in 1957) and political theory. In analysing situationist writing, one has the impression that one fine day the militants chanced upon the political dimension of contestation. On that day they decided that 'the revolution must be reinvented' and adopted the programme of workers' councils, forgetting or ignoring the fact that others before them had criticized the weaknesses in the Soviet revolution.[17] In declaring

---

[13] In addition to the text by Annie Kriegel already quoted, see also this phrase of Monatte: 'Syndicalism . . . has based its concept on work, on respect for work, on the usefulness of work, on its emancipation and organization', quoted by H. Dubief, *Le syndicalisme révolutionnaire*, Paris, Colin, 1969, p. 36. For the situationists, on the contrary, 'it is work itself, that must today be attacked . . . its suppression is the primary condition for the effective overtaking of the mercantile society'. *De la misère en milieu étudiant*, AFGES 1966, pp. 30–1 (first edition).

[14] M. Nadeau, *op. cit*, p. 62, footnote 31.

[15] R. Vaneigem, *op. cit.*, pp. 268–76.

[16] See what Vaneigem has to say on the subject, *loc. cit.*

[17] R. Navarri: 'Les dadaïstes, les surréalistes et la révolution d'octobre' in

that revolutionary organization must be formed on the model of the workers' councils and must be accompanied by criticism of everyday life, the situationists were unaware that they were taking up again the methods of analysis used by the anarchists, especially in relation to the Russian revolution. These methods of analysis, transmitted through Voline, Emma Goldman, Rudolf Rocker and others, were later incorporated into the doctrine of the German–Dutch ultra Left, in Gorter, Pannekoek, Otto Ruhle. In particular, the idea that the collectivization of the means of production leads to state capitalism was strongly defended by the leaders of the *Allgemeine Arbeiter Union-Deutschlands* (AAUD) from 1924 onwards. It was in order not to be swallowed up by the Comintern that the movement made itself felt through the *Kommunistische Arbeiter Partei-Deutschlands* (KAPD), the AAUD and later the AAUD.-E (unitary) in Germany. If then the slogan of workers' councils, both among the situationists and among the militants of the 22 March Movement, shows a degree of anarchist inuflence, yet it is only an indirect influence acting through the German ultra Left, through the workers' councils' movement, in short mediated by Marxist leftism.

In the same way, the slogan of self-management, propagated by the French leftists, in spite of its Proudhonian and Bakuninist echoes, is a part, as they interpret it, of the tradition of the 20th century, a tradition which is in itself ambiguous, in that it lies on the frontier between liberal socialism and authoritarian Marxism.[18]

Furthermore, the intensive propaganda of the anti-authoritarian view in favour of self-management is in itself marked by a certain ambiguity. Unconsciously, the militants are aware of this; they are reluctant to supply any doctrinal reference, and they refuse to explain whether what they mean by self-management is the setting up of autonomous groups of politically conscious workers or an abstract notion which would have only the negative virtue of excluding all

---

Europe, 461–2, September–October, 1967. The themes of the socialism of the workers' councils had already appeared in the early 1960s; see, for example, No. 6 of *L'internationale situationniste*, August 1961.

[18] D. Guérin demonstrates clearly that the idea of self-management, common to the Italian anarchists and to the group of *Ordine Nuovo* did not mean the same to both groups. This was the cause of the break between the anarchists and Gramsci and his friends after the sit-ins in 1920. *L'anarchisme*, Paris, Gallimard, 1965, pp. 129–31.

other solutions, especially Leninist ones. This is one authentic aspect of *leftism* which rejects all proposed solutions as illusory. Anarchist or pseudo-anarchist themes are used as outlets, as alibis rather than as an ideology.

Another aspect of anti-authoritarian leftism which lies even closer to the meeting point of anarchism and Marxist socialism is its immense confidence in the creative capacities of the masses. This gives rise to denunciations of the unions, which are relegated, together with the political parties, to the ranks of reformist instruments and to the demand that the workers should be organized on their work sites, outside the unions or party networks.[19] Strikers must be led not only to create spontaneously their own forms of organization and struggle (factory committees, action committees, strike committees), but also to overcome the stultifying obstacle presented by the traditional organizations which, according to the leftists, try to 'profit from' the movement of contestation and to channel it along the lines of reform. Hence the common concern of the militants of the 22 March and of the Situationist International, to objectivize the revolutionary process, to make the May strikers realize that 'they are making the revolution',[20] but not by 'injecting' this realization 'from the outside' as Lenin recommended, but by revealing it, as a catalyst, 'from within'. The entire tactics of the anti-authoritarian groups and all their efforts, too, to take their place in the revolutionary current of the 20th century stem from this need.

[19] The most radical criticism of trade-unionism has been put forward by Benjamin Peret who was himself a surrealist rather than an anarchist. He urged the 'destruction' of the unions as long ago as 1952 and his writings are fairly well known to the groups of the Anarchist Federation. B. Peret and G. Munis, *Les syndicats contre la révolution*, Paris, E. Losefeld, 1968. The problem is a far older one since, from the foundation of the CGT, the 'pure' anarchists opposed the idea that their comrades should join it. The creature capacity of the masses was stressed by Rosa Luxemburg and there is certainly a measure of 'Luxemburgism' in the French Left. At the very end of her life, she proposed 'the liquidation of the trade unions' and believed that workers' councils (*Arbeiteräte*) were the only bodies capable of establishing socialism (Congress of the Spartacus League, third session).

[20] In an 'Address to all Workers', the situationists described the current events as 'a revolutionary movement in which *only the awareness of what had already been accomplished was lacking*'; reproduced in R. Vienet, *Enragés et situationnistes dans le mouvement des occupations*, Paris, Gallimard, 1968, pp. 282–4 (italics supplied by the present author).

STARTING FROM SCRATCH

If one leaves on one side the purely 'university' phase of the movement of contestation, the action of the situationists was very limited indeed and mainly 'for the record'. In spite of their concern with the coherence of theory and praxis, they could not overcome the handicap of their small numbers: This was the price they paid for a much too elitist conception of their organization.

By contrast, the Movement of 22 March was at the centre of events. Its victories on the Nanterre campus and the militant fervour of its members made it the most active and popular of the groups.[21] Unlike the situationists, the militants of the 22 March invented their tactics, slogans and propaganda themes as they went along. The *enragés* and the situationists had the chance to put their ideas into practice in the first Committee of Occupation of the Sorbonne (14–17 May 1968) which, under their influence, set up total direct democracy in the Sorbonne, notably by calling a general assembly of the occupants every evening and submitting an exhaustive report on their activities for its approval. On 17 May, faced by the assembly's utter indifference, the committee resigned and was replaced by another one which did not go in for daily consultation but, surrounded by a host of 'technical' committees, was managed by a coalition of authoritarian groups. The militants of the 22 March refused to be integrated in organizational structures, however informal or democratic. They wanted to exist only as an informal group, perpetually inventing forms of action. They remained, therefore, one of those 'agitating minorities' of which Sorel has spoken, which aimed at inspiring revolutionary movement without any preconceived theory. The group would meet only to decide on a course of action and only those in favour of these actions would attend. The actions were to be *exemplary*, that is, they were to have the character of political escalation designed to induce others to follow their example. The occupation of one of the administrative buildings or the defence of a factory against the police were considered exemplary in that they enabled the movement to complete a stage in the battle against the capitalist state. Direct action of this kind went further than any proposed by the syndicalists in that it was inspired

[21] On the central role played by the movement of 22 March during the May–June revolt and their 'identification with the latest trends', see F. Arval: 'Sur le mouvement du 22 mars' in *France-Forum*, 90–91, October–November 1968.

by the example of urban guerrilla warfare and the tactics of systematic provocation.[22] The rejection of all organization and co-ordination with other groups arose out of a doctrinaire attachment to spontaneity and its advantages; meanwhile, the activism of the militants, their ceaseless propaganda among the strikers, was designed to create precisely that same spontaneity among the workers. The situationists, for their part, after the setback to direct democracy in the Sorbonne, organized themselves in the Committee for the Continuation of Occupations (CMDO) and revived total democracy within their own small committee. This committee also attempted to spread the doctrine of workers' councils verbally and in writing.[23]

Very soon, the need for some system, some coherence, even if only in tactical matters, arose. The discussions went beyond the temporary framework of the general strike – in a way they still continue. We must therefore ask what affiliations and influences these groups themselves acknowledge. This subjective aspect can help to reveal how effective was the part which anarchism has played in their ideas and tactics.

A first examination is not encouraging: in their desire to break with all systems, to set up pragmatic and spontaneous creation, the anti-authoritarian groups repudiate all the origins attributed to them. The members of the Situationist International go so far as to deny that they have any ideology at all since any ideology is alienating. They reject both spontaneity and anarchism.[24] But a more careful examination of their writings reveals explicit references to Bakunin (on authoritarian structures and bureaucracy); some recognize that 'anarchism had led in 1936 (in Spain) to a social revolution and to a

[22] The arguments about tactics and the attempts to systematize among the militants of 22 March are to be found in *Ce n'est qu'un début - continuons le combat*, Paris, F. Maspero, 1968.

[23] The history of the group of the *Enragés-Internationale Situationniste* and of the CMDO has been written by R. Vienet, *op. cit.*; pamphlets are reprinted in an appendix. The contents of these pamphlets can be compared with the very clear exposition of the political ideas of the situationists by Mustapha Khayati in 'De la misère en milieu étudiant', *op. cit.*

[24] See, for example, the strange pamphlet of 6 May 1968 in which the *enragés* jeer at the 'anarchists-à-la-Cohn-Bendit', reproduced in R. Vienet, *op. cit.*, pp. 260-1. In number 12 of *L'internationale situationniste*, which was published after the 'events', the situationists denied that they were 'spontaneists'. Pinning their revolutionary hopes on the masses, but opposed to any vanguard, they relied nevertheless on the 'spontaneous' gift for organization of the workers whatever that might amount to.

rough sketch, the most advanced ever, of proletarian power'.[25]
What the situationists reject in anarchist theory is what they call
the separation between theory and practice; in other words, they
condemn anarchist ideology as being only an ideal and not a logically
deduced praxis. But anarchism, nonetheless, retains in their eyes the
merit of 'representing the refusal of existing conditions for life as
a whole'.[26] This avowal confirms the impression produced by the
study of situational themes: if they include some elements of anarchist
criticism, they also refuse in advance to cut themselves off from any
particular revolutionary theory or practice. As for the forms which
the revolutionary struggle should take, the situationists clearly
borrowed them from the revolutionary practice of the 20th century:
Guy Debord tells us that the workers' councils are 'the political
form, which has at last been discovered, in which the economic
liberation of labour [can be] brought about'.[27] In other words, the
situationists want to find their origins in a praxis which creates its
own theory, while the anarchist movement is regarded as imposing
on the workers an ideology which is only an ideology.

The leading actors in the 22 March Movement illustrate even more
clearly this ideological eclecticism and this mistrust of the 'great
family' of anarchism. The majority of them had fought at one time
or another in the small anarchist or anarchizing groups which had
left the French Anarchist Federation and had freed themselves both
sentimentally and politically from a particular anarchist 'dogmatism'.
These groups had wanted not so much to renew anarchism as to
renew revolutionary theory: in publications such as *Noir et Rouge,
Informations Correspondance Ouvrières, Socialisme ou Barbarie,* a complete
reconsideration was undertaken, starting with the revolutionary
experiences of the last decades. These journals published theoretical
and critical articles on the movement of workers' councils in Germany, on self-management in Yugoslavia and later in Algeria, on
the Spanish experiments in self-management, etc. In this crucible,
anarchism was smelted with other ideologies and practices. The
militants formed in this *milieu,* of which Daniel Cohn-Bendit is the
best-known, had broken their links with any school; this state of mind
enabled them to innovate, while keeping elements from the revolutionary saga of the past. Those who took part in the university
disturbances of 1967–68 had definitely sown their anarchist wild oats

[25] G. Debord, *La société du spectacle,* p. 75.
[26] *Loc. cit.,* p. 72.
[27] *Ibidem,* p. 97.

while gaining some knowledge of modern sociological analysis and adopting new ideas taken from non-anarchist horizons. Contacts with the Trotskyists, with the students from Berkeley or from the German SDS, added new elements to the old sediment. By this means they learnt of new forms of tactics such as permanent contestation, provocation at all levels of social life in order to 'unmask, to uncover the real mechanism of the capitalist system . . .'.[28] This generation admits that it owes to anarchism only the rejection of all dogmatism, of the authoritarianism of Leninist organizations.[29] And if they have retained from anarchism the ideas of organizing themselves into small autonomous groups and of self-management, it is also true that they have been inspired by the Marxist analysis of the relations of production and of classes. They have learnt the lesson of the Kronstadt revolt, of the occupation of factories in Italy in 1920, and of the confrontations on the campus of Berkeley. Daniel Cohn-Bendit states, for instance, that he was influenced by the Trotskyist criticism of Soviet society, by Mao Tse-tung on the question of the revolutionary alliance with the peasant masses, and by Marcuse when it comes to demonstrating the repressive nature of modern society or when the latter proclaims that everything must be destroyed in order that everything could be rebuilt later.[30] Therefore, indifferent to labels, the contestarians describe themselves as 'libertarian Marxists' when they are forced to answer this kind of question.[31]

THE TECHNIQUES OF CONTESTATION

After this rapid survey of the themes and sources of contestation, one can well ask whether the spontaneist groups reflect their time, if the practice of social conflict in recent years in France is in accord with their ideological postulates. In other words, was the course of

[28] Interview with Karl D. Wolff, president of the SDS in *L'homme et la société*, 8, April–May–June, 1968, p. 134.

[29] Interview with D. Cohn-Bendit in *Magazine littéraire*, 8, May 1968. The main reproach made to the anarchists of the older generation, was that they had withdrawn into the realms of philosophy and utopianism.

[30] *Op. cit.* It is remarkable that Daniel Cohn-Bendit says that he too was influenced by dadaism. As can be seen, the sources of inspiration of the contestarians were the same.

[31] Cf. for example D. and G. Cohn-Bendit, *Le gauchisme, remède à la maladie sénile du communisme*, Paris, Seuil, 1968.

social struggle carried on in an anarchist way? From the outset, one comes up against a formidable obstacle: the lack of accurate information, of research and monographs undertaken in satisfactory conditions. Every strike, every work-stoppage, every wage-claim of any size in the last decade would have to be the object of careful sociological study. We have some facts and, if they are carefully handled, they enable us to come to some conclusions which are really only hypotheses, to be verified in the future by historians and sociologists who will have at their disposal an infinitely richer documentation.

In most modern sectors of the economy, in the metallurgical, engineering, and petro-chemical industries, but also in banks, insurance companies, and advertising agencies, one sees in France a gradual change in the methods of social conflict. It is remarkable that though this change did not start in May 1968, neither did it cease after the end of the strikes in June 1968. It seems indeed that a movement, a trend, began in about 1966 and has spread for some years without allowing any conclusion to be drawn as to whether it was an ephemeral or a structural phenomenon. The main characteristics of what can for convenience's sake be called contestation are: work stoppage is most frequently decided for an unlimited period, accompanied by occupation of the sites; the demands concern not so much questions of working categories, but broader 'qualitative' issues such as the hierarchic structure in the enterprise, the wage system as a whole, management in and of the enterprise; the decision to strike (and its organization) is taken outside the unions, or, at least, does not arise simply on the initiative of the union delegates as in the case of the 'classic' strike; sometimes the strike takes place even against the advice of the unions; the organization of the strike does not take into account the distinction between unionists and non-unionists; often, direct democracy is introduced in the form of the general assembly of the strikers, deciding on all important issues, appointing commissions of work and delegates, subject to recall, whether or not they belong to a union; the new forms taken by social conflicts are found most often in firms in which there is a great turnover among personnel, where managerial authoritarianism is pronounced, where operations have been speeded up and where the Confédération Générale du Travail is relatively weak (and correspondingly the Confédération Française Démocratique du Travail is rather strong). The initiative is taken by the younger workers, in some cases the very young (under twenty).

To illustrate these general remarks, one can go back to the period before the general strike of May–June 1968. This strike was preceded, not to say prepared, by a movement of 'harassing strikes' which had already all the characteristics of the May 1968 strikes[32]: wildcat strikes (not supported by the unions), involving the occupation of the buildings, the locking up of the director, confrontations with the police, sometimes 'fraternization' with the students. There is one extremely concise study, written and published before the events of May 1968, on the synthetic textile factory Rhodiacéta, in Besançon, which was occupied by strikers on 25 February 1967. All the above-mentioned conditions were present there: in particular, a majority of the CFDT, high speed work, a 'rationalized' organization of work. The strike, moreover, was declared because of the conditions of work and hierarchic relations; wage claims were only secondary issues.[33] The period of occupation produced an indisputably libertarian atmosphere: continual comings and goings of families, visitors, students, passionate discussions in the general assemblies and commissions, plays staged on the factory floor, the creation of a library. The movement spread through osmosis to other factories in the region. The rise in wages (3·8%) granted on 22 March 1967 did not mark the end of the struggle.

Other strikes took place in 1967–68 which were very different from the traditional strikes declared by the union delegation under the very precise 'quantitative' slogan and for a limited period. These strikes which were described at the time as 'workers' *jacqueries*' (Jean Lacouture) took place in Caen, Mulhouse, Redon and Le Mans. Those in the area round Caen have been carefully studied.[34] There, too the reason given for the strike was the 'whole range of relations within the framework of the socio-economic structure'. What was contested in the first-place were relations within the

[32] The incidence of strikes which heralded a general strike was noted by several observers, cf. *Les événements de mai-juin 1968 vus à travers cent entreprises*. Centre National d'Information pour la Productivité des Entreprises, n.d. (July 1968). In spite of the attitude particular to this study, there is no reason to doubt the basic data, especially as they are corroborated by other written or verbal sources.

[33] M. A. Burnier, 'Besançon: occupation d'usine, colère froide' in *L'événement*, 15, April 1967. According to the author this was the first case of a factory being occupied in France since 1947.

[34] S. Pérignon: 'Action syndicale et décentralisations industrielles (les grèves de janvier 1968 dans la région caennaise)' in *L'homme et la société*, 9, July–September 1968.

factory; what was already demanded was workers' control. Here again the strike was from the outset unlimited in time, sites were occupied, confrontation with the *gardes-mobiles* was violent. Those taking part were young workers working at very high speed, with a very high turnover of personnel (20 to 25%). Again, the CFDT was firmly established and the CGT weak. One of these firms, Saviem, at Blainville-sur-Orne, was the first in the region in May 1968 to declare an unlimited strike.

By May this kind of strike had become usual. Its characteristics had been accentuated within a national movement which comprised nearly ten million strikers. The new forms of contestation have been sufficiently described, and need not be insisted upon here. The region round Nantes probably went furthest along the road of contestation. The Sud-Aviation factory at Bouguenais (a suburb of Nantes) was the first to come out on strike (14 May), to occupy the huge area covered by the factory, to lock up the management and to set up a defence of the plant. The development of the strike at Sud-Aviation is fairly well-known: the arguments, the topics discussed, the actions and attitudes of the strikers are familiar through innumerable documents and particularly films made on the spot. The experience of Sud-Aviation spread to the whole city of Nantes, to the extent that one could speak of the 'Commune of Nantes' and even of the 'Soviet of Rezé'.[35] What can be gathered from this experience is that there was a central strike committee at city level and that there were various local committees and managements which saw to it that the economic life of the city was carried on. For more than a fortnight, the city was in a state of quasi-self-management. Though we should have no illusions about the libertarian character of the General Strike Council, which was in reality an inter-union committee serving as an observation-post for the various unions, it remains nonetheless true that the running of daily life was taken over by the inhabitants themselves. It is, on the other hand, very much more difficult to pinpoint the influence of the anarchists (influential within the departmental union of the CGT-FO, led by an anarcho-syndicalist of the old school, Alexandre Hébert) and the

---

[35] See the remarkable study by P. Galard: 'Le second pouvoir du mai nantais' in *Politique aujourd'hui*, 8–9, August–September 1969. Cf. also an invaluable document: 'Nantes, toute une ville découvre le pouvoir populaire', in *Cahiers de mai*, No. 1, 15 June 1968 (a series of interviews with the strikers in Nantes during the occupations).

leftists in the student union (AGEN). The latter, it seems, were fairly close to the situationists.[36]

If one assumes that there was a continuity with the period preceding May 1968 there are indications which point to a persistence of new forms taken by the social struggle after the movement for the occupation of sites had been exhausted. Thus, in some firms, new institutions which appeared only in May–June 1968 have become permanent.[37] In many factories where this was not the case 'the psychology of the workers is still . . . marked by the struggle undertaken in 1968'.[38] Above all, we see the repetition of the abovementioned forms of social conflict. If one considers only cases which are known and publicized, one must mention the 'anti-hierarchical' strike at Coder in Marseilles which took place in June 1969, in which the Nox workshop constituted itself as a general assembly and decreed an unlimited strike in spite of the public and very firm opposition of the CGT.[39] In the same way, the steel works of La Sollac in the Moselle were occupied for a fortnight in March–April 1969 and an unlimited strike was declared in May 1969 in spite of the unions. The demands encompassed the whole wage system.[40]

In some cases, the 'wildcat' strike, occupation, 'qualitative' claims, in short the direct contestation of the managerial role in the plant took place without reference to May 1968. Even more novel forms of contestation appeared, such as the active solidarity and driving-force supplied in the negotiations by the strikers' wives.[41]

[36] P. Galard mentions the contacts between the students in Nantes and the situationists in Strasbourg before May 1968; during the strike one of the situationists went to Nantes and met the leaders of the Student Association. Cf. *Internationale situationniste*, 12, September 1969.

[37] Thus in the CSF of Issy-les-Moulineaux, the functional action committees continued to exist after the strikers returned to work, *Cahiers de mai*, 2, 1–15 July 1968.

[38] M. F. and R. Mouriaux: 'Le mai des prolétaires à Usinor-Dunkerque' in *Politique aujourd'hui*, 2, February 1970. Three conflicts have taken place in Usinor-Dunkerque since May 1968, two of which have involved occupying the buildings, *op. cit.*

[39] *Cahiers de mai*, 12, June 1969.

[40] *Ibidem*. The *Cahiers de mai*, are an inexhaustible source of information, all the strikes are mentioned by name and research on the spot has been undertaken among the strikers. Although this is a partisan journal, the facts as reported in it do not appear to suffer from this.

[41] This is what happened in the strike in the Penrroya de Largentière mines (Ardèche) which in February 1970 entirely paralysed all mining operations, see *Cahiers de mai*, 18, March 1970. It is very significant that the trade unions themselves had to have recourse to procedures (spontaneously in nearly all the

The uninterrupted wave of strikes makes one wonder whether this is not a definite innovation in methods of social conflict. Only the future can show whether the unions will be supplanted by new structures such as factory committees, or a French equivalent of the British shop-stewards. It must be realized that, for the last three years, wherever it has been possible to observe the development of a strike, it has been noticeable that the traditional framework has tended to disappear: the radical contestation of all aspects of power within the factory, the attempts at self-organization, even self-management, criticism of the very role of the unions, the unleashing of conflicts in whole sectors, are the distinctive signs of a mode of action which may well be described as libertarian.

NEITHER MARXISM NOR ANARCHISM

It is undoubtedly true that for some years now libertarian themes and practices have been on the upsurge. But the question which I asked at the beginning of this article cannot be answered definitively. Is this simply the rebirth of anarchism or does it go further? Some authors have tried to make an elegant synthesis by speaking of *libertarian Marxism*.[42] Others distinguish between the petit-bourgeois anarchism, turned back on the past, which disappeared at the end of the last century and the anarchism orientated to the future which appeared in France in 1968.[43] This in my opinion, is to draw too quick a conclusion while we are still too near to recent events, the echoes of which have not yet died away. One thing is certain, however, namely that Marxist ideologies of bolshevik inspiration (Stalinism, Trotskyism, Maoism) have had little influence on recent social conflicts in France.[44] But anarchism as a social movement has

plants) such as a referendum to decide the outcome of the strike. The same thing happened in the case of the recent vote held by the CGT on 4 January 1970 in the EDF (Electricité de France).

[42] This is true of D. Guérin. See his interview, already quoted, in *Le fait public*.

[43] Tom Nairn, 'Why it Happened', in Angelo Quattrocchi and Tom Nairn, *The Beginning of the End*, London, 1968. This is also, on the whole, the thesis of Edgar Morin, quoted by Nairn.

[44] The lack of impact which the Trotskyist and Maoist groups had on the events of May–June has not been sufficiently noticed. They were unable to implant their ideas (and more understandably their organization) either in the occupied factories or in the innumerable action committees which sprang up

not been able to arise from the ashes; in this sense, one must agree with recent historians of anarchism who see no traces of its survival except in the vast realm of ideas.[45] Yet even if one agrees with this view it cannot be denied that some themes are perennial. Nevertheless it is also true that the identification between the ideology of the anti-authoritarian groups and the spontaneous action of the anonymous masses has given rise to a way of thinking and of action which is almost unprecedented.[46] Thus the question remains: are we witnessing in France the last spasm of the old practices which would mark the end of a diffuse tradition of 'violent' social revolts and movements (the Commune, the strikes in 1919–20, 1936, 1947)?[47] Or, on the contrary, are these the prologue of a new revolutionary project which seeks by original means (which mingle old and new elements) to 'transform the world' and 'to change life'? The sole aim of this article is to pose the question clearly by illustrating it from the French experience of generalized contestation.

---

the day after 13 May 1968. Later, they joined the fashion of the day, underplaying their slogans on the formation of a revolutionary party, and fell back on forms of action advocated by the 22 March Movement. There were even cases of unnatural marriages taking place between Maoism and Spontaneism (e.g. the 'Mao-Spontex' group). On the lack of impact of the authoritarian groups, see F. Arval, 'Sur le mouvement du 22 mars' quoted above, and my study, *Le projet révolutionnaire*, chapter 2.

[45] See for example, I. L. Horowitz, *The Anarchists*, New York, Dell Publishing Co., 1964, Introduction.

[46] As Claude Lefort so justly remarked about the student revolt in Nanterre in 1967–68: see E. Morin, C. Lefort, J. M. Coudray, *Mai 1968. La Brèche*, Paris, Fayard, 1968, p. 45.

[47] It must be remembered that membership of the trade unions in France does not exceed 20% of the active population. Thus the trade unionists were unable to channel the revolt towards reform until after an outburst which lasted three weeks or more. For, although the unions (including the CGT) in periods of social unrest become in France as they do in other countries 'a restraining factor' (the term is G. Lefranc's in 'Visages du syndicalisme français' in *Revue de défense nationale*, January 1969), the unions are too numerous, and have too little influence over the bulk of the workers, to play a regulative role as well as in Great Britain and the USA.

(*Translated from French*)

Michael Lerner

Anarchism and the American Counter-Culture

NINE YEARS AGO GEORGE WOODCOCK SURVEYED THE 'GHOST OF THE historical anarchist movement' and concluded that there was 'no reasonable likelihood of a renaissance'. History showed that 'the movements which fail to take the chances it offers them are never born again'. Seven years later, when identifiably anarchist tendencies re-emerged in the youth movements in England and Holland, Woodcock wondered 'whether I had been rash in so officiously burying the historic anarchist movement'. He decided that he had not been rash because of the differences between the new anarchists and the old. The new anarchists represented no 'knock in the coffin' but 'a new manifestation of the [anarchist] idea'.

Woodcock described the new anarchists as 'militant pacifists' who had 'forgotten Spain and had no use for the old romanticism of the *dinamitero* and the *petroleuse*'. He pointed to the difference between the old days when one 'joined' an anarchist party and the current situation in which the young '*became*' anarchists. Finally, Woodcock discerned no obvious signs of an anarchist revival in the United States.[1]

ANARCHISM RENASCENT

It was not only the professional observer of radical and anarchist movements who did not foresee what was in the making in America.

[1] In 'Anarchism Revisited', *Commentary*, August 1968, George Woodcock reviews the analysis he made in his major study, *Anarchism*, New York, World, 1962; Meridian edition, 1967. Although Woodcock saw no 'obvious' anarchist revival in the United States, he agreed with Jack Newfield (*A Prophetic Minority*, New York. New American Library, 1966) that anarchism was an important influence in the new radical thought of 1966–67. Yet the quiet anarchist influence on intellectual currents that Woodcock had in mind is very different from the explicit and often violent manifestations of the anarchist idea and practice that have emerged in the past two years.

A whole school of political observers, sociologists, and political scientists forecast at the start of the 1960s a convergence of political systems, an end of ideology, and a decrease in the salience of political issues as technicians of government assumed control. For all these people the emergence of the first American youth movement, massive and militant, with the children they had raised as they wrote their predictions in its ranks, was probably the biggest surprise of the decade. If black militance was also unforeseen, it was more easily explicable in familiar neo-Marxist metaphors than the aspirations of youth. One could still try to argue that the decisive fact was that a 'student class' seven million strong had exceeded some critical mass on the campuses. But the pioneers of LSD – Ken Kesey and his Pranksters – and the hippies, street people, and flower children fit uncomfortably into Marxist categories. And it was they who were leading the students in building what Roszak has aptly named the 'counter-culture'.[2]

Blacks wanted 'in'; once-Marxist theorists understood that. Hippies, less understandably, wanted 'out'. They showed no ambition to battle for control of American capitalism and to make it serve the working class. They spoke in embarrassingly utopian terms of changing people's minds – attributable, doubtless, to their drug excesses. Drug-induced or not their words were indistinguishable from those of anarchists as dissimilar as Tolstoy and Bakunin who thought that the revolution had to be in men's minds. 'There will be a qualitative transformation, a new living, life-giving revelation, a new heaven and a new earth, a young and mighty world', Bakunin wrote, a vision that the songs of the counter-culture described precisely.

How would the transformation of minds be effected? The Beatles gave an early, widely disseminated answer – 'All You Need is Love'. Some historic anarchists might have agreed. But this answer set the youth culture far from Bakunin, who had concluded: 'Let us put our trust in the eternal spirit which destroys and annihilates only because it is the unsearchable and eternally creative source of all

[2] Theodore Roszak, *The Making of Counter Culture*, New York, Anchor, 1969, has written a pioneering but flawed study of the counter-culture. The problem is that his dislike of drugs, violence and even rock music impinges upon his perspective – he denounces what he does not like often without providing a careful analysis of the phenomena. Thus Ken Kesey and Timothy Leary are blamed for leading young people into drugs, while neither they nor the drug phenomenon are adequately analysed. Violence in the counter-culture is, similarly, deplored without being examined.

life.'[3] Those words still would not ring true in the counter-culture today. But the interesting point is that many of the young are moving ever closer to Bakunin's view than to the love tactics espoused a few years ago. For the espousal of a neo-anarchist world view by intelligent young people in the historical situation of the 1960s seemed *prima facie* even less likely than the emergence of the youth culture itself.

Woodcock's observations provide a useful guide for dating the speed with which anarchism as a potent if often unlabelled force in the American counter-culture has developed and matured. He wrote in August 1968, just before the role of the Yippies at the Chicago police riot catapulted Abbie Hoffman, Yippie leader and author of *Revolution for the Hell of It*, to national prominence. The growing acceptance of violent tactics can also be dated from the period of Chicago, Nixon's election, and the battle over People's Park in Berkeley. There is even an ironic hint of change in organizational structure: only a few months ago Abbie Hoffman suggested that his friends should consider forming a more formal party complete with membership cards. The rash of bombing and burning of buildings testify that the *dinamitero* and the *petroleuse* are not forgotten. Whatever the utility of Woodcock's distinction between social movements resurrected and reincarnated, the new American anarchists have begun to resemble their forebears in depth and detail.

Some of the most significant similarities between the new anarchism and the old seem to include the new acceptance of violence, the rejection of majoritarianism, the insistence on the moral responsibility of the individual, the radical critique of the technological state, the asceticism towards property, and the desire to simplify life.[4] The next three sections of this essay attempt to describe this nucleus of anarchist tendencies as it has re-emerged in the counter-culture. The fifth section suggests some psychosocial factors in the specific American situation that may help to account for the re-emergence of anarchist tendencies.

A caveat before proceeding: this description and analysis is highly problematic. My views, while often stated unequivocally, are just what they seem – views; moreover, I hold other more sceptical views that often prevail over those described here. But I am an

[3] Woodcock, *Anarchism*, p. 151.

[4] *Ibid.*, Woodcock suggests that these were important elements in historical anarchism.

American youth as well as an academic, and though I am uncomfortable either as a participant or as an unengaged observer, I feel the arguments for the new anarchism to be persuasive to an important part of me – an important fragment of my identity. Take as an example the analysis of personal violence advanced in what follows: by turns I see it from different personal perspectives as psychologically sophistic and socially perilous or as psychologically accurate and socially important, as an intellectual game or as potentially prophetic. Since in childhood, adolescence and perhaps youth, games often prophesy, the analysis may be both playful and serious. In any case, it seemed valuable as an aid to understanding the ethos of the new anarchism to let the sympathetic fragment of me speak without burdening the product with predictable 'tough minded' criticisms that readers, according to their predilections, may provide.

Before proceeding to the discussion of violence I should say what I mean by 'counter-culture'. Counter-culture, as currently used, refers to norms and patterns of behaviour, emerging institutions (such as rock festivals and communes), and beliefs and artistic traditions that have coalesced to provide an opposing alternative to the cultural templates of the main culture. It is a term that can be broadly applied to radical students, hippies, motor cycle gangs, the homosexual Gay Power movement, women's liberation groups, the Maoist Revolutionary Youth Movement factions, the Black Panthers, Puerto Rican Young Lords, and lower class white Patriots. Though all of these groups join in opposition to the main culture, I will use counter-culture in its narrower sense below, as it refers to a *core coalition* of 'hippies' and the groups closest to them. Thus by counter-culture I mean the people who are living in the mountains and woods in California, Vermont, Oregon, New Mexico and elsewhere, the street people of New York and Berkeley, the mystics, the people whose lives centre on drugs and/or music, the commune dwellers, those who have given up professions for crafts, and the political action hippies such as the Yippies, the Crazies, the Molotov Cocktail Party, and the Motherfuckers. To this one would have to add those deprecatingly referred to, for want of a better term as 'life-style people' – the musicians, artists, students, and people proudly without occupational identity who populate counter-culture communities. The marginal groups that I would include as part of this core coalition are the cyclists who move in and out of hippie communities, some of the anti-draft resisters, and the Revolutionary Youth Movement I – the Weathermen. The Weathermen constitute a useful marginal case: whereas they regard themselves as Marxist, they resemble the political action hippies in their activities and outlook more than they resemble their friends in the more traditionally Marxist·Revolutionary Youth Movement II. I would tend to exclude from this 'core coalition' the Panthers, Young Lords and Patriots, some of the more traditional McCarthy and Vietnam summer activists, and the large body of students who smoke a little marijuana or dress a little hip but who have made no basic commitment to the values that the core coalition – for all its many divergencies – shares.

The core coalition is conscious of its centrality in the counter-culture and I think would be identified as central by others both inside and outside the broader collection of oppositional groups. I suspect one would also find a hiatus between the identification that members of the core coalition make with each other and the broader identification they have with the other oppositional groups. And I do not think it is an artifact of my classification but, rather, a significant empirical fact, that it is this 'core coalition' in the counter-culture that most closely resembles the historic anarchists.

ANARCHIST VIOLENCE

The most startling new resemblance between the counter-culture anarchists and the historic anarchists is the increasingly widespread acceptance of violence as a tactic. It is simply no longer true that the new anarchists are militant pacifists with no use for 'the old romanticism of the *dinamitero* and the *petroleuse*'.

Discerning increasing *acceptance* of violence is different from predicting that widespread utilization of violent tactics will necessarily follow from their acceptance. People are no longer shocked by talk and instances of violent political action, but there is a step from there to initiation of violence. Sporadic bombing and burning has already started in California, which has for years led the nation in these developments; now there are bombings of large corporate headquarters in New York as well. Whether the initiation of violence on a large scale will come next is something I do not think we can foresee.

The acceptance of violence is expressed in the counter-culture in characteristic ways. There are few written arguments for violence. One way new anarchists continue to differ from the old is in their indifference to formal ideology and written position papers (thus in one ironic sense they are proving the end-of-ideology theorists right). There are exceptions to the general indifference to formal ideology at the margins of the counter-culture. Revolutionary Youth Movement adherents – both the Weathermen and the opposing faction – write out their views, as do a generally older group of contributors to the *New York Review of Books*, who recently discussed the wisdom of anti-draft groups continuing to turn themselves in to the police after raids on draft centres. For the rest, the acceptance of violence is expressed in talk, action, film, and music. Timothy Leary has accurately described the rock musicians as the true prophets of the counter-culture. To hear vividly expressed the way in which the mood of the rock musicians (and their listeners) has changed, one need only listen to Mick Jagger of the Rolling Stones sing 'Street Fighting Man', or the Steve Miller Band sing 'Space Cowboy':

> Let me tell you people that I've found a new way
> And I'm tired of all this talk about love . . .
> You back-room schemers, star-struck dreamers
> Better find something new to say;
> It's the same old story, same old song
> And you've got some heavy dues to pay . . .
> . . . I've been travelling through space
> Since the moment I first realized
> What all you fast-talking cats would do if you could
> I'm ready for the final surprise . . .

Jagger, the Steve Miller Band, and groups such as the Jefferson Airplane, MC 5, the Doors, and Steppenwolf have come a long way from the Beatles' 'All You Need Is Love'. The Beatles made one attempt to stem the turn towards violence with a cautionary song called 'Revolution' which says in part: 'But when you talk about destruction – Don't you know that you can count me out.' But even the Beatles were ambivalent, for after the word 'out' comes a whisper hissed '*in*!' And the augurs seem to be that soon Jagger and the Steve Miller Band will seem tame. There is a new band called 'Up' that plays with bayonets attached to the necks of its guitars.

The turn towards violence is not the only politically significant development in the counter-culture since the Chicago confrontations. Another important trend that has mixed significance for the turn towards violence is the movement of many radicals and hippies out of the cities and into communes in the country. The move to the country started well before 1969 and was partly a response to dissatisfaction with the cities. But its accelerating course also shares with the new acceptance of violence a common genesis, the deep sense of frustration at the intractability of the main culture that developed with the death of Robert Kennedy, the defeat of Eugene McCarthy, events in Chicago, Nixon's election, the multiple indictments and jail sentences facing Movement leaders, and the Telegraph Avenue battle that marked the demise of the People's Park in Berkeley. There were two main responses to these signals of this beginning of what Abbie Hoffman warned would be a period of oppression. Some wished to stay and fight; others wished to move out and find the freedom to create the lives they wanted for themselves. Some even combined the two impulses by describing the move to the country as a necessary preface to a guerrilla offensive.

On the one hand the move to the country may decrease the likelihood of any real or large-scale guerrilla action in the cities growing out of the new acceptance of violence as a tactic. On the other hand, the life-style and convictions of many who have moved to the country and those who want to keep the cities as a base reinforce each other, and reinforce the acceptance of violence. In dress there is a similarity between the new backwoodsman and the new guerrilla. In action there is a relationship between the woodsman's acceptance of physical violence and the guerrilla's espousal of political violence. The two tendencies will reinforce each other most explicitly, of course, if one of the next moves of the legal authorities is a widespread crackdown on rural communes.

Many people in both New York and Berkeley are talking as though preparing for violence. Some groups, such as the Motherfuckers in the East Village in New York, have organized patrols to protect hippies from police harassment. Far more widespread is the toughness with which people are dressing – and this should be distinguished from the *mocking* adaptation of military and police uniforms by flower people that is still in evidence. The Weathermen, who take their name from Bob Dylan's line, 'You don't need to be a weatherman to see which way the wind blows', have begun to fling themselves against the police armed with sticks and chains and they are by no means as universally disavowed by the young as newspaper columnists would have one believe. The rumours that they plan to use guns next are not greeted with horror. On college campuses one hears admiring stories, perhaps partly true and largely apocryphal, of white Vietnam veterans becoming guerrillas in the North Dakota badlands, supplying themselves with arms by stealing trucks from army convoys. No film is more admired than Gillo Pontecorvo's 'Battle of Algiers', which convincingly recreates a terroristic, suicidal and ultimately successful urban guerrilla movement. One could multiply examples but the point is clear: whatever else differentiates the new anarchists from the old, the often romantic attachment to violence has reappeared.

Since this new acceptance of violence is likely to be condemned everywhere except where it is accepted within the counter-culture, let us look – if only to understand it better – at some of its characteristically anarchist qualities. But first note that one important thing has changed: very few of the new anarchists either wish to or believe they can destroy the state completely. What they hope to achieve by violence is either a fundamental modification of the state or (and this is more true of the commune dwellers) the *de facto* right of counter-culture communities to control their own affairs at a local level.

Some of the young who are 'into violence' have that clear predilection for physical assault that characterized a number of historical anarchists and – more generally – the self-selected storm troopers of every social movement. There are those who like to break heads, either as Weathermen or as policemen. Yet at the Berkeley campus of the University of California, one has a different feeling about the grim young men who warn motorists not to leave their cars in the pay parking lot that now stands where the community-built People's Park once stood. The story of People's Park tells something of the kind of scenario that increases acceptance of violence. In brief, street people and students turned some cleared land owned by the university into a very creative park. The university, to re-establish its 'conveniently forgotten' deed to the land, surrounded it with a chain-link fence, bulldozed it flat, and defended it with the aid of police. The defence of the bulldozed lot was bloody; several deputies have since been indicted for their treatment of students and street people. The university, which plans to build on the land eventually, then could find no one willing to touch the land except a parking-lot company, to which it leased the lot on terms that made it almost a gift. Now the young people picket the lot with signs advising motorists – 'Park at Your Own Risk'. The licence numbers of those who park in the lot despite the warning are listed on bulletin boards under the caption 'Actions Speak Louder Than Words'.

The reader of these broadsides is being invited to bomb the cars:

in one sense the grim young men are no longer militant pacifists. Yet if you ask these advocates of local terrorism about their view of modern war, many still reject it unequivocally. When it comes to opposing a reactionary and repressive state government, however, they believe that they must turn to violence to secure the kind of community they once fought peaceably for or else give up the quest. As Tolstoy said of Kropotkin: 'His arguments in favour of violence do not seem to me the expression of his opinions, but only of his fidelity to the banner under which he has served so honestly all his life.'[5]

Two further anarchist characteristics of much counter-culture violence are the scale on which violence is undertaken and the view of the violent act of rebellion as somehow sacred. It is well known that when violence becomes the policy of opposed groups there almost inevitably results an escalation in its savagery. Yet in no case can the violence planned by the new anarchists become the technological violence of the bomber pilot who flies miles above a country he may never have set foot in and releases bombs of terrible power and sophistication without feeling either anger or deep personal conviction. The pattern of violence predominant now in the counter-culture is reflected by the Weathermen who – like everyone else in the country – have access to guns. Yet more may be involved than a calculus of penalties when they attack the police with clubs and chains instead of guns, often expecting to be arrested and prepared to take blows just as they give them. Their medieval assaults resemble in their physical immediacy the jousts that Norman Mailer once proposed New York should hold in Central Park.

It can be argued that the recovery of the capacity for aggression on this insistently personal scale in the counter-culture is not, as some have wishfully thought, some aberrant development, but rather may be related to the recovery of the capacity for love, the lifting of various repressions, the recovery of the wish for primitive community, and so forth. In such a state a man may wish to stop inflicting constant small violence upon his woman, himself, and his friends, and may attempt to push the aggression outwards – perhaps the way primitive man did – fighting back against the enforcers of state justice instead of accepting their commands as a necessary price of civilization. An extreme and pathological example will show the 'transvaluation of values' in respect to violence that has taken place in the counter-culture: Charles Manson, who is alleged to have

[5] *Ibid.*, p. 223.

ordered the murder of Sharon Tate and her friends, is not *utterly* condemned by many I have spoken to. More recently, in fact, he has become a hero and symbol of revolt for some of the Weathermen groups. These people are not surprised, in particular, that his girls loved him, and that however crazy he was and however indefensible his alleged act, his violence and the gentleness of which the girls so often spoke were 'out front'.

The Weathermen and Charles Manson are the extremes. Everywhere in the counter-culture one finds people who are seeking to get back in touch with their capacity to shout, hit, face physical danger with courage, and feel. In many less destructive forms the recovery of the capacity for aggression on a human scale is a pressing concern. In California there are the cyclists, the serious admirers of Che Guevara, the new backwoodsmen, and the devotees of karate and other 'martial arts'.

It is not difficult to see how the task of integrating the acceptance of violence into one's life becomes a somehow sacred task. 'Ritualistic' murders and the explicitly sacred violence of karate are clear examples of the fact that this transformation of violence from profane to sacred does indeed take place. There is a subtler sense of sacred mission in the violence of the Weathermen, the terrorism in 'The Battle of Algiers', and more generally in the violence of the Arab commandos, who have become widely admired.

It is easy and perhaps wise to query critically any sanctification of violence. But before dismissing the new anarchist violence on these grounds one should inquire whether the way they make *their* violence sacred differs from the practice of the main culture. Robert Lifton, suggesting that nuclear technology has eroded the symbolic continuities that make men feel meaningfully connected with a past and with a future, has argued that men often deify the power that destroyed their old continuities. He discerns a religion of nuclearism in which people come to worship in some sense the awesome weapons that destroyed the old 'magical' guarantees that their lives had significance, much as Indians and Africans worshipped the 'white man's magic' that was more powerful than their own.[6] We even give to nuclear holocausts a name similar to that given to the God of the early Hebrews – thus Herman Kahn wrote a book called *Thinking About The Unthinkable*.

[6] Robert Lifton, informal remarks at the Wellfleet Psychohistorical Conference, 1969.

The middle and upper classes in the dominant culture have lost touch with personal violence. They bring up children out of touch with and neurotically afraid of their own anger. They are urged to accept surrogate violence – football, jets, nuclear weaponry – while advertising defines surrogate sex and surrogate lives that they may come in touch with through the use of the advertised preparations, potions, and charms. The characteristic of the main culture that the counter-culture has rejected most emphatically in its transvaluation of values is the acceptance of surrogate (or endlessly delayed) gratification as a substitute for personal and immediate gratification. As part of this pattern, the religion of nuclearism and the Sunday ritual of watching the violence of televised football are rejected and the feelings of sacredness are returned to acts of personal violence. This may not be a long step forward in some ways, particularly since personal violence can so easily escalate into technological violence regardless of whether the societal inequities protested against will be reduced by the escalation. Most would judge the return to personal violence as a step backward from any standpoint. But in other ways personal violence – if boundaries of its sacred sphere and non-lethal ritualization of its enactment become better defined – may be a more satisfying and less dangerous persuasion than the nuclearism that has tried to replace it.

Whether or not this argument holds, it remains true that historically anarchists such as Bakunin saw something akin to the sacred in the violent response of individuals to governmental oppression or dispossession, and this vision has returned in the counter-culture today.[7]

[7] The discussion above stressed the positive aspects of personal violence, such as the personal consequences of getting back in touch with anger. The potential danger of personal violence for the polity must be mentioned as well. By readily accessible techniques, the angry anarchist can move from clubs to bombs. There is increasing evidence of a trend in this direction in New York and California. Bombs are, of course, very much in the anarchist tradition. Yet their use allows one to move away from violence as an expression of personal anger towards violence as a dispassionate policy. When violence becomes policy and technology allows physical and emotional remove, the *personal* values of getting back in touch with the physical expression of hostility are sacrificed.

To *understand* the bombings it is important to recognize that to bomb buildings may be a sign of the psychological well-being of the bomber as easily as it is a sign of pathological hostility projected into the public sphere. One could suggest, only partly ironically, that the bombers may be young radicals who genuinely discovered 'the meaning of meaning it' in their commitment to radical social change. Strong object relationships, the quest for competence, and capacity

INDIVIDUAL AND MAJORITY

The return of the sacred to individual violence is part of a broader characteristic of the counter-culture: the return of the sense of sacredness of an individual life. In secular language the message is that *your* life is your most important possession and tool and that it is of the utmost significance how that life is lived.

Given the stress on the responsibility of the individual, it is not surprising that few in the counter-culture believe the wishes of the national majority should necessarily prevail. There is another reason

for realistic appraisal of the situation may have indicated to them that emotionally fulfilling personal violence was an impotent weapon against societal oppression. Though as members of the counter-culture they may have valued the immediate gratification that personal violence brings, they found the gratification lessened by the realization that personal violence became fantasy posturing – what Robert Brustein has called 'revolution as theatre'. They could not resign themselves to ivory tower dreaming as academics, guerrilla theatre playing at revolution, or retreat into fantasy. Thus they adopt what the main culture always urged – capacity for sublimation and delayed gratification. They become willing to behave 'appropriately', to bomb (though they find this behaviour intrinsically less satisfying than regressive personal violence) in the realistic quest for a broader societal good.

And yet they find themselves caught up in the process anarchists have always objected to: techniques of violence – technology – transform not only the weapons but also the fighters. Aggression that once served personal needs is transformed by realistic perception of the impotence of personal violence into a personally unsatisfying, brutalizing and depersonalized activity. This technological violence only brings gratification to the sublimated wish inasmuch as the technique successfully achieves the policy objectives.

Nor can one deny the psychological well-being of bombers on the grounds that they utterly misperceive the effects of bombing in the existing situation. *I* think they utterly misperceive its effects, which I think may well be disastrous. But though I may fear a right-wing reaction, the terrorists can guess that the Nixon Administration will over-react to a limited number of bombings and that the country will be radicalized by distaste for the Administration response. Though the odds may favour the first scenario, to expect or hope that the second is accurate is not delusional or crazy in any clinical sense.

What the observation that the bombers may not be crazy at all underlines is the fact that what is arguably healthy for some individuals may be disastrous for the society. Bombing may be an 'appropriate' extension of their commitment, yet others from no less valid a perspective can judge that it is a terrible error. The bombings fit the anarchist tradition but suggest an anarchist dilemma. For to bomb is to move away from personal towards technological violence; the technological means compromise the anarchist's personal and societal ends. This dilemma exists whatever one's view of the bombings may be.

(besides this emphasis on the authority of the individual) for the unpopularity of majoritarianism. Communists and socialists of preceding generations derived their sense of righteousness from their certainty that they spoke for the proletarian majority. But the new anarchists have had to recognize that what remains of the American proletariat wants what the swollen middle class has. Thus the anarchist vision of the good life has little prospect of gaining widespread support unless there is a fundamental change in men's minds.

Much of the music of the counter-culture refers to a dawn, a new age, an Age of Aquarius, where much that 'can't stand the light of day' will change. Some believe a new age is imminent; for most, the new age refers more to a time when they will have the space and freedom to consolidate their own lives and communities, rather than to a time when the entire society will be transformed. People of both views believe, however, that in the meanwhile the oppressed, indoctrinated, alienated majority has no moral right to impose its will on the only communities that have liberated themselves.

The strength of this rejection of majoritarianism is most visible in California. The popularity of Reagan's rightist government there is in no way seen by radicals as a reason not to oppose his initiatives against their communities. This is because they fundamentally believe, with Thoreau, that

> voting is a sort of gaming, like checkers or backgammon, with a slight moral tinge to it, a playing with right and wrong, with moral questions . . . I cast my vote, perchance, as I think right; but I am not vitally concerned that the right should prevail. I am willing to leave it to the majority. Its obligation, therefore, never exceeds expedience. Even voting *for the right* is *doing* nothing for it. It is only expressing to men feebly your desire that it should prevail. A wise man will not leave the right to the mercy of chance, nor wish it to prevail through the power of the majority.[8]

One finds in the counter-culture that distinctively anarchist combination of apolitical disdain for (and often ignorance of) the normal political processes combined with a passionate sense of the political responsibility of the individual. To the question 'what can one man do?' the anarchist – almost alone – answers 'everything', meaning

[8] Henry David Thoreau, 'Civil Disobedience', reprinted in Irving L. Horowitz, (ed.), *The Anarchists*, New York, Dell, 1964, p. 317.

that to take the step that might save others is the only way to re-possess one's own life. Thoreau went to jail on an assumption very similar to the assumption of the young men in the Resistance anti-draft movement. Dave Harris, once a president of the Stanford University student body in California, now husband of Joan Baez and in jail for resisting the draft, gave a talk that is widely viewed as one of the purest expressions of why people resist. The parallels between Harris's views and Thoreau's, and with the anarchist tradition more generally, are very striking:

Before I talk specifically about the draft, I'd like to begin at a general point. That general point has to do with what you and I possess as a tool. One of the things that you and I are constantly looking for in this world is a really adequate tool, something with which one can bring about a change in the world. . . . The tool that you and I have is the tool of a life. What matters is how that life is lived from day to day to day. . . . The most obvious assumption of military conscription in this country is that the lives of young people in this country belong not to those young people; the lives of those young people are instead possessions of the state, to be used by the state when and where the state chooses to use them. . . . What the draft card represents is a pledge. It's a pledge that all of you have signed to the American state. That pledge says, '*When and where you decide murder to be a fit international policy, I'm your boy.* . . .' What we see happening in a situation like Vietnam is not a mistake. It is not something that has fallen out of the sky on all of us. Rather, we see the American logic coming to fruition. We see a dispossessed people dispossessing other people of their lives. . . . The first problem that you and I have is repossessing that basic instrument called a life. . . . It is only when we begin to repossess those lives that you and I can ever talk about those lives having meaning or about living in a society that was really shaped by the meaning of those lives. . . .

The system of military conscription is not General Hershey. It is not Lyndon Johnson. . . . Military conscription is every man that carries a draft card. . . . The most elaborate bureaucracy for selective service in the world does not function without people such as you and me willing to sign our lives over to that system. Without you and me, it's nothing. I mean, the beautiful thing about American totalitarianism is that it's participatory. Which means that if you don't buy it, it doesn't move. And I don't buy it. I think you buy it when you carry a draft card. I think you become one more link in a whole chain of death and oppression on people's lives around the world.

The prevalence in the counter-culture of views similar to Harris's makes it significant that, of all the traditions that support radical thought, his views most precisely echo the anarchist idea. In the quoted section of his speech one finds the anarchist assumption that the individual is both responsible and free, the precarious anarchist wager that if one man opposes the system it is possible that others will and the system can be halted, the anarchist view that carrying a draft card is not only a dispossession of life but also reaches logical fruition in what is happening in Vietnam. Elsewhere in the speech one finds the anarchist assumptions that one can reliably distinguish between the gods of militarism and brotherhood and the anarchist millennial vision of a day in which 'a young child finds two words in a book, and the two words are "oppressor" and "oppressed", and he asks you what those two words mean and you can't point to a goddam thing in the world to tell him'.

It is not difficult to see the similarity between Harris's views of the nature and purposes of the state and those of Godwin and Tolstoy. Godwin wrote that

> The state of society is incontestably artificial; the power of one man over another must always be derived from convention or from conquest; by nature we are equal. The necessary consequence is that government must always depend on the opinion of the governed. Let the most oppressed people under heaven once change their mode of thinking and they are free. . . . Government is very limited in its power of making men either virtuous or happy.[9]

Similarly, Tolstoy wrote:

> The modern state is nothing but a conspiracy to exploit, but most of all to demoralize its citizens. . . . I understand moral and religious laws, not compulsory for everyone but leading forward and promising a more harmonious future; I feel the laws of art, which always bring happiness. But political laws seem to me such prodigious lies. . . . I regard all governments, not only the Russian government, as intricate institutions, sanctified by tradition and custom, for the purpose of committing by force and with impunity

[9] Woodcock, *op. cit.*, p. 63.

the most revolting crimes. And I think the efforts of all those who wish to improve our social life should be directed towards the liberation of themselves from national governments whose evil, and above all whose futility, is in our time becoming more and more apparent.[10]

Finally, one finds in Harris's talk the joyous anarchist acceptance of the role of a criminal in an immoral society. Harris's words on this point find resonance throughout the counter-culture:

What we in the Resistance have said about that act of refusing to co-operate with military conscription is not that we see it as a final act. . . . It's one little thing. It's one step. But it's a first step. To take that step means for most of you taking on what's probably a wholly new social role. That's called the role of criminal. It's funny. You know, as you grow up, you always have this feeling that you are growing up towards something, that somewhere out there there's this like true occupation, that there's your thing sitting out there, and finally approaching twenty-three I have found my thing in being a criminal. It's really too much. And being under sentence now for three years in the federal prison, the one thing I can say is that I find no more honourable position in modern America than that of criminal. . . .[11]

The acceptance of the role of criminal or identification with criminals in a society that the counter-culture feels has dispossessed people of their lives is widespread and utterly fundamental. Bob Dylan has a verse that goes 'There must be some way out of here, said the joker to the thief', and the thief turns out to have the answers. More recently The Band did a song 'I'm a Thief and I dig it'. When asked by their elders what they are doing inside the jails, the counter-acculturated can only reply, with Thoreau, 'What are you doing out there?'

This acceptance of the role of criminal is connected to the pervasive 'no' with which the counter-culture confronts the dominant culture. But the *quality* of this 'no' is akin to Bakunin's acceptance of creative destruction. Listen to Michael K. Ferber, a Boston draft resister, who gave a talk at the Arlington Street Church in Boston called 'A Time to Say No'.

[10] *Ibid.*, pp. 224–5, the first and second parts of the quotations are from different sources in Tolstoy's work.
[11] David Harris, untitled, Resistance xerox.

But what I want to say now goes beyond our saying No, for no matter how loudly we say it, no matter what ceremony we perform around our saying it, we will not become a community among ourselves nor effective agents for changing our country if a negative is all we share. Albert Camus said that the rebel, who says No, is also one who says Yes, and that when he draws a line beyond which he will refuse to co-operate, he is affirming the values on the other side of that line. For us who come here today, what is it that we affirm, what is it to which we can say yes?[12]

Bakunin's creative destruction has been replaced by a refusal to co-operate that is still pacifist in Harris's and Ferber's acts but is increasingly accompanied by a willingness to resist actively or even violently elsewhere. The similarity between Bakunin and Harris is that both say no in order to create a 'life-giving' alternative. One is reminded of Joan Baez's quite literally life-giving suggestion, made before her marriage, when she was asked what women could do to fight the draft. She replied that women should try to say yes to men who say no, which was, in the end, what she did.

TECHNOLOGY VERSUS THE SIMPLE LIFE

Anarchism first emerged as a protest movement paralleling the rise of the modern state. From the start it was fundamentally more radical than socialism or communism because it accepted the consequences of the criticism it made of the modern state: anarchists were not only willing but eager to return to a simplified and primitive life.[13]

What the anarchists opposed in the post-feudal state was not its imperfect functioning, which liberals decried, nor simply its class biases, which communists opposed, but the structural prerequisites of its functioning. The anarchists were prescient enough to see that these structural necessities – centralization, bureaucratization, specialization, and the subordination of the individual to market forces (whether free or controlled) – would remain even if socialists succeeded in achieving equitable distributions of wealth. The claims

[12] Quoted in Erik Erikson, 'Reflections on the Dissent of Contemporary Youth', *Daedalus*, winter 1970, p. 165.

[13] Woodcock, *op. cit.*, especially 'Prologue'.

that the capitalists made upon individual prerogatives in terms of the greater efficiency and security of the commonwealth might even be intensified in the socialist state – much as, de Jouvenel points out, the mass armies of modern warfare were unthinkable before the emergence of modern democracy.[14] The claim of the modern state that it represented the people only reinforced its controlling power. Only the anarchists asked whether the affluence, efficiency (for what?) and security (for whom?) that the modern state provided was worth the surrender of individual prerogatives. Anarchists alone can afford to make such a radical criticism of the nation-industrial-and-now-technological state for they alone are prepared to live with the alternative.

Let us examine some of the aspects of this willingness to return to a simpler life. First, there is a question (disputed also *among* the anarchists) whether they would give up all of the fruits of technology or only those whose production intolerably oppressed men. Some anarchists present and historical have believed that men should return to a totally primitive life, using only tools and techniques that they can make or use with their own hands. A surprising number of the historic anarchists took no such extreme view: 'If only it be understood', Tolstoy wrote, 'that we must not sacrifice the lives of our brother men for our own pleasure, it will be possible to apply technical improvements without destroying men's lives.'[15] Godwin had a similar vision, based on the optimism of many early anarchists that technology would one day liberate rather than enslave men.[16] Whether and in what way technology may some day liberate men (or whether it is doing so already) is a very difficult question. Jacques Ellul has argued very persuasively that it may be impossible to put an end to the incredible ways technology bends men's lives to serve its logic.[17] Yet Ellul's argument contradicts *some* of the evidence of my senses that some men are pulling themselves free and that with the advent of a guaranteed income in the United States more and more will have the freedom to live as they wish to. In any case, many anarchists of all periods have believed that not all technology need be thrown away. 'It is not for nothing that mankind, in their slavery, has achieved such progress in technical matters', Tolstoy

[14] Bertrand de Jouvenel, *On Power*, Boston, Beacon Press edition, 1962, pp. 7–11.

[15] Woodcock, *op. cit.*, p. 231.

[16] *Ibid.*, p. 88.

[17] Jacques Ellul, *The Technological Society*, New York, Knopf, 1964.

said.[18] And Timothy Leary foresees advances in communications and in production technique that will allow profound decentralization of production and decision-making, much as Simone Weil once imagined factory work being done by villagers in their homes and brought to central assembly points on days of festive gathering and learning.[19]

I said it was 'surprising' how many anarchist theorists have hoped that much of technology could be salvaged because contemporary anarchists are often charged with hypocrisy if they reject society while accepting some of its benefits. The answer to this charge seems to me three-fold: first, as suggested above, they may visualize a state in which a non-oppressive decentralized technology has been salvaged or invented; secondly, they generally say they are willing to accept a simpler life if more technical production would require intolerable oppression; and thirdly, since many, as I have also indicated, have modified their expectations and no longer expect to overthrow the state but rather hope to live on its boundaries or in its interstices while working to provide for their minimal needs, why is it at all hypocritical to purchase what they want from the main culture? Their dream of a change in men's minds, after all, is a hope that others will come to recognize sufficiency as a better guide to the good life than affluence, and a vision of a world where men toil only to meet their minimal requirements.

Another argument made against the return to the simple life is that one gains no freedom at all but rather becomes enslaved to labour, ignorance, and disease. This argument has significant force if you are speaking of anarchists who wish to give up everything, though even then one can ask whether the labour, ignorance and disease of primitive society *as modern men would recreate it* would be so terrible or worse than the price technological society exacts. The argument has little force against the modern anarchist vision of a technology of sufficiency.

Another common argument against the return to primitive life is that all one will find is the lawless rule of the strongest and a tyranny of opinion – harsher than the tyranny of law – that George Orwell believed characteristic of anarchist communities.[20] There is some

---

[18] Woodcock, *op. cit.*, p. 231.

[19] Simone Weil, *L'Enracinement*, Paris, 1949, see also M. M. Davy, *Simone Weil*, Paris, 1961, 'l'organisation du travail-vivant', pp. 98–103.

[20] Woodcock, *op. cit.*, p. 84, draws together Godwin's observation and Orwell's comment (in an essay on Swift): 'When human beings are governed

contradiction between the two fears; do we fear that nothing will constrain men or that they will be utterly constrained? Probably the latter fear is the more realistic. William Godwin *expected* that in anarchist communities

> opinion would be all sufficient; the inspection of every man over the conduct of his neighbours, when unstained by caprice, would constitute a censorship of the most irresistible nature. But the force of this censorship would depend upon its freedom, not following the positive dictates of law, but the spontaneous decisions of the understanding.[21]

What we must ask is whether conformity to communal opinion or assent to communal authority is more burdensome than obedience required under threat of punishment to the political justice of the state. I think the answer is highly dependent on the situation and the frame of mind of the participants. But the fact that in many anarchist communities people willingly *assent* to stricter codes of behaviour than would be required by law in the dominant culture does not seem to me to be a persuasive argument against the greater freedom anarchist communities allow. The view that anarchists have less liberty than others assumes what John Schaar has so tellingly criticized – a necessary opposition between liberty and authority. The anarchists appear to redefine authority (with Schaar) as assent to those who have shown by example and wisdom that they *deserve* to be emulated.[22] And anarchist communities frequently possess the rare ethical homogeneity that makes assent to exemplary authority most consonant with liberty.

A final argument in favour of an anarchist decentralization of authority and readjustment of the economy to minimal needs seems far-fetched, but it may turn out not to be. One can at least hypothesize that given the historical correlations between the centralization of power and the proliferation of lethal weaponry and between spiralling consumption and destruction of the environment, there may be no alternative to decentralization and a technology of

---

by "thou shalt not," the individual can practice a certain amount of eccentricity; when they are supposed to be governed by "love" and "reason" he is under continuous pressure to make him behave and think in exactly the same way as everyone does.'

[21] *Ibid.*, pp. 83–4.

[22] John Schaar, 'Notes on Authority', *New American Review*, New York, New American Library, January 1970, No. 8, pp. 44–80.

sufficiency. This is a hypothesis that will be empirically tested, one way or the other. And even if we became convinced that the hypothesis was correct, whether we would wish to *adapt* the anarchist alternative instead of accepting the consequences of affluence and centralized power would be a question of normative values.

These questions keep returning us, however, to the large problem of how the anarchists would restructure the entire society if the minds of men were to change and it was in their power to do so. What is actually true of a great number of people in the counter-culture is that they have discovered they *can* live lives of sufficiency around the edges of the affluent society, either working or scavenging or stealing, according to their ethics, to provide themselves with what they need. The choice of this life of sufficiency is a choice many of them make *over* lives of great affluence. Thus they are at the centre of the anarchist tradition of an active preference for the simple life and of a general asceticism towards property – even when this asceticism is not required, and in fact is discouraged, by the economics of the main society.

DIFFERENCES, SIMILARITIES AND PSYCHOSOCIAL FACTORS

Up to this point I have stressed the similarities between the new and the historic anarchists. But, as Woodcock has pointed out, the differences are very substantial.[23] The new anarchists are from the middle class rather than the aristocracy or the peasant or factory poor. There are fewer working intellectuals, such as Proudhon, and this is both the source and symptom of a further difference: the new anarchists are even further than the old from the communists and socialists in their rejection of doctrinaire formulations. This 'apolitical' quality of the new anarchism makes it the unlabelled refuge of many Movement people who tire of the endless factionalism that divides American socialists and Marxists; it also helps to account for the distinctive quality of diversity without factionalism that characterizes the core of the counter-culture.[24]

The anti-doctrinaire position reflects a broader characteristic of the counter-culture – its suspicions of 'rationality', 'objectivity', and the intellectual posture more generally. This does not mean that

---

[23] Woodcock, 'Anarchism Revisited', *op. cit.*, makes the two points that follow.
[24] David Apter suggested this.

people do not read, nor that they do not reason. It means instead that they sense a resistance in culturally defined reality, with its self-serving definitions of 'rationality' and 'objectivity', that militates against their discovery of another set of truths. Hannah Arendt once said you cannot expect people to reason when they see reason is being used against them as a trap. This describes the experience of those who ponder these questions in the counter-culture. As a result there is a defiant espousal of absurdity, subjectivity, mysticism and magic, things that are seriously explored but also serve as a shield behind which those who do reason can seek new mappings of reality unencumbered by old definitions of intellectual responsibility.

Whatever the reasons for the surface appearance of anti-intellectualism in the counter-culture, it constitutes another difference between the new anarchists and many of the historic anarchists, and it has opened anarchism to a far broader spectrum of the young than historic anarchism drew upon. From abroad it may not be apparent that, although the centres of the counter-culture are coastal, it is a phenomenon that permeates the country: there are small communities of dissidents in almost every major city. Many become acquainted with drugs and the mores of the counter-culture in such small communities and then flee to the coastal centres. In California and New York a large portion of the counter-acculturated appear to come from central American cities and small towns that they were too 'pathological' to 'adjust to'.

Some differences between the new anarchists and the old come from the *similar* totality of their opposition to very *different* societies. This totality of opposition is also what distinguishes the new anarchists from the liberal-radicals who worked for McCarthy and from the doctrinaire Marxists. The core of the counter-culture is the sector which carries through most completely the transvaluation of values (that is why the term *counter*-culture seems so apt). Many of the counter-culture's characteristics derive from needs and wishes to reject completely the arrangements of the main culture. The Marxists and the liberal-radicals alike accept many characteristics of the technological state. They hope to retain the state apparatus and to turn it to their own purposes, a strategy the anarchists reject.

An example of differences between new and old anarchists arising from similar opposition to different cultures is the unpopularity today of any notion of a 'scientific' anarchism such as Kropotkin espoused. This is not because of any impossibility of formulating a 'scientific' argument for anarchism in the existing situation, but rather because at this time social scientific analysis is seen as part of the ideological arsenal of the state, whereas in Kropotkin's time tradition was the weapon of the state and scientific argument the preferred tool for social criticism. Today the metaphors used to argue for anarchism tend to be mystical, playfully irrational, or reactionary (harkening back to an earlier Utopia). This 'difference' between the new and old anarchists emerges from a constant core of opposition to the dominant system of apologetics.

Other elements in the new anarchism derive from the rejection of social arrangements that have no parallel in the arrangements the old anarchists rejected. The rejection of existing arrangements has a further characteristic: the new anarchists often find two alternative courses of action that are completely opposed but that share as their common denominator contempt for the 'appropriate' behaviour defined by the dominant culture. I think this accounts for the polar contradictions sustained without evidence of internal tension in the counter-culture. Practitioners of opposite ways of life recognize that they are similarly motivated.

For example, one finds in the counter-culture an intense attention to pure foods, air, and water and painstaking attention to the significance of the view that 'you are what you eat'. People go to great lengths to secure foods that have not been adulterated with chemicals. On the other hand one finds – sometimes even in the same people – an equally intense willingness to accept violent alterations in body chemistry that accompany experimentation with drugs. The dominant culture says that 'appropriate' behaviour involves unquestioning consumption of some chemically treated foods and pills that put you to sleep, cheer you up, tranquillize you, and make you feel normal, but panicky avoidance of other pills and drugs that 'inappropriately' change experience. Those who reject this have only two alternatives – to go all the way towards pure foods, or all the way into chemical experimentation (or both).

There is a similar reaction to dominant cultural definitions of 'appropriate' relations between men and women. The official ideology is a rather openly hypocritical assurance of 'equal opportunity' in work and 'mutuality' in sex. The counter-culture moves again toward the polarities: on the one hand, there is women's liberation and the convergence of sexual styles; on the other hand there are many communes in which women quite happily take an utterly subordinate and very stereotyped-traditional 'feminine' position. In sex one finds a greater insistence either on real mutuality or the very explicit acceptance of what the dominant culture defines as 'exploitation' – listen to the Rolling Stones and consider their popularity.

The dominant culture discovered that some self-knowledge was therapeutic and adapted psychoanalysis to its adjustive needs. In the counter-culture one finds often frightening inward trips with drugs and meditation, on the one hand, and a fierce rejection of analytic reductionism or the use of interpretation as a put-down on the other. The reaction against psychoanalytic concepts is in part taken in order to discount the self-serving psychological analysis of social deviance that the main culture employs as one of its chief propaganda weapons against the counter-culture. But in part it reflects the conviction that psychoanalysed but existentially un-examined life is not worth living.

A final example might be the counter-culture reaction to an utterly pervasive technology. The polar responses of the counter-culture are to reject technology completely for the simple life or to explore its vast potentials for play and exploration. Ken Kesey was one of the first to explore what could be achieved by joining the drugs technology made available with the incredible playful effects that could be produced with tape recorders, slide projectors, movie cameras, and so forth.[25]

Though historic anarchism may have shared the complete opposi-tion to existing society that characterizes the new anarchists, there are some psychological qualities in the new anarchists that appear to be expressions of contemporary development. One cannot ignore the very obvious fact that the emergence of the new anarchism parallels a general loosening of repressions in American society and a corollary change in the epidemeology of mental problems: today we hear relatively less about problems of repression and more about problems of ego-boundaries. This also parallels the rise of the use of drugs both in the dominant culture and in the counter-culture. Sick people are less often those trying to hold in too much and more often those who cannot hold in anything or feel they have nothing to hold things in with. Thus people in the counter-culture speak of 'freaking out' when the centre will no longer hold and of trying to 'get my head together' when trying to repair themselves. To say someone is a very 'together' person is a high compliment: it means

[25] See Tom Wolfe's brilliant recreation of Ken Kesey's early LSD experiences in *The Electric Kool-Aid Acid Test*, New York, Bantam edition, 1969.

he is able to maintain fluidity, flexibility, and capacity for regressive play and insight while still staying in one piece.

Difficulties in holding things in or knowing who one is arise particularly in adolescence. At that time, Erikson and others suggest, a capacity for regression and for some identity diffusion is a prerequisite for further differentiation of psychic capabilities and of a higher reintegration of these capabilities in adulthood.[26] It is the young who sometimes cannot hold together in the uncertainties of this period and it is also the young who are attracted at this time to anarchist communities. These communities offer a complete break with parental values and freedom 'to do what you want'; on the other hand the communities provide – as Godwin would have predicted – comfortingly forceful pressures towards a conformity to which the young person has assented.

In such communities people can experiment with regression and alternative identity fragments. Consider in this connection the role of drugs. It is universally recognized in the dominant culture that drugs contribute to pathologies of adolescent regression and identity confusion. The problem is that this truth is beaten into the ground. In the comic strips one finds Colonel Lee rescuing a good young boy from evil hippies while elsewhere on the page Rex Morgan, M.D., warns a father that his daughter may be addicted to one of the 'psychoto-mimetic drugs – so called because they mimic psychoses'. Psychologists patronizingly inquire why the young *need* to take drugs, and case histories of clearly pathological need are represented as the norm. Rarely does the dominant culture explore the possibility that drugs handled with some adequacy may contribute to psychological development. If 'thinking about thinking' and 'consciousness of consciousness' are attributes of post-formal cognitive development, why is it out of the question that drugs may facilitate progress in these areas?

Since the dominant culture refuses to explore this possibility the counter-culture, naturally, explores it with a vengeance. Where this exploration is going one cannot pretend to know, particularly since the cutting off of the supply of marijuana by the Nixon Administration has been followed by an epidemic of heroin use in urban high schools. The significance of drugs here is that they are widely credited in the counter-culture with putting people back in touch with feelings, sensations, capacities for play and visions of a freer way of life that were buried long ago. Even coming out of drugs or

26 Erik Erikson, *op. cit.*, pp. 162–3.

going beyond drugs may result in a belief in the possibility of living with fewer institutional and psychic mechanisms of repression. Thus I think one source of the idea of anarchist community is the drug-released vision of political and psychic life lived with fewer controls.

This observation is related to a point Keniston makes in describing what he believes is the emergence in post-industrial society of a post-adolescent stage of life that he calls youth. The specific psychological characteristics of 'youth' are many, but among them is a questioning 'post-conventional' morality that leads the young to question authority critically before obeying it. One can object to euphoria over this 'further' development of morality on the grounds that it would be disastrous for the society if it became widespread; that it would result in chaos or ... anarchy. Keniston's interesting and tentative response is that individuals who have passed safely through the regressions of adolescence and who have begun to reintegrate a more highly developed personality may have a capacity to sustain forms of social organization that less developed people could not sustain. Specifically, one might cite a critical morality, a cognitive capacity to see situations from the position of the other, and less anxiety over absence of institutional constraints as relevant to this capacity to sustain relationships with others in different ways. Thus chaos might *not* be the consequence in a population where higher levels of personality development were common, precisely because of the prevalence of a new capacity to enjoy anarchic communal relationships.[27]

My final obervation, then, is that – even if technological society does not require a turn to anarchism as the only alternative to annihilation or poisoning – technological society may, with its demands for highly developed workers, help to create men who *need* (as well as are capable of) interpersonal and ethical relationships of a different sort. The argument is both metaphysical and tendentious; but it is not at all impossible that technology will again – as it seems to have done in the past – participate in changing the life cycles of men who then bend technology to their new needs and capacities. If the counter-culture is at all prophetic of the way needs and capacities will change, the anarchist model and anarchist values may have more to do with the shape of future society than we have expected.

---

[27] Kenneth Keniston, 'Psychological Development and Historical Conditions', 1970 Yale, mimeograph. For the argument that the 'higher' psychological development *might* be socially disastrous, see Michael Lerner, 'Respectable Bigotry', *American Scholar*, Fall 1969.

J. Romero Maura

The Spanish Case

SPAIN IS THE WESTERN COUNTRY WHICH, SECOND ONLY TO PORTUGAL, holds the record for the most unmitigated, the most lasting and – by its own standards – the most successful domination of the extreme Right. None should be surprised, then, that after thirty-one years of determined authoritarian rule, Spanish anarchism should not be a significant force at present. Like all revolutionaries everywhere and always, Spanish anarchists in the past managed to gather some strength only when there was a degree of freedom allowing them to organize politically, unheard of in General Franco's regime, or else when dictators were afflicted by impotence in certain geographical areas, or by glaring imbecility, none of which has been the case in post-civil war Spain.

If it is impossible to say anything much about anarchism in Spain today, it would also be entirely futile to venture a forecast of future developments. Such an exercise would be totally sterile since it is not known what Spanish workers actually feel, how they perceive their own past, and what their expectations are for the future. It is not merely a matter of censorship; in fact the powers that be are only marginally better informed than the general public, because the best way of finding out about political attitudes is to study political behaviour, and this is hard to do when it is as seriously constricted as is the case in Spain. Indeed, blatant ignorance of what is going on in the minds of the ruled is a permanent feature of modern autocracy; the rulers may manage to turn this into an asset by capitalizing on fear of the unknown, but they cannot hope to free themselves of it. As for the interested observer, he will find it all the more difficult to prophesy in this case, because the difficulties resulting from a lack of data are supplemented by the impossibility of guessing what the masses, at present in a state of complete political demobilization, will do when mobilized in a society so different from that of pre-Franco Spain[1]

[1] For an attempt at establishing what elements of Spanish working-class

However, in this collection of essays dealing with the present and the future of anarchism, it may be useful to look back into the history of modern Spain – though exactly how useful will depend on the similarity of conditions then and now, and on the adaptability of anarchism to changed conditions, neither of which aspects can be treated in this essay, or indeed at all, it would seem, given the present state of the bibliography on these matters.

Recent literature – most of it with leftist overtones – has widely discussed a number of important issues related to the experience of Spanish anarchism. Interest has focused especially on problems connected with the seizure of power,[2] with anarchist participation in the Civil War governments of Largo Caballero and Negrín,[3] with the performance of anarchist collectivization.[4] 'Liberal' scholarship has also shown a certain amount of interest in the problems raised by anarchist revolutionarism in connection with the survival of the liberal state of 1931–36.[5] Issues have been clarified, and some books have brought fascinating new material to light, but on most counts the evidence remains inconclusive, and without much more new evidence the discussion can be very unrewarding.

The present essay will attempt to formulate a hypothetical

---

tradition have survived in the latter part of the Franco regime, see Jon Amsden, *Industrial Relations in Contemporary Spain: A Study of the Bargaining Process and Worker Participation under National Syndicalism* (Ph.D. Thesis, London, 1969, Unpubl.).

[2] Most of the Trotskyite literature deals with this problem. The main arguments of the Trotskyite approach in: *La Révolution Espagnole, 1936–9*, supplément à *Etudes Marxistes*, Nº 7–8, Paris, n.d., 1969.

[3] This subject is central to two of the best works on Spanish anarchism in the 1930s: John Brademas, *Revolution and Social Revolution. A Contribution to the History of the Anarcho-syndicalist Movement in Spain, 1930–1937* (D.Phil thesis, Oxford, 1953, Unpubl.) and César M. Lorenzo, *Les Anarchistes Espagnols et le Pouvoir, 1868–1969*, Paris, 1969.

[4] Collectivization has given rise to interminable arguments but little work on sources. The most comprehensive bibliography (until 1967) in Frank Mintz, 'La Collectivisation en Espagne, 1936–1939; Esquisse Bibliographique', in: *Archives Internationales de Sociologie de la Cooperation et du Développement*, Nº. 22, Suppl. à *Communauté*, VII–XII, 1967. The best summary, in F. Mintz, *L'Autogestion dans L'Espagne Révolutionnaire*, Paris, 1970. See also: Hugh Thomas, 'Anarchist Agrarian Collectives in the Spanish Civil War', in Martin Gilbert, ed., *A Century of Conflict, 1850–1950: Essays for A. J. P. Taylor*, London, 1967, pp. 245–63.

[5] Stanley Payne's *The Spanish Revolution*, London, 1970, provides the most complete analysis from this point of view.

explanation (given the state of our knowledge of Spanish anarchism, it is bound to be hypothetical) of a rather different problem, namely how it happened that the anarchist movement was so successful in building up a *mass* organization, largely based on industrial workers, with such powerful and sustained revolutionary drive.

This is in many ways a crucial question. And it is curious that those studying the elements required for revolutionary movements to emerge and prosper should have paid so little attention to the fact that many of the conclusions drawn from a variety of European and American experiences are – as we shall see – invalidated by the Spanish anarchist case-story. It is curious, but at the same time readily understandable, since the prevailing explanations of the anarchist phenomenon in Spain muster a whole range of causes with one thing in common: their specificity. And this supposed uniqueness of the Spanish background is held to make the example of Spanish anarchism irrelevant, unsuitable for generalizations deduced from more 'normal' experiences to be checked against. Although a detailed criticism of the predominant explanations would require more space than we have available, it can easily be shown that they are wholly inadequate.

THE SPANISH ROOTS

The main explanations why anarchism developed in Spain and nowhere else to the same extent may be grouped in five categories. The first of these seeks the answer in the specificity of the Spanish character. This romantic view of people living to the south of the Pyrenees has the virtue of fomenting tourism to Spain, but though explanations of this kind have been put forward by some serious writers,[6] they do not merit much attention, if only because the indigenous middle classes in Spain have never turned anarchist and do not seem ever to have been less attached to their worldly goods and interests than middle classes elsewhere.

The second and more serious explanation rests on the backwardness of the Spanish economy. According to this view, the small size of Catalan industries, a high illiteracy rate among the workers, the

[6] This view crops up from time to time in well-known books by Brenan, Borkenau and some others. Talk about the 'age-long ideas of death as liberation' in Spanish culture is still very fashionable (see e.g. G. Hills, *Spain*, London, 1970, p. 372); the argument can be found fully developed already in Chateaubriand and is no more adequately supported now than it was then.

latifundia of Andalusia, were breeding-grounds of anarchism.[7]
Apart from the fact that these conditions were by no means specifically Spanish, there is no clear pattern in Spanish conditions to make
this a generally valid explanation. The size of industries and the
modernity of the different industrial sectors have not been found to
relate consistently to the expansion of the different trade-union
denominations outside Spain.[8] Inside Spain, there is no evidence
either to support such a view.[9] As for illiteracy rates and the southern
latifundia, the success of the socialist *Federación Nacional de los
Trabajadores de la Tierra* in certain Andalusian provinces in the early
1930s is but one of the factors disproving an explanation couched in
these terms.[10]

Another common explanation is based on the idea that there must
be some sort of causal relationship between the fact that industrial
working-class anarchism was strongest in Catalonia and the emergence there of a powerful middle-class nationalist movement.
Nowhere is the argument put very clearly, but its major tenets may

[7] This hypothesis is summarized in most of its aspects in Pierre Vilar, *Histoire
d'Espagne*, Paris, 1958, pp. 80–1; J. Vicens Vives, *Cataluña en el siglo XIX*,
Madrid, 1961, pp. 254–60.

[8] Claude Willard, in *Les Guesdistes*, Paris, 1965, part III, has found no clear
correlations in this sphere, in his study of French socialism prior to 1905. On
the other hand the areas and industries where revolutionary syndicalism was
most widespread in Russia (see Paul Avrich, *The Russian Anarchists*, Princeton,
1967, chapters 3 & 8) would also seem to disprove the common interpretation
that socialism alone was equipped to penetrate the great modern industries.

[9] The evidence is very fragmentary. But there are too many examples to the
contrary. The union of typesetters was for a long time the socialist stronghold in
Madrid and the anarchist one in Barcelona. At the turn of the century, broadly
speaking, the miners of Asturias were socialist and the surface workers anarchist
(see David Ruiz, *El Movimiento Obrero en Asturias*, Oviedo, 1968, p. 100); it
seems, however, that at the start of the Civil War, a large proportion of Asturian
miners was anarchist (see C. M. Lorenzo, *Les Anarchistes*, p. 175, note 26); the
Catalan miners who rebelled in January 1932, were anarchists. In the early 1930s
the dockers of Barcelona and Gijón were anarchists, while those of Seville were
communists. Apparently the two main nuclei of anarchism in Madrid were the
construction workers ... and the employees of the Telephone Company. In
Barcelona and the rest of Catalonia, they do not seem to have controlled the
large textile mills and metallurgic plants any less than they did the small factories.

[10] For the progress made by socialism in Andalusia during the years of the
dictatorship, see Joaquín Maurín, *Los Hombres de la Dictadura*, Madrid, 1930,
pp. 197–9. On the FNTT, see G. Jackson, *The Spanish Republic and the Civil
War, 1931–1939*, Princeton, 1965, pp. 29, 79, 112. But the indispensable work on
this is Edward Malefakis, *Land Tenure, Agrarian Reform and Peasant Revolution in
Twentieth Century Spain* (Ph.D. Thesis, Columbia University, 1966).

be reduced to three points. First, there is the supposed influence of the autonomist views of the dominant Catalan culture; anarchism in Catalonia is considered to be a working-class translation of these views into a doctrine of social extremism. While the influence of Pi y Margall's theories on many of the early anarchists cannot be doubted,[11] it should not be forgotten that, because it was largely based upon a nationalist consciousness, Catalan autonomism tended to be despised by the internationalist-minded anarchists. Working-class ideals of self-government do not seem to have been stronger in Catalonia than in some other areas of Spain where there was no middle class with nationalist aspirations. The second tenet of this explanation is founded on the empirical fact that the Catalan middle classes failed to lead working-class discontent – the argument being that left-wing middle-class politicians, who in other countries and other parts of Spain were at the head of the socialist parties, failed in Catalonia to take up that leadership because of their exclusively nationalistic preoccupations. It is true that they failed, but not that they did not try hard.[12] Finally, the anarchist determination to have nothing to do with political power is held to reflect the Catalan nationalist indifference to national politics and to political power in itself. However fashionable it may have become to ascribe such indifference to the nationalists,[13] it simply was not so: the nationalists never gave up trying to influence Madrid; they never stopped sending deputies to the Cortes and they frequently exhibited what to many seemed an immoderate lust for power both in the times of the *Mancomunidad* and in the days of the *Generalidad*.

A fourth explanation of the Spanish anarchist phenomenon alleges that anarchism was the explosive result of a lack of political

---

[11] For a summary of this, see Federico Urales, *La Evolución de la Filosofía en España*, edited and with an introduction by R. Pérez de la Dehesa, Barcelona, 1968.

[12] The nationalist Left, from its formation as an independent political party in 1905, never stopped trying to carve out for itself a working-class base. Some of the foremost figures of this Left, like Corominas, Layret and Companys, had close personal relations with certain anarchists. But they failed. The best outline of the politics of the Republican Left is in Amadeu Hurtado, *Quaranta Anys d'Avocat*, 3 vols., Mexico, 1956, Barcelona, 1964, 1967.

[13] This indifference of nationalists to national politics is one of the main myths of the Left about modern Spain. It is all the more curious since most relatively elaborate analyses reject it. The argument, complete, is in A. Ramos Oliveira, *Politics, Economics and Men of Modern Spain – 1808-1946*, London, 1946, pp. 380-93.

freedom. The safety-valve metaphor is popular but based on a mis-representation of Spanish modern history, while failing to take into account the plain fact we have already referred to, that anarchism and other revolutionary movements have only been strong in conditions where other, more moderate political alternatives *were* available.[14]

The fifth interpretation of libertarian strength and influence in Spain ascribes the phenomenon to the disillusionment of the workers with a liberal-democratic constitution which gave the workers no real power.[15] This explanation, even if it works in the context of restoration politics, obviously fails to account for the fact that anarchism was never as strong as under the Second Republic of 1931–36, when the constitution did afford the masses a significant measure of real power.

In the beginning, there was Giuseppe Fanelli, the ex-Mazzinian, one of Garibaldi's Thousand and a follower of Bakunin. He gave social context, as well as under economic conditions, not obviously different from what, in other parts of Spain and elsewhere, allowed the rise of flourishing socialist and communist organizations. Naturally, this neither proves nor disproves that anarchism could have thrived just as well under very different conditions, as did its Marxist competitors. But it is clear from what we have pointed out that Spanish anarchism, with its revolutionary virulence, was *not* the only form which working-class social consciousness and political discontent could possibly have taken under the then prevailing above mentioned conditions – which is what the standard explanations in fact imply.

The explanation of Spanish anarcho-syndicalism's success in organizing a mass movement with a sustained revolutionary *élan* should initially be sought in the very nature of the anarchist conception of society and of how to achieve revolution. The rest of this essay will attempt to outline the ways in which that conception was generated, why it made the formation of a mass revolutionary movement possible and, last but by no means least, how strict adherence to the original conceptions in matters of organization allowed the movement to retain its drive over a long period of time.

[14] It is ever more difficult to find in the books of professional historians over-simplified versions of the restoration as a period of unmitigated *caciquismo*. But the official Spanish historiography continues to stick to this version. Outside Spain, one example of this version is J. Connelly Ullman, *The Tragic Week: a Study of Anticlericalism in Spain, 1875–1912*, Harvard, 1968.

[15] See Payne, *Spanish Revolution*, p. 21.

ORIGINS AND BACKGROUND

There is a widespread impression that anarchism always fascinated
the Spanish masses and that it remained more or less unchanged in
Spain since the times of the First International. But this is a distorted
view of what actually happened. Anarchism did not become a mass
movement in Spain until the final years of the first world war. Its
basic outlook changed radically in the course of time, and it is only
once the anarcho-syndicalist conception had crystallized that
Spain's libertarians succeeded in transforming their movement into
a mass organization. The Spanish anarcho-syndicalist formula was
the outcome of a long, painful and complex process of theoretical
adjustment of the original libertarian doctrines.

In the beginning, there was Guiseppe Fanelli, the ex-Mazzinian,
one of Garibaldi's Thousand and a follower of Bakunin. He gave
birth to the first Spanish group of the International in 1868. At its
Congress of Córdoba in 1872, the 'Spanish Region', firmly in the
hands of the anarchists, had already a membership of 25,000. It
would appear that by 1874 the 50,000 mark had been reached. On
9 January of that year, the International was outlawed by the government; it was to remain underground for seven years.

The anarchist doctrine of the first period was anarcho-collectiv-
ism: Bakunin's own doctrine. The general principles are well known
and need only to be summarized here: anarchists believed that the
only way of turning society into a just society was to overturn it.
It was essential to annihilate the power of the state. Revolution was
a matter of superior firing power and it was up to the workers to
organize to that effect. The anarchist revolution, when it came,
would be essentially brought about by the working class. Revolutionaries needed to gather great strength and must beware of under-
estimating the strength of reaction: here, Bakuninism – at least in
its pre-Nechayev phase – was far more realistic than Blanquism.

Since their doctrine obliged them to desist from any participation,
however indirect, in the established political institutions, so that
they could not set themselves up as an anarchist party, the Bakuninists logically decided that revolutionaries had better organize along
the lines of labour organizations. This was approved at the first
anarchist congress of the 'Spanish Region' in Barcelona in 1870.
The basic cell was to be the local craft union. All the craft unions of
different crafts in the same area were bound together into one local

federation. All local federations converged in the Spanish Federal Committee.

The leaders of the 1870 Congress foresaw what difficulties could arise from such a structure and they planned another parallel system of organizational linkage, whereby every local craft union would be linked to other unions of the same craft located elsewhere through a national federation of that craft. But the different national federations had no link with each other, and in fact this parallel structure never developed. In the following months, the structure of the Spanish Federation was modified in various minor ways, but the essential fact remained, namely that action in the Spanish Federation could only be co-ordinated through the area units (local, county, regional) instead of through corporative units of the same craft or trade. The Bakuninists intended to strengthen the Spanish Federation until it could destroy the bourgeois state. More and more workers would be drawn into the anarchist unions, where they would be educated for revolution. When revolution came, it would bring a stateless but strongly organized society, a society in which the idle would get nothing and the Federation would rule. Because of its educational role in the present and its executive role in a revolutionary society to come, the Federation was sacred. It had to be preserved above all. It was not to meddle, therefore, in routine affairs. It was not to lend itself to provocation. Partial wage claims and material demands were discouraged as pointless and could only be allowed as long as they did not endanger the Federation. Any untimely violent action would be thoroughly condemned and immediately disowned.

With this blueprint in mind, the leaders set about their task. By the time the Federation was declared illegal, as a part of the general European scare following the Commune, the main body of workers who had joined the International were the textile hands of the Catalan region. Their previously existing resistance associations had joined the Federation without really changing their basic reformist outlook. With but few exceptions, revolutionary activities were limited to revolutionary indoctrination. During the years in the underground, the leaders fought hard to preserve what they could of the Federation. They knew that only with a return to legality could it hope to prosper, and any talk of countering the legal ban with reprisals was short-lived and easily silenced. When it was allowed to function openly again, the Federation had some 3,000 members.

The leaders reorganized along the same lines as before 1874. At the Seville Congress of 1882 the Federation had a membership of almost 60,000 workers throughout Spain. But this time the overall picture was totally different. For, instead of being concentrated in the industrial areas of Catalonia, anarchism was now almost equally strong in the North East and the South. A few thousand Andalusian landless labourers were recruited into the reborn organization. The second period of the Spanish Federation began auspiciously.

Yet catastrophe was round the corner. In the previous period, the leadership had found it relatively easy to compromise with the practical reformism of the Catalan affiliated unions: peaceful demonstrations or strikes for better wages may have appeared to true anarchists a rather fruitless exercise, but it did not endanger the Federation. In the South, however, as Salvemini was to tell Italian socialists a little later with regard to the *mezzogiorno*, there was no room for reformism. To the militants there, the only therapy of any use was the seizure of the land, since the one great malady was land hunger. This was made plain by a large peasant uprising in the South at the end of 1882, known as the Black Hand episode. The leaders of the Federation could not take the side of the impatient Andalusians and, anxious above all to protect their organization, they branded the rebels as common criminals. The Federation's decision was perfectly coherent with its theoretical premises, which did not allow for anything other than doctrinal education before the actual dawning of revolution. Many southern leaders appreciated this, and their answer to the decision which disowned them partly took the form of a theoretical revision of Bakuninism. In a very short time, they were converted to anarcho-communism, the doctrine whose main advocates were Malatesta and Kropotkin.

Anarcho-communism retained intact the view that revolution was ultimately a matter of superior firing power, but attacked Bakunin's collectivism on the grounds that it was egoistic and soulless. Future society would be communist, and the Federation itself would disappear. The new doctrine was also rather more doubtful than Bakunin had been about the revolutionary role of the working class as such and insisted more than he had done on the importance of revolutionary ideals and values.

It is only natural that the militants of the South should have embraced a doctrine denying any future usefulness to a Federation which weighed them down in the present. The controversy opposing anarcho-collectivists and anarcho-communists lasted from 1882 to

1888. It was basically a conflict between Catalan and Andalusian anarchists. When reconciliation came at the Valencia Congress of 1888, it took place over the dead body of collectivism. In fact, the collectivist leaders of Catalonia themselves had grown tired of the reformism of their federated unions. These had been successful, annoyingly so, since they had attracted some of the most unrevolutionary workers – republican, even catholic or Carlist workers – who joined in because of the prospects of immediate material rewards. The trade unionist mentality, as Lenin was to call it, was becoming ever stronger. In despair, the militant leaders became convinced that it was impossible to organize revolutionaries along the pattern of labour organizations, and that trade unions would never become revolutionary even if they were led by anarchists. At Valencia, therefore, they practically dissolved the Federation.[16]

Spanish anarchists then opted for the obvious alternative: revolutionaries would organize as groups of like-minded men bent on revolution. These groups would not be a party, because discipline was not thought necessary. While militants might carry on struggling within the unions as much as they pleased, meaningful revolutionary action would be the province of the *grupos de afinidad* alone.

The militants withdrew from the unions, to a very large extent it seems. This isolated them. Their publications were little read and their revolutionary preachings went unheeded. Then the idea came naturally to some, that the toiling masses could not fail to get the message if it was shouted loud enough. The hope that deeds would do what words had failed to do set off a wave of terrorism. Most anarchists, and the entire leadership, were opposed to bomb throwing; but they had lost all power to make the hot-heads obey them. Ruthless repression destroyed the last remnants of organization in the mid-1890s. Many of the ablest leaders fled the country, never to return. Then came the colonial wars against the Cuban and Philippine rebellions, and the Spanish–American war of 1898. Only after that was over and constitutional liberties were restored, could the anarchists come back into public life.

[16] The main secondary sources for the period 1868–1874 are: Casimiro Martí, *Orígenes del Anarquismo en Barcelona*, Barcelona, 1959; José Termes Ardévol, *El Movimiento Obrero en España: La Primera Internacional 1864–1881*, Barcelona, 1965; Clara E. Lida, *Orígenes del Anarquismo español: 1868–1884* (Ph.D. Thesis, Princeton, 1968, unpublished). For the period 1874–1888, Max Nettlau's, *La Première Internationale en Espagne 1868–1888*, is essential, edited by Renée Lamberêt, Dordrecht, 1969. For the Black Hand, see C. E. Lida, 'Agrarian Anarchism in Andalusia' in *International Review of Social History*, *XIV*, 1969, part 3, pp. 315–52.

If there was one thing the experiences of the 1890s had impressed on the few remaining anarchists, it was that terrorism was not the proper instrument to awaken the anaesthetized workers. On the other hand, it simply would not do just to preach revolution. What then? The answer was brought from neighbouring France by returning libertarian émigrés: the general revolutionary strike. At the turn of the century, Catalan anarchists fervently advocated the general strike as the 'only possible' road to revolution.

The adoption of the formula of the general strike in Spain at that time was in many ways a much more superficial phenomenon than has been supposed. Catalan anarchists remained anarcho-communists, and therefore retained their basic distrust of the revolutionary potential of trade unions. They also stuck to their insurrectionist conception of the final battle. Their general strike would essentially amount to an armed mass rising. The important thing, here, is that their enthusiasm for the general strike showed that anarchists in Catalonia had realized at last that participation of the masses in the revolutionary venture from the very beginning was essential.

The general strike was tried in February 1902. Barcelona's hundred and fifty thousand workers struck for a week: but the strike was no more than an exhibition of strength and dignity, followed by a peaceful return to work. Then, in the 1903 elections, the workers of Catalonia voted massively for the Republican Party and for its leader in Barcelona, Alejandro Lerroux. The anarchists mistakenly thought that the workers followed the latter because of the demagogy of his public speeches rather than because of his reformist policies. This misapprehension led them to deduce that they ought to look more revolutionary than Lerroux: a new terrorist phase began.

The outcome was, once more, that the workers turned their backs on such dangerous preachers and maintained their allegiance to the Republican Party, which seemed to them their only effective protector against an exasperated police force. By 1907, the anarchists in Catalonia were more lonely and forsaken than they had ever been, more so even than in the 1890s, for this time, thanks to Lerroux, they were not even persecuted, and instead of being pitied victims, many were taken for provocateurs.[17]

[17] For the terrorism of the 1890s, the best sources are still R. Mella and J. Prat, *La Barbarie Gubernamental en España*, Brooklyn – in fact Barcelona – 1897, and the *roman à clef* of R. Sempau, *Los victimarios*, Barcelona, 1901. For the evolution of the syndical and labour movement in those years, there are hardly any secondary sources. For the terrorism of the first decade of the century, a synthesis in my article in *Past and Present*, December, 1968.

The leadership realized its mistake: the workers' infatuation with Lerroux showed in fact how far they were from sharing the anarchists' longing for revolution. At the same time, more and more anarchist sympathizers in the workshops protested against those they disparagingly called 'the philosophers', i.e. the promoters of that anarchist intransigence which had substantially contributed to the exodus of non-anarchist workers from anarchist-dominated craft-unions. The anarcho-communist tactic of not caring about the unions at all, or else of infiltrating them only to blow them up in an attempt to throw them into the revolutionary battle without giving the least thought to the daily struggles of the members had, together with the adverse economic situation, destroyed the Barcelona craft unions. Every day employers were growing stronger and more insolent.

SOLIDARIDAD OBRERA TO CNT

In order to put a stop to this, a group of militants held several informal meetings, convening thereafter a more formal one where they proposed that a Federation of working-class associations in the Barcelona area should be formed. The proposed aims were the betterment of present conditions and the education of the workers for their future emancipation. The idea was welcomed with unexpected enthusiasm in working-class quarters. So much so that the organizers, after a year of preparatory work, convened a Catalan Congress of the working class. A Catalan Federation, named *Solidaridad Obrera*, was the product of this congress. On the crest of the wave, the organizers convened a further meeting in order to turn the organization into a nationwide one: in October 1910 the CNT was born.[18] The Spanish anarcho-syndicalist formula had been found. Authors who have studied this evolution see the events of 1907–10 either as a resurrection of Bakuninist tactics or as a Spanish importation of French revolutionary syndicalism. It is essential to understand that it was not so.

In spite of the surface similarity of the 1870 and the 1907–10 strategies of fighting for revolution from within the unions, the

[18] Since there are no monographic studies on the penetration of revolutionary syndicalist ideas in the Catalan anarchist movement of that time, the best basic sources are the collections of *La Huelga General*, in Barcelona, *El Trabajo*, of Sabadell and *Solidaridad Obrera* also of Barcelona.

founders of *Solidaridad Obrera* and of the CNT contributed something essential which was wanting in Bakuninism: a philosophy of the daily struggle. It was normal that in 1908–9 the anarchist militants, who were workers also, should decide to devote all their efforts to putting an end to the anaemia of the unions and the defencelessness of their class; but they now had a theory which made this not only possible but advisable, even necessary. The theory was that of French revolutionary syndicalism, whose conception of direct action dignified the daily struggle of the workers against their employers by making the smallest act of factory indiscipline a revolutionary act. Direct action meant *ouvriérisme*, the refusal to co-operate in any institutional mechanisms of solving labour problems, whose function was to cloak the inevitable antagonism between the classes. Strikes, boycotts, sabotage and the label were to be the normal weapons for pressing their demands. Every concession wrested from the employers or from the state would thus be war booty and not a conciliation bonus. 'Revolutionary gymnastics' would temper the revolutionary character of the workers in readiness for the last assault.

But here the similarity between French revolutionary syndicalism and Spanish anarcho-syndicalism ends, for even though the latter aspired like the former to the general strike, the anarcho-syndicalists did not see in it a panacea for a practically bloodless revolution. The old collectivist and communist conception of the final struggle as an armed insurrection was not abandoned. *In this respect,* Pierre Monatte's utterances at the Amsterdam Congress were bound to seem nonsensical to the men of *Solidaridad Obrera* who agreed all the way with Malatesta.[19] When the militants set about inaugurating their brand-new strategy, the French CGT was becoming increasingly reformist. Victor Griffuelhes would soon be out, and under Jouhaux the CGT was soon to corroborate once more what the social-democrats had always been saying and what the experience of Spanish Bakuninism had indeed borne out, i.e. that revolutionaries cannot organize in trade unions and yet expect to constitute a truly revolutionary organization.

In the first years, the CNT managed to preserve its revolutionary temper, but it did not really get off the ground. By the beginning of the first world war it had not yet reached the modest peak figures attained in the early 1880s by the Spanish Federation. It had been

[19] See the *Freedom* pamphlet: *The International Anarchist Congress held at Plancius Hall, Amsterdam, on August 26–31, 1907*, London, 1907.

outlawed for three years (1911–14), because of its militancy, directed not only against employers but also against the colonial policies of the restoration. But these were very important years for the CNT, because they produced a generation of young, tough and able syndicalist leaders.

Then, with the war, food prices shot up, with wages lagging far behind; the industries of neutral Spain were working three shifts for the Allies, and the conditions were next to ideal for a powerful and militant trade-union movement to take root. The CNT, with only 15,000 members in 1915, grew very quickly. In Catalonia alone, there were more than 70,000 members by mid-1918. An organization that size could not keep on growing without giving itself a new structure. It was the problems raised by the transition from minority unionism to mass-unionism that compelled the Catalan Region of the CNT to convene the June 1918 Congress in Sans. The Congress decided that the workers should be organized locally on a product basis: craft unions would disappear and all the workers involved in a given industrial activity would be grouped in one union, e.g. the *sindicato único* of the building trades, of metallurgy, etc. Then, following the pattern laid down by the Spanish Federation in the 1870s, it was decided that the different unions should be organized on a territorial basis. All *sindicatos únicos* in a given town would be grouped in the local federation; then there would be county federations grouping the representatives of the local federations; all county federations would be bound together in a Catalan Regional Confederation. The Congress then voted the suppression of union dues on the grounds that union funds lead to union bureaucracy; whenever necessary, strike funds would be raised *ad hoc* by the federations and only a very small levy should be paid by members for the sustenance of the Confederal press and of the only paid full-time official of the Confederation in Catalonia: its secretary.

The Madrid Congress of December 1919 confirmed the outlook of the Sans Congress. A proposal to create National Federations of Industry following the traditional socialist model was rejected as unrevolutionary. It was decided that only the secretaries of the Regional Federations and the secretary of the National Committee of the CNT, should receive any remuneration at all, however meagre. In order to nip bureaucratic tendencies in the bud, and in order to enable members of the National Committee (NC) to go on working in their normal factory jobs, it was decided that the NC would always reside in a given region; the National Congress of the

CNT would each time designate the region, and the NC would be appointed by the members of that region from amongst themselves. This structural peculiarity was to be preserved right up to 1936, with only minor modifications. Major changes in the formal disposition were approved in later Congresses, but the organization went on working along the lines laid down in 1918–19.[20] The militancy of the CNT is so well-known that there is no need to go into details here. Its membership figures were very impressive: more than 700,000 members by the end of 1918 and more than a million two years later. But these were the years of the revolutionary tide in Europe. When it receded, the strength of the CNT dwindled also: the years 1921 to 1923 were terrible ones for Spanish anarchism. The economic crisis produced by the loss of export markets spawned a three-cornered terrorism, opposing trade unions, employers and the state, which helped to provoke the dictatorship of Primo de Rivera. Between 1923 and 1931 the CNT all but disappeared. When the Second Republic was inaugurated in April 1931, the political pendulum throughout Europe had swung to the Right, and economic conditions did not seem to favour a rebirth in Spain of a strong revolutionary CNT. Besides, the Socialist Party had held throughout all the years of the dictatorship a monopoly of organized labour and had a well oiled machine together with a substantial share in the new government. But the CNT emerged stronger than ever: half a million members in June 1931, more than double that figure in 1932, one million six hundred thousand members by July 1936.[21]

Designed not to stifle the revolutionary *élan* of its members, the

[20] The structure given to the CNT in 1918–19 had its origins in the Spanish Bakuninist Federation and in the French CGT. But it was a peculiarity of the CNT to refuse to organize Federations of Industries. The Madrid Congress of 1931 decided that these Federations should be formed, but the extremists prevented the ruling from being put into practice. A further point which needs stressing is that – in spite of the lack of adequate statistics on Spain – the experience of the French CGT in its first period seems to prove that the scarcity of strike funds did not have an adverse effect on the effectiveness of the strikes (see comparative figures in Carl Landauer, *European Socialism: A History of Ideas and Movements*, Berkeley, Los Angeles, 1959, I, p. 347).

[21] Little is known about the CNT until 1917. For the period prior to 1923, the best sources are: M. Buenacasa, *El Movimiento Obrero Español: 1886–1926: Figuras Ejemplares*, Paris, 1966; Albert Balcells, *El Sindicalismo a Barcelona, 1916–1923*, Barcelona, 1965. For the period of the dictatorship and the republic, apart from the aforementioned works by Brademas and C. M. Lorenzo, see the books by José Peirats, *La CNT en la Revolución Española*, Toulouse, 1953, vol. I, and *Los Anarquistas en la Crisis Española*, Buenos Aires, 1964.

structure of the CNT actually helped in a very direct way to foment it. The *sindicato único*, by placing all the workers in a given factory under the one umbrella of a single union, imposed the militancy of the majority of unskilled workers on the labour aristocracy. The territorial basis of organization linkage brought all the workers from one area together and fomented working-class solidarity over and before corporative solidarity. In this, the Spanish experience vindicated Fernand Pelloutier's passionate defence of the revolutionary virtues inherent in the territorial formula of the *Bourses du Travail* – something the history of the Italian *Camere del lavoro* had already corroborated.[22]

Quite as important, if not more so, were the effects of the policy of the non-remuneration of the Confederation's officials. This, together with the paucity of union funds that had to be administered, prevented the formation of a middle-class bureaucracy within the trade union movement similar to that which developed in other European countries. In fact, it prevented the formation of any bureaucracy whatsoever, and all the consequences that go with bureaucratic hypertrophy, which were analysed all too aptly by sympathizers of revolutionary syndicalism in Europe.[23] The non-remuneration policy operated a selection of leaders among the most dedicated, men who owned nothing and remained entrenched in their *refus de parvenir*.[24]

There was another aspect where the organizational pattern of the

---

[22] For the *Bourses du Travail* and the underlying conception, see Fernand Pelloutier, *Histoires des Bourses du Travail*, Introduction by G. Sorel, Paris, 1902; also, Paul Delesalle, *Les Bourses du Travail et la CGT*, Paris, n.d. For the *Camere del lavoro* and the specifically Italian aspects, an essential work is G. Procacci, 'La Classe operaia agli inizi del secolo XX', in *Studi Storici, a III*. N°. 1, 1962. See also, I. Barbadoro, 'Problemi e Caratteristiche Storiche de Movimento Sindicale Italiano', in *Rivista Storica de Socialismo, ci*, 19, 1963.

[23] The warnings by the theoreticians of revolutionary syndicalism on the dangers of party bureaucracy were not taken seriously by the men of the Second International. However, it should be remembered that Robert Michels, author of the great classic on this subject, was a revolutionary syndicalist of sorts from the very beginning. Another interesting book in this context is Arturo Labriola, *Il Socialismo Contemporaneo*, Rocca San Giovanni, 1914, where he speaks of the dangers, for the socialist revolution, of the formation of a 'new class' (p. 281).

[24] Another important consequence of the policy of non-remuneration of union officials was that all the positions were always occupied by members of the unions and that for them to remain at their post, not only was their capacity taken into account, but also they had to be re-elected as representatives of their local union.

CNT reinforced its revolutionary tendencies, and this was the very looseness of its organizational links. In-built indiscipline, for all its obvious defects, had the advantage of neutralizing in advance any attempt by governments to penetrate the leadership, and to bribe or threaten individual leaders who had few means of enforcing moderating policies. Provocation, of course, was more easily engineered, but then it was always so easy to provoke the CNT. . . .

Social democratic and communist contemporary critics of the CNT have been joined by all later historians of the movement in branding its endless sequence of general strikes and risings as an irresponsible wastage of its revolutionary potential. There can be no doubt that vast strikes like the second *Canadiense* strike of 1919 in Barcelona, or the Saragossa strike of March–April 1934, where enormous energy was spent on the liberation of a few jailed militants or for the reinstallment of a few dismissed workers, did temporarily weaken the actual strength of the CNT. But a closer analysis of the history of the Confederation would seem to suggest that the above-mentioned critics are mistaken in thinking of the revolutionary potential of the CNT masses as a fixed stock which could have been administered in a much better way. In fact, everything points to the conclusion that all this revolutionary potential was generated *in the course of* and thanks to that apparently wasteful activism.

This is not so contradictory as it sounds, if one takes into account what is known of the dynamics of certain groups with a strong subculture. The lack of CNT direct participation in political institutions, and the ways in which it was structured contributed to keep the influence of well-intentioned middle-class sympathizers to a minimum.[25] *Ouvriérisme* was not only a slogan but also a reality. Then, constant activity in common originated a maximum of interpersonal communication not only among the leaders but also between them and the rank and file, and among all the members; this contributed very powerfully to the diffusion of the values of the CNT subculture, and strengthened its cohesion. Common efforts and sufferings – 'revolutionary gymnastics' – welded the group together

[25] The only instance of a continued collaboration between middle-class individuals and the CNT involved the left-wing lawyers. But this was a very limited phenomenon. Besides, when it organized, the CNT, unlike Italian syndicalism, had no middle-class intellectuals in its leadership. Unlike the French CGT it did not even have bourgeois intellectuals who, without being members themselves, could give theoretical coherence to syndicalist practice. This phenomenon, which has its parallel in the late date at which the Spanish Socialist Party started to recruit intellectuals, has not yet been explained satisfactorily.

as a whole, while repression in turn triggered off inside the CNT the familiar defence mechanisms consisting in the inversion of values, self-assertion and the like.[26]

The logic of maximum dramatization not only forged a militant spirit, the like of which the parties of the Second and Third International could never induce in their mass following; it also had a very direct effect upon the dominant orientation of the CNT leadership. Indeed, while the organizational features of the CNT account for the dedication of its leadership, the reasons for the systematic exclusion of the more moderate elements in favour of the more violent men lies here. The mechanics of elimination of the less extremist were always the same: the more violent would die or go to jail as a consequence of some direct action; the compassion and the indignation of the confederal masses would explode in a wave of protest; violent protests would bring to the fore a group of violent leaders. But even when the membership could not be induced to demonstrate massively or riotously, the more moderate leaders could not prevent the extremists from elbowing them aside by making full use of the organization, and of the confederal press and strength, for 'free-the-prisoners' campaigns and for raising funds to help prisoners and their families and pay for their legal expenses. That is how Seguí lost control to the terrorists in the early 1920s, how the *Treintistas* were ousted from the CNT in the early 1930s, and how the FAI gained control of the CNT during the Republic by means of its *Comités pro-Presos*.[27]

REFORMISM AND REVOLUTION

What has been said so far should provide, it is to be hoped, a coherent framework to explain how the Spanish anarcho-syndicalist

[26] This outline of the dynamics of subcultures follows the model described by A. K. Cohen in his classic book: *Delinquent Boys. – The Culture of the Gang*, Glencoe, 1955. A synthesis of later literature on the subject is in M. E. Wolfgang and F. Ferracuti, *The Subculture of Violence – Towards an Integrated Theory in Criminology*, London, 1967.

[27] Not only the better known leaders of the FAI needed to be capable of facing up personally to violent situations. See for example the case of Emilio Boal (Buenacasa, *Movimiento*, pp. 251–7) and that of Mariano Vázquez (M. Muñoz Diez, *Marianet: Semblanza de un Hombre*, Mexico, 1960). The best study of the process by which the gunmen imposed their will on the moderates in the first years after the first world war is Angel Pestaña, *Lo que Aprendí en la Vida*,

formula emerged and how the first group of toughened and dedicated militants was formed; also, how they managed to capture the leadership of a working class which craved material betterment, and how the organizational and tactical methods of the CNT resulted in keeping the revolutionary flame alight. This, however, leaves two critical questions unanswered: firstly, why were the CNT masses converted to a revolutionary approach in the first place? And secondly, how was it that the CNT masses, or indeed the CNT leaders, did not abandon the Confederation as a consequence of the inadequacy of the anarcho-syndicalist conception for understanding the nature of modern society, and coping with it.

The first question is easier to answer than the second. There is little doubt that the economic, social and political conditions prevailing in Spain during the years 1917–20 provided an ideal soil for the revolutionary seed to germinate in. From October 1917 to the retreat of the Red Army before Warsaw in 1920, the 'revolutionary tide' welled up as strongly in Spain as elsewhere and this is not surprising.[28]

The second question in fact raises the problem why the reformist social democratic, or alternatively the communist conceptions did not impose themselves on the CNT as they managed to do in most of the rest of Europe. This question appears regularly in the literature on Spanish anarchism, and is based on the false assumption that the anarcho-syndicalist conception of the workers' struggle in pre-revolutionary society was completely at odds with what the *real* social process signified (hence the constant reference to 'religious' 'messianic' models as explanations).

There are several reasons why the reformist conceptions of European social democracy should not have struck the CNT members as being in anyway superior to their own. The parties of the Second International largely shared the belief that trade union demands, if successful, would weaken capitalism because the very nature of capitalism made it impossible for all or a substantial part of these demands to be granted. Hence the emphasis on exclusively

Madrid, n.d. 1933. For the failure of *Treintismo* and the use of the *Comités-pro-Presos* by the FAI, see Brademas, *A Contribution . . .*, chapters 3 and 4.

[28] Salvador Seguí was without a doubt the ideal leader of the CNT in the period of its initial growth, when it had to transform the essentially materialist aspirations of new members into a revolutionary spirit. Inevitably, he was pushed aside later. There is no detailed biography of Seguí; the best source is J. Viadiu *et al.*, *Salvador Seguí, su vida, su obra*, Paris, 1960.

material demands, in what Edouard Berth called *le socialisme du moindre effort*. When it was discovered that capitalism could afford to concede much more than had been thought, the leaders generally had no difficulty in pesuading their followers that they should stick to a reformist line; for the main propaganda plank of socialist organizations had always been the claim that only they could achieve material betterment for the working class.[29] Perhaps the weakness of Spanish capitalism reduced the prospects of reformism in Spain, but it is probably more important to point out that the demands of the CNT went much further than those of any social democrats: with its emphasis on true equality, *autogestión* and working-class dignity, anarcho-syndicalism made demands on the capitalist system which it could not possibly grant to the workers, at any rate nowhere to the same extent as the measure of improvements conceded in the sphere of better wages and more security. Its own subculture thus protected the CNT against reformism.

The attitude of the CNT to the problem of collaboration with the state and with bourgeois institutions inoculated it against reformist influence. Initially, the social democrats and the anarchists had agreed that the state was the instrument of bourgeois domination. In due course, Millerandism and other forms of less direct collaboration showed that the bourgeois state would become less bourgeois if the workers were prepared to fight for a share in it. The reason why this was never apparent to the CNT is because the CNT put the onus on the state of proving its reformist virtues while making it almost impossible, through continued harassment, for the state to do just that. The impasse was not merely the result of anarchist demands being such as were almost impossible for the state to grant, but also of a situation where anarchist principles of non-collaboration with public labour institutions like the *Instituto de Reformas Sociales* prevented these from being useful. Meanwhile the CNT commitment to electoral abstention provided political parties with little incentive to antagonize their middle-class voters by sponsoring policies which would not yield any immediate returns at the polls. Under these conditions, what few pro-working-class laws were enacted were naturally seen by the CNT as symptoms of the enemy's weakness or fear, and received with marked ingratitude.

There were, in other parts of Europe at the beginning of the

[29] For an excellent synthesis of aims and methods of recruitment of English and German unions, see Arnold J. Heidenheimer, 'Trade Unions, Benefit Systems and Party Mobilization Styles', *Comparative Politics*, I, 3 April 1969.

century, organizations and militants to whom the reformist policies of social democracy appeared far from commendable. There, revolutionary conscience took the form of bolshevism or of revolutionary syndicalism; by 1920 at the latest, the second of these was dead and the former alone remained as a revolutionary party. The basic reason why Spanish anarcho-syndicalism did not follow the same process seems perfectly clear; its underlying conceptions did not let it down in the way that the conceptions of revolutionary syndicalists failed them elsewhere.

Although too little is known as yet of the growth and decay of French and Italian revolutionary syndicalism, one thing is plain enough, namely that their conception of the revolutionary general strike was a dangerous myth. The general strike of the syndicalists was not, as is so frequently claimed, an economic strike. It was to be a general *prise de possession*, accompanied by a degree of violence. But the idea of the general strike was conceived as an alternative to armed insurrection, after the French Commune seemed to have proved categorically, once and for all, that armed insurrection was bound to be defeated by the armies of the bourgeois state. French and Italian syndicalists thought that the general strike, by atomizing violence and preventing through sabotage the co-ordination of the state's effort, would make the use of conventional armies against the workers impossible. This was an illusion, as is shown by the ease with which statesmen have dealt with general strikes since as long ago as 1904. Already in 1901, Jaurès had warned the CGT leaders that they were being irresponsible by letting the workers think that they could attain the syndicalist revolution without having to fight arms in hand: 'la grève générale... ruse avec la classe ouvrière'.

Anarcho-communists in the Italian USI realized the dangers of this mistake, but for all Armando Borghi's efforts they could not impose their views on a movement they did not control. In Spain, however, this misjudgement never gained ground. As has already been pointed out, the founders of *Solidaridad Obrera* and of the CNT had an anarcho-communist background, so much so that – contrary to the programme of revolutionary syndicalism elsewhere – their avowed aim was to the end *comunismo libertario*. They never relinquished the anarcho-communist conception of the final battle as one which would be decided by sheer force. In this way, failed CNT uprisings could be accounted for in terms of excessive rashness, but not of a gross misconception of the nature of the struggle – a vital difference this, since failures due to mere rashness are more likely to result in prudence than in desertion.[30]

From this perspective it is easier to understand that communism was not to find in Spain the opportunities it had in France to capitalize before the Polish fiasco on the disillusionment of revolutionaries with the syndicalist strategy of the general strike. The CNT was, of course, impressed by the October Revolution, to the point of actually joining the Red Trade-Union International. But the Confederation was only impressed in so far as it seemed that the revolution in Russia meant power to the people and the Soviets: had not the *April Theses* and *State and Revolution* been regarded by many in Russia itself as quasi anarchist pamphlets? Then CNT travellers

[30] Jacques Julliard in *Clemenceau Briseur de Grèves*, Paris, 1965, pp. 123–40, has shown how the CGT lost its impetus and its revolutionary leadership already with the fall of Griffuelhes and his replacement by Niel in 1909. But the syndicalist *conception* of the revolution was still strong in the French working-class movement until the events of 1920 and the consequent disillusionment; the standard work on this is Annie Kriegel, *Aux Origines du Communisme Français 1914–1920*, Paris, 1964, 2 vols. The Italian case is more complex and has been studied less; the defeat of the syndicalists in the Congress of Rome of 1906 represents for the PSI something like the fall of Griffuelhes for the CGT. Although the first great defeat of revolutionary syndicalism as a strategy was the *Settimana Rossa* of 1914 (see L. Lotti, *La Settimana Rossa*, Florence, 1965), and this was at the origin of the sharp turn in the strategy of many revolutionary syndicalists (see Renzo de Felice, *Mussolini, Il Revoluzionario*, Turin, 1969, chapters 8–10; Orietta Lupo, 'I Sindicalisti Rivoluzionari nel 1914', in *Rivista Storica del Socialismo*, X, 32, 1967, pp. 43–82), the events of 1920 in Turin seem to prove that the ideals of revolutionary syndicalism had not then died out totally (although Paolo Spriano's monograph, *L'Occupazione delle Fabriche*, Turin, 1964, would appear to disprove such a view). The ambiguity of the conception of violence in Georges Sorel no doubt reflects the *fausse conscience* of the revolutionary syndicalists with regard to the problem of revolution. Although the writings of Griffuelhes express no uneasiness at all in that respect, some of the closer studies of the way in which revolution would take place do reflect unease. Thus, both Emile Pouget and Pataud (*Comment Nous Ferons la Révolution*, Paris, s.d. – 1907) and Arturo Labriola (*Riforme e Rivoluzione Sociale. – La Crisi Pratica del Partito Socialista*, Milan, 1904) were ultimately confident that the discoveries of science would miraculously prevent the revolution from being a blood-bath. The warnings of Jaurès are reprinted in the book edited by Hubert Lagerdelle, *La Grève Générale et le Socialisme: Enquête Internationale*, Paris, 1905, which is the best compendium of the positions in Europe on the subject of the general strike. Much before Briand in France and Canalejas in Spain proved how right Jaurès had been, Giolitti had shown in 1904 how easily a government could deal with a revolutionary general strike (see G. Procacci, 'Lo sciopero generale del 1904', in *Rivista Storica del Socialismo*, v. 17, 1962, pp. 401–38).

brought back bad news from the USSR and anarchist literature started telling dire tales of what was actually happening there. The fate of the *Makhnovshchina* was publicized and anarcho-syndicalists in Spain could not but trust anarchist witnesses of bolshevik crimes against the revolution.

Only a reduced group of militants was seduced by the bolshevik efficiency in seizing power and was convinced of the need for a strong, disciplined, closed organization. They were among the most popular and the most respected. But the 'anarcho-bolsheviks', as they were known, made little progress. The organizational structures of the CNT and the attitudes within it did not favour their endeavour; neither did the history of communist parties. To revolutionaries in Spain, the October Revolution had been an affair of the masses, and, for all their supposed strategic superiority, communist parties outside Russia had achieved very little after 1917. The Comintern produced a whole generation of militants at least as devoted and able as those of the CNT and the FAI, but communist parties never managed to overcome what Rosa Luxemburg had called the pedantic social-democratic separation of politics and labour.[31] In view of the record of communist parties in Austria, Germany and elsewhere, anarcho-syndicalists may be forgiven for thinking in the 1930s that the only difference between the second and the third Internationals was that the former was reformist and said so, while the communists were reformist but denied it.[32]

When in July 1936 the generals rebelled, the CNT, though caught unprepared, reacted without hesitation. From that moment on and until Franco's victory speech of April 1939, nearly three years elapsed. None had foreseen such a protracted war. But the Spanish anarcho-syndicalists were taken even more by surprise by the length of the conflict than anyone else. Like Lenin in 1917, they had failed to realize that what they rightly saw as a necessarily armed struggle would not simply be a successful insurrection but a terrible Civil War, which in many ways was also an international one. The very need to fight such a war was an even more shattering blow to

[31] See Rosa Luxemburg, *Grève de Masse, parti et syndicats, 1906*, in R. L. *Oeuvres*, Paris, 1969, I, pp. 91–174.
[32] Synthesis of the criticisms of the communists formulated in the 1930s by the anarchists, in the pamphlet: *La CNT y los Comunistas Españoles. – Intervención de V. Orobón Fernández*, n.p. n.d. For the anarcho-bolsheviks, see C. M. Lorenzo, *Les Anarchistes*, pp. 58–62; Ricardo Sanz, *El Sindicalismo y la Política. – Los 'Solidarios' y 'Nosotros'*, Toulouse, n.d.

the hopes of Spanish anarchists than it was to the Russian bolsheviks. What happened thereafter is, in its outline, well known, and has been dramatically summed up by one of the FAI leaders: 'When it actually came to building revolution, our pre-revolutionary education proved a liability.'[33] But that is another story.

[33] Jacinto Toryho, *La Traición del Señor Azaña*, New York, 1939, p. 25.

David Stafford

Anarchists in Britain Today

The State is not something which can be destroyed by a revolution, but it is a condition, a certain relationship between human beings, a mode of behaviour. We destroy it by contracting other relationships, by behaving differently (Gustav Landauer).

IN 1965 IT WAS POSSIBLE FOR THE AUTHOR OF AN ARTICLE ON THE anarchists in Britain to begin by observing that anarchists no longer figured in the popular consciousness and that the existence of anarchists could occasion as much polite surprise as the continued existence of the Independent Labour Party.[1] This present article and its inclusion in a special issue on Anarchism is perhaps in part a proof that this situation is no longer true, and that anarchism has recently attracted sufficient attention to justify a new and closer look at anarchists in Britain today. It would hardly be rash to argue that whatever else may be true of the Left in Britain in 1970, the anarchists' presence deserves to provoke much less polite surprise than it may have done five years ago.

This article is not, however, a description of the shape and variety of anarchists and anarchist groups to be found in Britain today. It is rather an attempt to describe one particular facet of anarchist thought which has characterized anarchism in the 1960s and to relate this to the 'anarchization' of the New Left described by James Joll in his concluding article. It is to that extent an extrapolation and abstraction from a very wide range of alternatives and undoubtedly presents a picture which many anarchists would not recognize or would repudiate. But anarchism has no single comprehensive viewpoint and an article which pleased all would perhaps be a wasted effort. Instead, a description is offered which it is hoped will provide an illustration of certain noteworthy recent processes amongst anarchists apparent to an outside observer.

In the 1960s it was possible to distinguish three distinct phases or elements in the development of the New Left. The first phase, represented by the *Universities and Left Review*, the *New Reasoner*, and *New Left Review* up to *circa* 1962, originated in the climate produced by the traumas of the 20th Party Congress of the CPSU, of Hungary and Suez in 1956, and the overwhelming conservative victory of

[1] Adam Roberts, 'The Uncertain Anarchists', *New Society*, 27 May 1965.

1959. What this New Left did was to re-emphasize the moral concern and imagination of socialism and to reject the reduction of social issues to simple political formulae. It attempted to establish a new ethically based politics for the Left. In rejecting Gaitskellism, one of the effects of the critique of the New Left was to focus attention on the distorting influence within the socialist movement of the Labour Party's commitment in 1918 to nationalization and state control – in other words on the confusion between socialism and state control, in part a reflection of the paternalistic *credo* of the Fabians. The editorial of the first issue of *New Left Review*, in January 1960, placed the emphasis squarely on the need to rediscover a lost libertarian tradition within the socialist movement, and significantly began with a quotation from William Morris's *Commonweal*, the organ of the Socialist League within which, throughout the 1880s, the anarchists had been active, and control of which they succeeded in capturing in 1889. The editorial defined the task of the New Left in the following terms:

'We are convinced that politics, too narrowly conceived, has been a main cause of the decline of socialism in this country, and one of the reasons for the disaffection of socialist ideas of young people in particular. The humanist strengths of socialism – which are the foundations for a generally popular socialist movement – must be developed in cultural and social terms, as well as in economic and political. . . . The task of socialism is to meet people where they are, where they work, where they are touched, obtained, moved, frustrated, nauseated – to develop discontent and, at the same time, to give the socialist movement some direct sense of the times and ways in which we live. . . . The present form of nationalization is not a socialist form: it does not give ordinary men and women direct control over their own lives. Nor does the "public corporation" form of nationalization confront – as a socialist measure should – the urgent problems of a modern industrial society: such questions as bureaucracy, the distance between men and decisions which affect them, the problems of over-centralization, and the vested power of the new property classes. Here, a whole neglected tradition within socialism needs to be imaginatively rediscovered.'[2]

Socialism therefore was no longer defined as political action within

[2] *New Left Review*, No. 1, January–February 1960.

the framework of centralized parliamentary politics and Whitehall. It was multi-level and multi-faceted, and the implications for socialist action were further spelled out by E. P. Thompson:

> 'We can only find out how to break through our present political conventions, and help people to think of socialism as something done by people and not for people or to people, by pressing in new ways on the ground. One socialist youth club of a quite new kind, in East London, or Liverpool or Leeds; one determined municipal council, probing the possibility of new kinds of municipal ownership in the face of Government opposition; one tenants' association with a new dynamic, pioneering on its own account new patterns of social welfare – play-centres, nursery facilities, community services for and by the women – involving people in the discussion and solution of problems of town planning, racial intercourse, leisure facilities; one pit, factory, or sector of nationalized industry where new forms of workers' control can actually be forced on management. . . .'[3]

This quotation of Thompson's, however, points to a characteristic of the New Left which belongs essentially to the second phase in its development. The regenerating activities of the first phase, for all it was a reaction to the Labour Party of Gaitskell, were confined within a certain framework; that of seeking to create a nucleus of the converted in order to change the socialist movement from within by means of rational persuasion. The task was defined almost solely in terms of education, of spreading the faith gently; and of eventually persuading a renewed Labour Party to see the light – 'the most urgent task for socialism today remains the clarification of ideas'; the need was to marry the two elements of a socialist movement – 'the theoretical analysis which gives the movement perspective, the clarion call to moral principle . . . which gives the movement guts'.[4]

A change took place with the emergence of the second phase. This was marked by the espousal of direct action politics characteristic of the crusade against the bomb, a crusade initiated by the Direct Action Committee against Nuclear Weapons and continued by its better known successor, the Committee of 100, which was founded in 1960 and whose activities first came to the eye of the general

[3] *Ibid.*, no. 6.
[4] *Ibid.*, no. 1.

public in 1961 with major sit-downs in London, at Holy Loch, and at US air bases. The very fact of the existence of the Committee of 100 was an illustration of the kind of politics pointed to by the New Left – and which of course had always been advocated by anarchists: an *ad hoc* spontaneous organization, unhampered by an authoritarian structure, applying direct action pressure for change. The Committee of 100 was an anarchist phenomenon – but in its early stages it failed to prescribe an anarchist programme. Indeed, there was a great deal of confusion within the Committee's own ranks about the objectives of direct action. Should it simply be propagandist or should it have more ambitious aims such as the disruption of the functioning of the state? In this debate it was the adherents of the second broad view who triumphed, and from 1962 onwards the Committee of 100, both under the influence of anarchists within its ranks and through a process of self-generating anarchism, widened the scope of its activities, and acting in accordance with the spirit of the slogan 'Ban the Bomb means ban the State', inaugurated a campaign of direct action which involved activities such as persuading workers not to work on military projects, revealing to the public the existence of regional seats of government in the event of war, and various forms of sabotage such as the obstruction of government communications.

After the Cuban missile crisis of 1962 and the Test Ban Treaty of 1963 helped to defuse the anti-bomb issue and to separate the various elements which had conjoined in the anti-bomb movement – pacifists, anarchists, left-wing socialists, and the vast mass of simply worried citizens with no particular political allegiance (most of whom had in fact dropped out in the early stages or had confined their activities to the more respectable Campaign for Nuclear Disarmament) – the Left was itself somewhat disarmed by the victory of the Labour Party at the elections of 1964 and 1966. For a while voices were muted while the Left gave the labour government the benefit of the doubt. The truce did not, however, last long, and by 1968 there existed a critical mass, totally and apparently finally disenchanted with the parliamentary politics of the Left, waiting for the necessary catalyst. This was provided primarily by the Vietnam war; the Tet offensive of January 1968 and the May Days in Paris of the same year appeared to put revolution on the agenda, and did put *Black Dwarf* (and latterly the *Red Mole*) on the newspaper stands. The Vietnam and French issues served together with the growing adulation of Che Guevara, admiration for the revolutionary movements of the underdeveloped world and the impact of radical movements in the United States to create the third phase of the New Left – which was characterized by an emphasis on violent, liberating, revolutionary action. Conjoined with the libertarian vision and the belief in direct action as a valid – indeed the only valid – means of political expression, came a revolutionary romanticism recalling that of Bakunin, which has often verged on nihilism and irrationality; and indeed it is significant that Bakunin began to be quoted favourably perhaps for the first time for a hundred years outside the context of the anarchist movement itself and that, as James Joll points out, it is Bakunin of all the anarchist writers who has attracted the attention of the New Left. Cohn-Bendit, for example, describes himself as 'a Marxist in the way Bakunin was'.[5]

Thus the main components of the New Left syndrome at the end of the 1960s and the beginning of the 1970s may be described as a belief in the need for or alternatively the imminence of a revolutionary overthrow of society; the desirability and feasibility of a libertarian structure of society which will avoid the authoritarianism of the so-called socialist societies (the arguments of the New Left reflect, in their attitude towards the communist states, a great deal of the convergence theory – 'the bureaucratic societies of East and West are coming to resemble one another more and more. Their industrial workers face increasing managerial domination and alienation in their work. The work itself becomes more and more fragmented and more and more meaningless'[6]); and the preparation for this through a form of action involving people at all levels of society in various ways without the centralizing action of any one organization or party. Avoidance of the Leninist model of the centralized political party will guarantee that the aims of revolution will be consistent with its ends: '. . . the new style of revolutionary politics is people doing things for themselves. . . . It will be a revolt from belief which breaks up all the repressive institutions of our society today – the state, the education system – and replaces them by popularly administered, democratic worker control organizations in all the different institutions of social life. . . . What we have got to do is build a movement which already shows you, in anticipation, the

[5] *Anarchy*, No. 99, May 1969. And see also R. Lowenthal, 'Unreason and Revolution', *Encounter*, November 1969.

[6] *Solidarity*, Vol. 2, No. 12. The *Solidarity* group is the most libertarian of the non-anarchist groups of the New Left, and has been responsible for publishing, *inter alia*, the writings of Kuron and Modalewski; it also has links with the French *Socialisme ou Barbarie* group.

sort of institutions that will characterize the best revolutionary society ... one avoids the system by creating institutions which can replace it.'[7] As a recent commentator on the characteristics of the New Left has remarked,[8] 'it is the style of action and the utopian goal that define the movement.'

The creation of the elements of the new society within the framework of the old and particularly within the framework of the revolutionary movement itself is of course a straight anarchist concept (as James Joll points out) which was laid down categorically in the Sonvillier circular of 1871 and the resolution of the St Imier Congress of 1872 which, together, form the founding charter of the European Anarchist Movement, and which was the main issue on which Marx and his supporters disagreed with the anarchists; and this kind of thinking about the form of present political action has cast a new perspective upon the past in which the history of socialism moves far from the traditional orthodox Marxist interpretation, to one much closer to, though not wholly identical with, that of the anarchists, so that the guiding landmarks of the socialist tradition consist of the Paris Commune, Rosa Luxemburg, the Makhnovites, the Kronstadt mutiny (which provides a stick with which to beat the Trotskyites), and the workers' uprising in Budapest in 1956.

This adoption by the New Left of concepts and of a utopianism traditionally associated with the libertarian and anarchist tradition, upon which a great deal has been written and which hardly needs expanding,[9] brings us to the main concern of this article – what of the anarchists themselves? What happened to the anarchists in the 1960s and where do they stand now, and what is their relationship to the New Left?

There is no doubt that the number of anarchists has increased in the last ten years, just as public and mass media interest in their activities has. While it is imposssible to state with any precision how many anarchists there are, a rough guide can be obtained from the circulation of the two main anarchist journals, the weekly *Freedom* and the monthly *Anarchy*, both of which are published by the Freedom Press founded in 1886 by the group centred round Kropotkin, which is now based in the East End where, at the beginning of

[7] Robin Blackburn, quoted in the *Listener*, 22 January 1970.

[8] Lowenthal, *op. cit.*

[9] Although his observations are confined to the United States, Jack Newfield's *A Prophetic Minority* gives a valuable insight into some of the features of the New Left described here.

the century, anarchism found its strongest support. Whereas in 1965 it was estimated that these two journals each had a circulation of between 2,000 and 2,500, in 1969 *Anarchy* was selling about 3,500 copies, and *Freedom* over 4,000. In 1962 six anarchist groups, all in London, were listed in *Freedom*; in November 1968, 85 groups were listed, from all over the country, which contrasts strikingly with the position in 1964, when the Anarchist Federation of Britain was set up as a co-ordinating body, and could count under its umbrella twelve regional federations and groups. The growth in anarchist numbers has been matched by the growth of interest in them by the mass media, including radio and television interviews with anarchists and articles in glossy magazines and the serious weeklies. Perhaps most notable of all was a *Times* first leader in 1968 under the title 'Give flowers for the rebels failed'[10] – which, as Colin McInnes remarked,[11] was probably the first time the newspaper had dealt with anarchism since Kropotkin worked on its staff in the 19th century. Moreover, as Nicolas Walter points out in his article, the 1960s have seen a general recrudescence of academic interest in anarchism, and anarchists themselves tend to consider that it has been a 'good decade', with anarchism at last treated seriously, direct action widely accepted as a form of political action, the 'permissive society' at least half-established; and participatory democracy a slogan on the lips of all good people.

There has therefore undoubtedly been a growth in the number of anarchists in the course of the last ten years as well as a greater diffusion of basically anarchist ideas and attitudes. Yet here we come to a paradox which immediately strikes the outside observer. While the New Left has adopted many concepts which belong essentially to the anarchist tradition, and while it has espoused a revolutionary romanticism which comes close to that of Bakunin, many anarchists themselves have been engaged in a fundamental rethinking of traditional anarchist dogma which involves a *rejection* of these self-same characteristics. While the New Left has been moving closer to the anarchists, the anarchists have been moving away from their traditional posture; and if one of the characteristics of the New Left in the 1960s is what has been described as 'The Balkanization of Utopia',[12] then one of the characteristics of the anarchists has been its abolition.

[10] *The Times*, 3 June 1968.
[11] *The Times*, 6 June 1968.
[12] *The Guardian*, 19 April 1965. See also *Solidarity*, Vol. 3, No. 9, June 1965:

When, in the 1880s, anarchists came to a pessimistic conclusion about the prospects of revolution, many of them adopted a nihilistic position which led them to acts of terrorism which still colour the popular image of the anarchist as an individual (preferably Central European) with a bomb in his back pocket. 'Propaganda by the deed', a term which mistakenly became identified with such attacks, was the symptom of a deeply pessimistic view of revolutionary possibilities, a view which led other anarchists to relapse into Bohemianism or into the creation of their own isolated and free communities. The pessimism apparent throughout the spectrum of the Left at the end of the 1950s produced on the contrary a fundamental re-examination of very basic anarchist dogmas and the influential diffusion of the concept of 'permanent protest', a form of anarchist theory based on a sceptical evaluation of the prospect of revolution and on a belief in the need for a more pragmatic perspective. The viewpoint of 'permanent protest' is most strongly represented in *Anarchy*, established in 1961 as a monthly journal for the discussion of anarchist theory in the light of modern sociological, psychological, anthropological and educational theory. It has in some part served to meet the complaint echoed by an observer of anarchist literature in 1961, that 'what is sadly lacking today is a statement of modern anarchist ideas in the light of a changed society and of the findings of psychological and sociological knowledge about the needs and behaviour of man'.[13] Its editor expressed the viewpoint of 'permanent protest' in an article in *Freedom* in June 1958:

[Twentieth century anarchism] is one which recognizes that the conflict between authority and liberty is a permanent aspect of the

'There is no road to Utopia, no one organization, or prophet, or Party, destined to lead the masses to the Promised Land. There is no one historically determined objective, no single vision of a different and new society, no solitary economic panacea that will do away with the alienation of man from his fellow men and from the products of his own activity.... The "balkanization of Utopia" need convey no disparaging overtones of incapacity or futility.... Starting from many different premises, various groups are making fundamental critiques of established society ... these critiques are slowly converging.... They are preparing a resurgence of libertarian thought and action based on more genuinely socialist objectives than at any previous period of history. The era of closed ideologies (including totalitarian "revolutionary" ideologies) is slowly coming to an end ... the "balkanization of Utopia" ... is the sole guarantee that "Utopia", if we ever get near to it, will be worth living in.'

[13] *Clare Market Review*, 1961. George Woodcock has described *Anarchy* as the best anarchist review to appear since the 1890s in France.

human condition and not something that can be resolved by a vaguely specified social revolution. It recognizes that the choice between libertarian and authoritarian solutions occurs every day and in every way, and the extent to which we choose, or accept, or are fobbed off with, or lack the imagination and inventiveness to discover alternatives to, the authoritarian solutions to small problems, is the extent to which we are their powerless victims in big affairs. We are powerless to change the course of events over the nuclear arms race, imperialism and so on ... precisely *because* we have surrendered our power over everything else. . . . The vacuum created by the organizational requirements of a society in a period of rapid population growth and industrialization ... has been filled by the State, because of the weakness, inadequacy or incompleteness of libertarian alternatives. . . . This is the implication of Gustav Landauer's profound contribution to anarchist thought: 'The State is a condition, a certain relationship between human beings, a mode of human behaviour; we destroy it by behaving differently.'[14]

This quotation of Landauer's is to be found constantly reiterated in the columns of *Anarchy*. By taking this as the cornerstone of their view of anarchism, those who have adopted the viewpoint of 'permanent protest' have firmly re-focused attention on practical anarchist alternatives to specific issues within the framework of society as it now exists: 'The task of the anarchist is not ... to dream about the future society; rather it is to act as anarchistically as he can within the present society'[15]; or, put even more starkly and in even less utopian terms: 'the choice between libertarian and authoritarian solutions is not a once-and-for-all cataclysmic struggle, it is a series of running engagements, most of them never concluded'. It is a position too which underlies the observations of George Woodcock, the anarchist author of a history of the anarchist movement, *Anarchism* (1962), who, writing about the revival of anarchism at the end of the 1960s, concluded that the constructive insights of the anarchists could, provided they were separated from the tactics to which they were traditionally welded, 'wield some positive and beneficial influence in the shaping of society ... not an anarchist utopia, but a world that will really exist as the product of the vast

[14] Colin Ward, 'Anarchism and Respectability', *Freedom*, June 1958.
[15] G. Ostergaard, *Anarchy*, No. 20, October 1962.

technological changes of our age'.[16] One must, however, immediately add that there are many anarchists (indeed probably a majority) who do not subscribe to these views; and to some extent the division of function between the weekly *Freedom* and the monthly *Anarchy* reflects a division between 'traditionalists' and 'reformers' within the anarchist ranks, with the former adopting a more revolutionary stance towards immediate issues of the day, while the latter concentrate on practical and pragmatic approaches to various social issues. In the eyes of many anarchists, especially those associated with *Freedom*, *Anarchy* has succeeded in making anarchism respectable, which is apparently a bad thing, although, as one anarchist put it, respectable means 'able of respect', and this *Anarchy* has done.

This is a departure from classical anarchism which brings 'permanent protest' anarchism close to the doctrines of the Sarvodaya movement – a belief in the 'withering away' of the state rather than an abolition (although there is the important difference that the doctrine of Sarvodaya is based on the time-consuming process of developing moral and ethical awareness of the people before they can be capable of living in an anarchist society – this latter concept itself being distinguishable from the extreme versions of permanent protest theory). The Gandhian fusion of ends and means is comparable to the standpoint of English anarchists who look to the quotation from Landauer as a guide to action.

This conception of anarchism which sidesteps the dilemma which the anarchists have traditionally posited between apocalyptic revolution producing on its morrow the perfectly functioning anarchist society on the one hand, and opting out and seeking personal salvation on the other, was forcefully expressed in an article in *Anarchy* in 1967.[17] The author suggested that revolution and evolution were not mutually exclusive processes but descriptions of one process moving at different rates; revolution and reform were extremes on a scale of evolution. The great danger for anarchists, he argued, was to assume that after the revolution *stasis* could exist. On the contrary: 'We will always see revolutionary changes as a future ideal.... Therefore our basic goal must be continuing evolution. All the "classical" anarchist ideals must be borne in mind, even if they do at present seem utopian, but these should not prevent us from making piecemeal changes right now. The argument

[16] George Woodcock, 'Anarchism Revisited', *Commentary*, New York, No. 46, 2 August 1968.

[17] *Anarchy*, No. 74, April 1967.

for piecemeal "social engineering" has been stated too conservatively by Karl Popper . . . but it is probably the best we can hope for in view of the "social inertia" inherent in any society composed of organic entities', and the writer concluded with the following observation: 'Rebellion must be a permanent feature of anarchist thought and action, but rebellion is not at variance with making small changes today which are themselves preconditions for wider changes. Rebellion can be consistent with encouraging *some* trends in existing society, and often this encouragement can only be effective from within. To stand outside and criticize everything may keep oneself "pure" but it is not itself helping any revolution. Positive alternatives which can capture the imagination of the existing populace must be proposed and fought for.'

For an anarchist to advocate Popper (albeit a less conservative version) compounded the crime of attacking fundamentalist dogma, and the article produced predictable charges of Fabianism and gradualism. Yet such criticisms were off the mark if they were intended as criticisms of the 'permanent protesters', for the point about this particular school of thought (and it should be emphasized again that this represents only one tendency amongst anarchists) is that, unlike the gradualists or Fabians, they do not believe that one will ever reach the desired goal; anarchism will be a condition towards which they will always work, but precisely because it is a condition reflecting relationships between human groups and individuals rather than a structure imposed upon them it must remain as a model and no more. There can be no such thing as an anarchist society: or if there can it is such a remote goal that, in Herzen's words, it becomes a deception.

One of the implications of this view, which places emphasis on action here and now in areas where change in an anarchist direction can be achieved, is that anarchists must utilize the contributions of, and work at least to some degree with organizations and pressure groups which are not anarchist. Anarchists have traditionally participated in left wing movements such as the labour and anti-militarist movements, but a notable feature of anarchist activity in the last ten years has been a willingness to participate in or support movements or organizations which in no sense could be said to have any kind of specifically revolutionary perspectives – e.g. pressure groups such as the National Council for Civil Liberties. It was suggested at the 4th Congress in 1967 of the Anarchist Federation of Britain that it should become affiliated, and many individual anarchist groups have actually done so. The role of the anarchists is seen as that of enlightened members of the public exerting their influence as individuals in the community by example and argument, rather than as members of an anarchist 'party' which seeks to influence by reason of its numerical strength – although the danger of participation in such organizations is acutely felt by more traditional anarchists sensitive to charges of reformism and concerned primarily with the preservation of 'pure' anarchist ideas. This tendency to adopt a less intransigent attitude to such non-revolutionary and reforming organizations and movements undoubtedly reflects a changed social basis and can be seen in the concern shown by a journal like *Anarchy*, which reflects what would be normally associated with the progressive middle-class social conscience. A breakdown of issues dealt with in *Anarchy* since 1961 would show a deep concern with what have in 1970 become known as 'quality of life' issues. Long before most people had probably heard of ecology, the problems of environmental control, urban renewal and town-planning had been covered in detail in its columns, and the review has paid a great deal of attention to the radical criticism of modern American urban and technological society by the communitarian anarchist Paul Goodman. In the words of one of its contributors, the emergence of the technological society implies new forms of action for the anarchists:

. . . in the United States and in many countries of Europe, a new historical context is emerging for anarchist principles. The distinguishing features of this new context [are] the development of gigantic urban belts, the increasing centralization of social life into state capitalism, the extension of automated machinery to all areas of production, the breakdown of the traditional bourgeois class structure . . . the use of 'welfare' techniques to stifle material discontent, the ability of the bourgeoisie – more precisely, the State – to deal with economic dislocation and crisis, the development of a war economy, and the realignment of imperialist nations around the United States – what is crudely called the Pax Americana . . . new problems have arisen to which an ecological approach offers a more meaningful arena of discussion than the older syndicalist approach. Life itself compels the anarchist to concern himself increasingly with the quality of urban life.[18]

[18] Lewis Herber, 'Ecology and Revolutionary Thought', *Anarchy*, No. 69, 1966.

Education, penal reform, and sexual liberation are all issues in which an anarchist approach has topicality within the context of an increasing shift within society away from authoritarian attitudes, and these issues too have been dealt with in depth, frequently on the basis of contributions from writers who would not necessarily accept the anarchist label. *Anarchy* has moreover shown no hesitation in dealing with subjects proverbially problematic for the Left in general, such as the myth of the working-class as the agency of revolution (an article suggesting that the myth be recognized as such, in *Anarchy*, no. 68, October 1966, brought forth fury upon the head of its author, but despite this it is probably true to say that most anarchists do not subscribe to the myth, and look – as indeed the classic anarchist writers have done in the past – not to the working-through of the proletarian dialectic but to the actions of individual *déclassés* for the motor of revolution); and for anarchists in particular, such as the relevance of anarchism within an increasingly centralized and technological society which would appear to render its prescriptions even more utopian than they ever were. However, such objections raise no insuperable problem, for the anarchist would reply that precisely *because* of the growth of technology anarchist critiques are more important than ever for the maintenance of a healthy society; moreover, the anarchist will argue that technological development makes an anarchist approach not only more desirable but more feasible, that the progress of modern industry is favourable to decentralization,[19] and that modern technology increases the potential for disruption of the state. Thus anarchism does not reject technology; rather, it propounds a technology of decentralization in which 'it should be possible for very small units to maintain their own source of energy, their own small-scale industrial units, their own computerized agriculture, and so on'.[20]

The impression that present-day anarchist concerns reflect those of an educated and socially conscious minority is reinforced by the knowledge that a high percentage of the readership of the anarchist press consists of people involved in education. A postal survey of the readership of *Freedom* in 1960 revealed that the two occupational categories within which anarchists were most strongly represented were education and the printed word, while the most popular

[19] Colin Ward, 'Industrial Decentralization and Workers' Control', *Anarchy*, No. 20, December 1961.
[20] Paul Goodman, 'The Black Flag of Anarchism', *New York Times Magazine* 14 July 1968.

newspapers for anarchists were the *Guardian* and the *Observer*, and the most popular weekly the *New Statesman*; and a third of those who replied from Britain had voted in the election of 1959. Granted the disadvantages of a postal survey and that only 25% of those circulated bothered to reply (a total of 470 out of 1863 questionnaires) the figures suggest a significant change in the nature of anarchist support since the earlier years of the century when it was to be found amongst the mainly Jewish working-class population of London's East End. And although these figures are ten years old it is unlikely that the kind of readership has changed very much, with the possible exception of an enlarged student readership. There is no doubt that in Britain – as elsewhere – the social basis of the movement has shifted significantly since the heydey of the classical anarchists, and that anarchist ideas find their greatest support in highly developed societies amongst the middle class.

The remarks above, however, rather beg the question of why today the main focus of serious anarchist thinking reflects such a low key and such a pragmatic approach; for they simply shift the answer one stage further back and then not very satisfactorily, not only because there are no reliable readership statistics which can be compared over a period of time, but also because even if there were, they would provide no explanation of the process of rethinking amongst anarchists who have pioneered the way and who themselves have developed from positions of strict orthodoxy. A journal does not choose its readership, and thus we are brought back to consider the changing nature of anarchist ideas and the context within which the theory of 'permanent protest' has grown.

It has become a commonplace that the issue of the bomb in the early 1960s was the single main catalyst for the emergence of the New Left and for the appearance of extra-parliamentary direct action politics. The Committee of 100 reflected an anarchist philosophy, and 'the effect of its activities [was to] give British anarchism a bigger push forward than anything else that has happened since the last war'.[21] Anarchists who were active within the Committee however were far from satisfied with the limited aims it set itself in its early stages (and had always been cool towards the Campaign for Nuclear Disarmament and the original Direct Action Movement with its lack of comprehensive theoretical framework to relate the campaign against war with the struggle against the state). Part of this critical response was due to the fact that the Committee's campaigns of

[21] Nicolas Walter in *Anarchy*, No. 13, March 1962.

'direct action' (sit-downs, etc.) were more properly to be designated acts of 'propaganda by the deed' (where the emphasis is on propaganda rather than obstructive or revolutionary action), which failed to isolate the central problem – to the anarchists – of the state[22]; where direct action properly speaking was engaged upon it simply revealed the minority nature of the movement. An editorial in *Freedom* in 1961 explicitly criticized the Committee on these grounds: '"Our criticism" of the Committee of 100 . . . is that so far . . . they have tended to foster the illusion that the violence of our existing social system can be destroyed by massive non-violent demonstrations of civil disturbance, legally – that is, openly organized. We consider this to be a naive, utopian approach . . . we anarchists believe in paralysing the machinery of the State when we are strong enough to do so . . . [and] . . . we must undermine the authority of Government by solving more and more of our daily problems ourselves at district and street level.'[23]

The Committee of 100 belonged to and was recognized by the anarchists as belonging to the tradition of minority dissent, not to the tradition of majority revolution. After the first flush of enthusiasm had worn off and in the context of discussions to define a clear theoretical position, the Committee of 100 moved towards the anarchists and extended its activities to action directed against the state machinery *per se*. A first step was taken as early as 1961, when an industrial sub-committee was set up to formulate policies of industrial direct action, and the campaign was enlarged in the following years with the espousal of more openly illegal activities – in 1963 the publication of secret information about regional seats of government (Spies for Peace), and later on the encouragement of disruption of government telecommunications, as well as demonstrations against germ warfare at Porton and against the Greek state visit of 1963 which led to the infamous Challoner affair.

In a policy statement of 1964 the Committee of 100 clearly related its campaign against the bomb to a wider struggle against the distribution of power within society, and while it was careful to make it clear that this did not mean a wholesale concession to anarchist anti-statism, yet in part the statement reflected anarchist opinion: 'We have found that we cannot oppose nuclear war without

[22] For an extreme example of the argument that the anti-bomb movement was futile, see an article 'Anarchists and the H-Bomb', in *Freedom*, 24 July 1960.

[23] *Freedom*, 23 December 1961. As with most views expressed in *Freedom*, this was one which did not escape criticism from many anarchists.

addressing ourselves to the causes of war; that we cannot advocate non-violence without considering all the causes of violence; that we cannot resist the "defence" policy of the Government without coming up against the problem of the allocation of power in our society.'[24]

The 'anarchization' of the Committee of 100 was an admission of failure, a failure which its more perceptive anarchist critics had admitted much earlier; that is, failure to change the nuclear facts of life.[25] Not only did the Committee fail to persuade anyone to disarm unilaterally during the heydey of the mass sit-downs, but the entire nuclear issue was itself defused (although this did not become immediately apparent) after the Cuban missile crisis of 1962 and the Test Ban Treaty of 1963 (a CND policy statement of that year, 'Steps towards Peace', accepted American and Russian nuclear weapons). The failure of the mass campaigns and the defusing of the central nuclear issue itself were to become instrumental in forcing a change which directed militant attention towards authority in all its guises, and particularly towards those areas in which the individual came into direct contact with it – in the factories, in the council house queues, etc. '. . . It has become clear that we cannot shock people into changing their conventional attitudes to life by exposing the danger and the immorality of the bomb alone . . . there must be complementary activity to build a public awareness of the wrongs running right through society. . . .'[26] Thus, while the anti-bomb movement and particularly the Committee of 100 gave anarchism a push forward, paradoxically it may be suggested that it was only *after* these movements had passed their peak and after their failure had become apparent that this became really true (and it was *after* the Cuban missile crisis of October 1962 and *after* the realization of their impotence to affect policies that feeling within the Committee crystallized into a more specifically anarchist direction).[27]

The decline and fall of the 'Ban the Bomb' campaign could only serve therefore to reinforce and to strengthen the ranks of those anarchists who were already sceptical of the possibility of revolutionary action (or action on any 'macro' issue). As one contributor

---

[24] *Resistance*, August 1964.

[25] Nicolas Walter, 'Damned Fools in Utopia', *New Left Review*, No. 13/14, January–April 1962.

[26] 'What has it got to do with the Bomb?' *Anarchy*, No. 26, April 1963.

[27] See D. Shelley, 'Anarchists and the Committee of 100', *Anarchy*, No. 50, April 1965.

to *Anarchy* put it, 'Our preoccupation with crisis-oriented projects will only lead to our defeat in the long run if not in the short run.'[28] Thus the main focus of their activity and intellectual inquiry became directed at issues such as housing, where direct action in 1965 in the case of the King Hill Hostel for homeless families led the Kent County Council to modify its policies, and workers' control.[29] Leaving aside the issues of workers' control and the anarcho-syndicalist strain within anarchism,[30] the kind of action in which anarchists now find themselves engaged in is perhaps best exemplified in their contribution to the squatting campaigns which flowered for a brief period in London and elsewhere in 1969, where anarchists were possibly more active in relation to their resources than any other political group.[31] For the anarchist, squatting is perhaps one of the best examples of direct action, for it is here that the victim of social injustice takes redress into his own hands and expropriates or lays claim to unused property and defies the powers-that-be by cutting through bureaucratic red tape; and although they recognize both as failures in any absolute terms, anarchists will tend to cite the anti-bomb movement and the squatting campaign as the two main examples of relatively successful anarchist action over the last decade. Moreover, the 1969 campaigns evoked memories of the far more militant and widespread squatting campaigns of the immediate postwar years (1945–46), and this provided anarchists across a wide spectrum with the opportunity for an unequivocal response which many of them must have welcomed at a time when issues which were providing rallying cries for the New Left provoked little more than opportunities for dissension amongst or abstention by the anarchists themselves. The third phase of the New Left

[28] Robert Swann, 'Direct Action and the Urban Environment', *Anarchy*, No. 41, July 1964.

[29] Both were subjects to which complete issues of *Anarchy* were devoted: *Anarchy*, No. 2, April 1961 on workers' control; *Anarchy*, No. 23, January 1963 on housing.

[30] The anarcho-syndicalist tradition is represented by the Syndicalist Workers' Federation, which sprang in 1954 from the Anarchist Federation of Britain, which the anarcho-syndicalists succeeded in 'capturing' after a split within the anarchists at the end of the second world war. Its newspaper, *Direct Action* (previously entitled *World Labour News*), was published up to 1968, and the Federation appears now to be defunct. This tradition has adherents in the anarchist ranks and has been left aside in this article only because there has been no striking change in its traditional position. It should, however, be emphasized that the advocacy of workers' control is not confined solely to this group.

[31] Richard Boston, 'Housing In', *New Society*, 6 March 1969.

erupted in 1968 with the Tet offensive and the Paris students and workers, and the syndrome it produced embraced the slogans of workers' and students' control as well as unequivocal support for national liberation movements in the third world (e.g. S. America, Palestine, and in 1969, in Ulster). But the majority of anarchists refused to identify with the Vietnam Solidarity Campaign, the spearhead of the big anti-Vietnam war demonstrations, on the grounds that total identification with Ho Chi Minh was as reprehensible as that of the supporters of the war with Washington. 'Neither Washington nor Hanoi' and a 'Plague on both your houses' was the anarchist slogan. Their stance was hardly one, with its qualifications, which could offer much competition in a climate of growing militancy characteristic of the New Left as a whole. Indeed, the October 1968 Vietnam demonstration was condemned by one writer in *Anarchy* on the grounds that it had no defined purpose and was not even a form of direct action. Interestingly enough, a conclusion similar to that drawn by others at the height of the 'Ban-the-Bomb' campaign was drawn by the writer concerned: 'It is surely by constant confrontation and transformation in the institutions in which people really live, rather than by apocalyptic encounters in the political superstructure, that real and lasting changes will come about. "Student", "Consumer", are actual experiences, roles; "politics" is an abstract sphere of activity which has been drafted uncomfortably on top of these. To fight – even to win – in its arena, is no guarantee that people's real lives will be changed one iota.'[32] Not only did Vietnam fail to provide a focus of concern for the man in the street, but it was an issue – in anarchist eyes – which attracted the 'political hitchhikers of the Left', and this reminded at least some of the older anarchists of their conflicts with the communists and Trotskyites in the Spanish Civil War, and of the need to beware of the enemies on the Left. As one anarchist put it, 'the New Left is simply the old Left in a new guise'; or as another put it 'there are always New Lefts and most of them peddle Marxist theories with reformist tactics'. (One should note here, however, that some anarchists have taken a less equivocal stand on libertarian movements: at the International Anarchist Conference held at Carrara in August 1968 a British delegate said, in the course of an attack on the old-established bureaucracy of the international anarchist movement that 'our aim is not the struggle for anarchism as an abstract ideal but a revolutionary movement with the most libertarian character

[32] *Anarchy*, No. 96, February 1969.

possible. That is why we prefer to work with large numbers of revolutionaries some of whom might not bear our anarchist label, rather than with certain bureaucrats for whom the only thing that made them anarchists was the use of the label itself.'[33] Thus a 'rightist revisionism' which opens up the possibility of co-operation with reformist campaigns is matched by a 'leftist revisionism'. The characteristic of both is a preparedness to work closely with non-anarchist, but libertarian movements; and both are suspect to the traditionalist.)

The May Days in France also appear to have produced a series of contradictory responses. Some anarchists believe that no revolutionary situation ever existed in France; others that it did, but that it was betrayed – as ever – by the communists, and hence that, provided the dangers are avoided, revolutionary action is on the agenda for Britain; others believe that the revolution was crushed by the power of the state – which conclusion can produce either a lowering of perspectives, or, to those unable to cast off their ideological baggage, a bloody-minded attitude of 'let them try it here'.

Thus the squatting campaign was wholeheartedly welcomed by the anarchists. The contrasted reaction of the New Left, however, served to reveal, firstly, the extent to which the New Left remained wedded, despite the borrowed anarchist vocabulary, to older and traditional Marxist concepts, or at least to a neo-Leninism (unlike the American New Left the British New Left seems strikingly devoid of any domestic concern and its ideology is primarily that of foreign revolutionary movements – although the Ulster issues might change this); and secondly the degree to which the very premisses of their ideas set anarchists apart, as they have always done, from the concerns which move the rest of the revolutionary Left. The anarchists' concern was with the homeless; that of the New Left was with revolution; and thus squatting was to be treated warily, for 'instead of the vanguard, squatting concentrates on the homeless. Instead of politicization it reduces itself to an emotional appeal.'[34] Indeed, the

---

[33] *Freedom*, 21 September 1968: *Black Dwarf*, 22 September 1968.

[34] *International Socialism*, No. 41, December 1969. The *International Socialism* group is very deeply distrusted by the anarchists, who strongly criticize their 'exploitation' of the squatting campaign. It would be misleading to suggest that this was the only view expressed by the New Left, for in some ways it is uncharacteristic in its emphasis on the revolutionary role of the working-class, a subject on which the New Left as a whole is remarkably unclear. It can be usefully contrasted with the remarks of Marcuse on the disappearance of the old industrial working-class and the existence of a diffuse and dispersed mass

New Left was right on its own terms to keep the anarchist squatters at arms length: for in 1970 some of the leading squatters have come to agreements with local councils which have led them to evict groups who have refused to move from the property concerned. This, indeed, signified anarchist concern with the individual family rather than with the abstracted revolutionary proletariat and its vanguard; and the criticism of the New Left on what was to the anarchists one of the most promising movements of social protest to have developed since the issue of the bomb faded out in the mid-1960s, provides an appropriate note on which to end, for it illuminates the point at which anarchism appears as the successor of 19th century liberalism in its primary concern with the freedom of the individual (and in its commitment to the rational exchange of ideas freely expressed; most serious anarchists deplore the present-day vogue for irrationality, illiteracy and inarticulacy characteristic of many activists), and thus diverges radically from other movements of the contemporary revolutionary Left. Paul Goodman's strictures on the activities of the SDS at Columbia University could well have been delivered by the English anarchists on the activities of the International Socialists in the London Squatting Campaign: 'the concept of radicalizing is a rather presumptuous manipulation of people for their own good . . . it is authoritarian for people to be expended for the cause of somebody's strategy' [35] Sharing with other Leftist groups the secular ideals of communism and socialism, anarchists have consistently refused to acknowledge the need for a revolutionary vanguard or of a centralized revolution to bring this new society about, and have, at least in theory if not in practice, rejected the intellectual arrogance of the Leninist tradition. The problem of transition has, however, traditionally been fudged either

---

base, which implies 'not . . . a large, centralized and co-ordinated movement, but local and regional political action against specific grievances – riots, ghetto rebellions and so on; that is to say, certainly mass movements, but mass movements which in large part are lacking political consciousness and will depend more than before on political guidance and direction by militant leading minorities . . . the strength of the New Left may well reside in precisely these small contesting and competing groups active at many points at the same time, a kind of political guerrilla force in peace or in so-called peace . . . [foreshadowing] what may in all likelihood be the basic organization of libertarian socialism – namely councils of small manual and intellectual workers, soviets, if one can still use the term. I would like to call it organized spontaneity.' *Black Dwarf,* 28 March 1969.

[35] Goodman, *op. cit.*

by arguing that the revolution would be a mass-movement, or, alternatively, that a form of minority revolutionary action could be devised which would preclude the dangers of authoritarianism (Bakunin's arguments here were more than unconvincing, and it is significant that it is Bakunin of the anarchists who has been taken up by the elitist New Left). If neither alternative is valid – and even if one were valid, the implicit anarchist contention that political action is by nature conservative would surely preclude the development of an 'anarchist society' – then logically anarchists should abandon all pretensions to a programme of secular salvation. Some anarchists are now beginning to argue this, and to provide a valuable contribution to radical social criticism; and it is this development which is most worthy of note amongst anarchists in the last decade. George Molnar, an Australian anarchist whose writings have been extremely influential amongst some British anarchists, has put it this way . . . 'the conflicting strains in anarchism cannot be resolved until anarchism is altogether purged of its association with a programme of secular salvation. In order to uphold consistently the libertarian and anti-authoritarian aspects of anarchism it will have to be understood that these aspects cannot be secured by converting society to them: that universal liberation is an illusion; that revolutions *always* involve seizing and exercising power; that "the abolition of the State", in the sense extolled by classical anarchism, is a myth. If, as anarchists have always argued, many little reforms will not eliminate authoritarianism, neither will One Big Reform. The muck of ages, as Marx called it, clings to revolutionaries as fast as it does to the orthodox, and anarchist revolutionaries are not exempt from this mournful generalization. It is only too evident, in any case, that the critical aspects of anarchism will not attract large numbers of people, that anarchism is not something which can assert itself over the whole of society. Anarchism, consistently interpreted, is permanent opposition.'[36]

[36] *Anarchy*, No. 4, June 1961.

Chushichi Tsuzuki

Anarchism in Japan

IT WOULD SEEM CURIOUS TO AN OUTSIDE OBSERVER THAT THE
DISSOLUTION of the *Nihon-Anakisuto-Renmei* (Japanese Anarchist
Federation) should be formally announced in January 1969, at a time
when militant students were determined to defend their 'fortress', the
Yasuda auditorium of Tokyo University, which they had occupied
for several months, against an attack by the riot police. The anarchists
themselves called the dissolution 'a deployment in the face of the
enemy'. Yet they had to admit at the same time that they had reached
a deadlock in their attempts within the Federation to formulate new
theories of anarchism and to hit upon new forms of organization for
the new era of direct action which they believed had begun.[1] Indeed,
they remained very weak numerically, and they had only a limited
direct influence among the student movements which appeared in
their eyes to have ushered in this era.

It has been said that acceptance of democracy in post-war Japan
encouraged the spread of anarchism as a sentiment, and this, in
turn, rendered anarchism as a movement 'superfluous'.[2] One of the
stalwarts of the *Tōdai-Zenkyōtō* (Council of United Struggle, Tokyo
University) cheerfully declared that they were 'aristocratic anarchists'.
Their struggle, he said, was 'not the one fought by the maltreated,
nor even on their behalf, but was the revolt of the young aristocrats
who felt that they had to deny their own aristocratic attributes in
order to make themselves truly noble'.[3] It has also been pointed out
that the concept of student power and the tactics of campus occupation were in the line of anarcho-syndicalism in spite of the professed
political sympathies (Trotskyism or Maoism) of the movement's
leaders. Yoshitaka Yamamoto, the leader of the *Tōdai-Zenkyōtō*
admitted that the term·anarchism had been used as an epithet as
derogatory as 'left-wing infantile disease' or 'generational struggle'.

[1] *Jiyū-Rengo* ('*Libera Federacio*'), 1 January 1969.
[2] Michio Matsuda, *Anākizumu* (*Anarchism*), Tokyo, 1963, p. 61.
[3] *Jōkyō* (*Situation*), No. 8, 1969, p. 37.

These, he said, had been freely levelled by the 'bureaucrats' of the Communist Party and the 'authoritarian' professors of universities (both formerly champions of the post-war democracy) against what he called 'incalculable human (revolutionary) passions'. He felt, however, that anarchism had been unduly neglected and ought to be re-examined.[4]

Indeed, there was an element of anarchism in all this. Anarchism, or rather nihilism, as a sentiment, however, flourished in post-war Japan not so much because of the apparent progress of democracy, as because of the fact that parliamentary democracy, still a delicate plant in a hostile soil, began to show signs of atrophy under the perpetual rule (or misrule) of conservative governments. Moreover, there was nothing novel in nihilism as such. As the pioneer anarchists sometimes remarked, the spirit of total negation can be traced to the influence among other things of Buddhism and of Taoism,[5] and it provided a moral seedbed for the introduction of anarchism as a body of European thought. This was a profound shock to the authoritarian government of Meiji, which drew its sustenance from another national tradition, that of conformity.

In the following account I propose to deal mainly with anarchism as an intellectual movement in Japan and its bearing on the students' revolt in the 1960s.

HISTORICAL BACKGROUND

It is noteworthy that anarchism in Japan has been closely related to the movement against war. In fact, it had its origin in an anti-war campaign during the Russo-Japanese war, when Shūsui Kōtoku, editor of the anti-war socialist paper *Heimin* (*Common People*), read Kropotkin while in prison. It is also significant that Kōtoku approached socialism and anarchism in terms not of working-class politics but of the self-sacrificing devotion of the high-minded liberals of lower Samurai origins. Within the short-lived Socialist Party of Japan, he led the 'hard' faction of direct actionists against the 'soft' parliamentarians, at a time when neither parliamentary action nor direct action in the form of a general strike was possible for the socialists. He was involved in a premature plot against the Emperor

[4] Y. Yamamoto, *Chisei-no-Hanran* (*Revolt of Intellect*), Tokyo, 1969, p. 195; *Asahi Journal*, 6 July 1969.

[5] For instance Shūsui Kōtoku in *Hikari* (*Light*), 15 December 1906.

Meiji, and in the treason trial of 1910–11, which was largely rigged by the prosecution, 26 anarchists (including three Buddhist priests) were indicted, 12 of whom, including Kōtoku, were executed.

Some anarchists were spared, simply because they were already in prison for other offences. Sakae Ōsugi, one of the prisoners, who was destined to succeed Kōtoku, came from a family of distinguished soldiers and had introduced himself as 'the son of a murderer' when he joined the anti-war movement led by Kōtoku. For some time after the treason trial he concentrated upon literary work, and in this less provocative way he was able to develop his own anarchist thought under the influence of Bergson and Sorel, Stirner and Nietzsche. The nature of the social system which would come as the result of economic progress, he argued, would depend upon 'an unknown factor' in man's reasoning to be developed by 'a minority who would strive for the expansion of each one's self'.[6] He applied his philosophy of life to the labour movement which, he declared, was 'an attempt on the part of the working man to regain himself' and consequently 'the problem of life itself'.[7]

During the first world war, the Japanese socialists and anarchists remained too powerless to raise even the feeblest voice of protest. The rapid expansion of industry during the war, and the inspiration given by the Russian revolution, however, led to a real awakening of the labour movement. Ōsugi flirted with the Comintern for a while, but soon broke with those who organized the clandestine Communist Party in 1922. This *Ana-Boru Ronsō* (dispute between the anarchists and bolsheviks) culminated in a bold attempt by Ōsugi to capture the nascent trade union movement for anarcho-syndicalism, but all his efforts in this line were frustrated by government intervention. Meanwhile, some anarchists, especially those organized in a secret society called *Girochinsha* (Guillotine Society), were driven to acts of terrorism. Ironically, Ōsugi himself fell victim to the 'white' terrorism of the military police which followed the Kantō earthquake of 1923. He was murdered in an army barracks.

Thereafter, there was a revival of anarchism as a form of reaction against the political achievements of 'Taishō Democracy' embodied as they were in the Universal Suffrage Act of 1925, which was accompanied by a safety measure, an act for the maintenance of internal security. While the inaugural conference of the Peasants-

[6] Ōsugi, '*Kusari-Kōjō* (The Chain Factory)', *Kindai-Shisō* (*Modern Thought*), September 1913.
[7] Ōsugi in *Rōdō-Undō* (*Labour Movement*), October 1919, June 1920.

Workers Party was dispersed by the police, anarchist stalwarts of various factions arrived on the scene to denounce the beginning of the workers' participation in parliamentary politics, and from this rather unseemly protest was born the Black (Youth) Federation. Sakutarō Iwasa, a veteran anarchist, who had set up a Social Revolutionary Party among the Japanese immigrants in San Francisco when Kōtoku visited there, now exerted a decisive influence upon the Federation. He was an exponent of 'pure anarchism', according to which all the socialist parties and trade unions would only assist the progress of capitalism with the ideology of class war, which was 'a sham'. 'The workers who work under big capitalists', he declared, 'are sharing and promoting their masters' exploitation.' They themselves would exploit the people if they were successful in revolution; only an anarchist minority could achieve a revolution for the people because they desired freedom and emancipation, but not power for themselves, and consequently would attain their aims by freeing other people from exploitation and from power.[8] By calling for a boycott of all forms of organization, however, Iwasa and the Black Federation crippled the newly created syndicalist federation, the National Association of Trade Unions, which had had an auspicious start with a combined membership of over 10,000 in 1926.[9]

Shortly afterwards, yet another syndicalist federation came into existence with the assistance of, among others, Sanshirō Ishikawa. Ishikawa's anarchist convictions, which dated from before Kōtoku's, had been strengthened by reading *Towards Democracy* and other writings of Edward Carpenter. 'I have for a very long time been dissatisfied with mere mechanical materialistic Socialism and the parliamentary movement', he wrote to Carpenter in 1909.[10] Like Ōsugi, he was spared because he had been in prison at the time of the treason trial. After his release, he spent eight years as an exile in Europe, mostly with the Reclus family in Brussels. With a knowledge of the French syndicalist movement, he now exhorted his followers to ally themselves with working-class organizations.

[8] Iwasa, *Kakumei-Dansō* (*Thoughts on Revolution*), 1958, quoted in Kiyoshi Akiyama, *Nihon-no Hangyaku-Shisō* (*Rebellious Thought in Japan*), Tokyo, 1968, p. 164; Iwasa, 'Kaihō-nitaisuru-Anakisuto-no-Yakuwari (The Anarchist Role in Emancipation), *Jiyū-Rengō-Shinbun* (*Liberal Federation Newspaper*), 1 May 1930, Matsuda, *op. cit.*, pp. 376, 382.

[9] Kensuke Yamaguchi, 'Nihon-niokeru-Anaruko-Sandikarizumu (Anarcho-Syndicalism in Japan)', *Shisō-no-Kagaku* (*Science of Thought*), November 1966.

[10] Ishikawa to Carpenter, 14 December 1909, Carpenter Collection, Sheffield City Library.

During the years of great depression, the syndicalist unions, formed mainly among the workers employed in small firms, fought a series of desperate struggles, the most celebrated of which was the workers' occupation of a dyeing factory in Tokyo in 1930, when an anarchist worker sat on the top of a tall chimney for 15 days with a black flag flying. After the Japanese invasion of Manchuria in 1931, government action against left-wing bodies became more ruthless and frequent. The tenacity with which the Left held out is attested by an attempt made in 1935 to form a united front, an 'alliance to smash Nazism and Fascism' as it was called, among the left-wing social democrats, bolsheviks, anarchists and syndicalists, though it was at once suppressed by the police. In the same year, the syndicalist unions received a fatal blow, the arrest of the members of a secret society called the Anarchist Communist Party, which had been formed to organize an armed uprising against the government. Characteristically, the 'self-righteousness and adventurism of the intellectuals' of the 'party' were condemned by the syndicalist workers.[11]

AFTER THE SECOND WORLD WAR

In 1945, unconditional surrender and the physical destruction of the country seemed to promise a new era when, free from the old government and the old ruling classes that had gone, as it seemed, for ever, the anarchists might be given a chance to try their ideas for the reconstruction of society. It was with such hope that the aged Ishikawa wrote an anarchist 'Utopia' entitled '*Gojūnen-go-no-Nihon* (Japan 50 Years Later)' shortly after the end of the war. In this work, democratic reorganization of post-war Japan, itself a pale imitation of the European experience of the last hundred years, is followed by a peaceful revolution; the extensive use of mutual exchange banks and the growth of mutualist trade unions lead to the emergence of a new society, in which the old Diet building is used only for meetings of the unions, and culture and the economy are conducted on a co-operative basis so as to enable each individual to live a life of artistic creation. Most of Ishikawa's fellow anarchists, however, do not appear to have shared his belief in nudity as the symbol of natural freedom nor his peculiar view that the emperor should be

[11] Yamaguchi, *loc. cit.*, 4.

maintained even in an anarchist Utopia as the symbol of communal affection.[12]

The Japanese Anarchist Federation came into existence in May 1946, at a time when millions of hungry workers were taking part in demonstrations all over the country demanding food and a 'democratic popular front'. The revived anarchist movement, however, failed to make an impression on the Left; their programme of action remained academic, in spite of some attempts made by syndicalist unionists to establish workers' control of production. The anarchists favoured 'a revolutionary popular front' but quarrelled among themselves over their attitude towards the Communist Party. Their organ, *Heimin*, unlike its predecessors edited by Kōtoku and Ōsugi, 'did not create a great social shock'.[13] It seems that the anarchists, lacking an adequate theory of transition, could not compete with the communists or socialists in practical proposals for the reconstruction of society. Thus they were driven either into political and industrial struggles outside their own ranks or back into the realm of the ideal, in which they were unrivalled. By the end of 1946 the tone of the *Heimin* had become more intellectual and idealist and more conspicuously anti-Marxist than before.

When SCAP (Supreme Commander for the Allied Powers) issued an injunction against a general strike prepared by a Joint Action Committee of communists, socialists and their trade union allies on behalf of the underpaid governmental workers, an industrial offensive which threatened the overthrow of the conservative government, the anarchist organ indulged in *Schadenfreude* by criticizing what they called 'the conservative nature of the strike of the bureaucrats (namely governmental workers)'.[14] SCAP sought to contain communist influence among government employees by depriving them of the right to strike,[15] to the relief of the government and to the delight of the anarchists, who insisted that the civil servants were 'the agents of authoritarianism'. The anarchists, it seems, failed to see the nature of the power wielded by SCAP, just as the communists had for some time after the war regarded the American forces as an army of liberation.

In the meantime, the pre-war debate on the difference between

[12] Published in *Shisō-no-Kagaku*, December 1966.

[13] Michio Osawa, 'Sengo-Nihon-no-Anakizumu-Undō (The Anarchist Movement in Post-war Japan) IV', *Jiyū-Rengō*, 1 October 1964.

[14] *Heimin-Shinbun*, 12 February 1947.

[15] *Ibid.*, 9 August 1948.

'pure anarchism' and anarcho-syndicalism was revived, and the resulting division within the handful of participants in the debate led to the dissolution of the Japanese Anarchist Federation in October 1950. The disintegration, however, should be considered against the background of the cold war and the change in American policy towards Japan. The implementation of the new democratic peace constitution gave way to measures for the swift recovery of the national economy which encouraged employers to take the offensive against the workers. The virtual suppression of the Japanese Communist Party by SCAP in June 1950 preceded the outbreak of the Korean war, and the conclusion of the San Francisco Peace Treaty in the following year cleared the way for the return of war-time leaders in almost all spheres of national life. Indeed, 1950 marked a turning-point in the post-war history of Japan, and the decline of anarchism was only part of the general crisis which threatened the Japanese Left about this time.

THE STUDENTS

The post-war student movement had consolidated its strength by 1948, when the students set up the Zengakuren (*Zen-Nihon-Gakusei-Jichikai-Sōrengō* or All Japan General Federation of Student Unions) with a militant tradition already established through a series of struggles against an increase in tuition and fees and against those whom they regarded as the enemies of peace and democracy. Their relations with the Communist Party were tenuous from the start, though their militancy was encouraged for a while by the latter when the party, confronted with the Cominform criticism of 1950, abandoned its previous policy of peaceful revolution and adopted one of guerrilla warfare and armed insurrection. It is, however, noteworthy that the students' demands for 'local communes' and their insistence that 'it was high time to take over university power by themselves' can be traced to their struggles of this period.[16] The Communist Party's futile policy of 'extreme-leftist adventurism', and its dismal failure, left the student movement in low spirits and confusion.

It was not until 1956, when the revelation of the Stalinist enormities in Russia stirred world opinion, that left-wing forces outside

[16] Akira Yamanaka, *Sengo-Gakusei-Undōshi* (*History of the Post-war Student Movement*), Tokyo 1969, p. 154.

the Communist Party found strength to stand on their feet again. In this year, what was called 'the second foundation congress' of the Zengakuren was held, and it was decided that the prime responsibility of the student movement was to promote the struggle for peace. In the same year, the anarchists revived their Federation with the *Kurohata* (*Black Flag*) as its new organ. Meanwhile, the cautious response of the Communist Party to the events of 1956 (they regretted that the criticism of Stalin had gone too far in Hungary) led to the rise of 'Independent Marxism' which politically took the shape of a Japanese Trotskyist Federation, formed in January 1957, soon to be known as the *Kakukyōdō* (*Kakumei-Kyōsanshugisha-Dōmei* or Revolutionary Communist League). In the following year, a muddled debate over the new draft constitution of the Communist Party further encouraged the 'Independent Marxists' as the draft appeared too 'nationalist' and conservative. Japan, it declared, was still a 'semi-dependent' country 'half occupied by American imperialism', and would require a two-step revolution: a people's democratic revolution through the establishment of a 'National Democratic United Front' (itself a re-statement of a similar 'front' advocated in 1949) which would allow an alliance with 'national' capitalists; and a socialist revolution which would follow. It was under these circumstances that the revived Anarchist Federation at its annual conference of 1958 reviewed its whole attitude towards revolution. The delegates argued that the people would soon be forced to choose between atomic death and social revolution, and peaceful co-existence would only serve the interests of the rulers of the two world states. They would support the militant students and workers 'from behind' with an advocacy of 'People's Direct Action' against the danger of a nuclear war.[17] The anarchists, however, remained a group of devotees without allies. The workers on the whole were engaged in their own struggles for higher wages, which they were assured as long as they would work for higher productivity; while the militant students came largely under the influence of the Trotskyist movement.

From the 'Renaissance' of the student movement there emerged greater militancy and vehemence in the 'Main Stream' or 'Anti-Yoyogi' faction (Yoyogi being the name of the district in which the headquarters of the Communist Party is located) of the Zengakuren. Militant students now declared 'the Kishi government, tied as it was to the forces of international imperialism', to be their 'enemy at

[17] *Kurohata*, 1 December 1958.

home', and sought to turn the peace movement into a class struggle. They saw 'the crucial phase of a decisive battle in class war' in every issue that cropped up. A pattern of protest was formed at that time, when the government, in a rash attempt to strengthen the police system, failed to pay due respect to parliamentary opposition, and thereby provoked extra-parliamentary opposition by the indignant workers and students. The crisis was overcome by an agreement among top politicians to drop the matter altogether: this was a 'compromise' (itself an immoral concept in Japanese terms) that appeared to the students to be a criminal 'betrayal' on the part of the working-class 'establishment', the Socialist Party and its ally the Sōhyō (Nihon-Rōdō-Kumiai-Sō-Hyōgikai or General Council of Trade Unions of Japan), the major trade union federation. The range of negation for the militants was thus greatly extended.

The pattern was repeated on a much larger scale, with more serious results in 1960, when the nation was given for the first time a chance to decide its attitude towards the Security Treaty (or military alliance) with the United States. The 'Main Stream' Zengakuren had tried to invade the premises of the Diet, and had been at logger-heads with a National Council of socialists, communists, Sōhyō, and some intellectuals, who favoured orderly petition against the treaty. In May when Kishi enraged his adversaries by rushing the controversial treaty through the Diet with the aid of the police, overthrow of his government and defence of parliamentary democracy became the immediate targets of the national movement. Huge demonstrations were organized almost daily around the Diet, and a series of protest strikes was staged by the Sōhyō and other unions, involving 4 to 6 million workers, with considerable public support. Although the magnitude and vehemence of the protest led to the cancellation of Eisenhower's proposed visit and also to the resignation of Kishi, the opposition forces failed in their primary object of destroying the Security Treaty. And what had become of democracy?

The Kurohata had been appealing for a general strike. Now the anarchist organ commented that 'we have learned by experience . . . that politics which plead for democracy in the form of political parties, parliament, and political power, must inevitably lead to dictatorship'. The Anarchist Federation had joined with the 'Main Stream' Zengakuren in demanding fighting rather than demonstrations, and in this, it claimed, they were supported by 'the people' who had 'surpassed' those who had in the past acted as their leaders. In this sense 'the anarchist revolution had begun', and had been suppressed by the National Council.[18] Hence the charge of dictatorship. However fanciful many of the anarchist claims may now seem, there is a grain of bitter truth in their allegation: belief in parliamentary democracy was now seriously shaken, and the gap between the militants and the existing left-wing parties was unbridgeably widened, especially as the communists condemned 'Trotskyist' tactics as responsible for the death of a Zengakuren student in a skirmish with the police.

The *Kurohata* also pointed out that the ruling party, the liberal democrats, had amassed many votes by bribery and other means and therefore the demonstrations around the Diet had also been directed against 'dirty politics.'[19] Yet there was a temporary lull after the storm. As 'doubling of income' and 'high economic growth' became not only the shibboleth of the government but also the signs of actual prosperity that marked the years after the 1960 struggle, the unbroken rule of the liberal democrats seemed assured in the Diet. At the same time the oposition parties consoled themselves with the modest achievement of retaining one third of the Diet seats, which would enable them to forestall an attempt to eliminate the peace clause of the constitution. The Zengakuren militants busied themselves with endless debates over the niceties of revolutionary theories and tactics which divided and subdivided their forces into warring sects.

The anarchists seem to have had second thoughts on the Zengakuren sects and the movement of the 'New Left' in general, which they thought were making their leaders into 'little Stalins'. They were particularly suspicious of the Trotskyist *Kakukyōdō* (Revolutionary Communist League) whose allies among the students, the *Marugakudō* (*Marukusushugi-Gakusei-Dōmei* or Marxist Student League), had captured the Zengakuren executive. In fact, at the general election for the House of Councillors in July 1962, the Trotskyists put forward one of their leaders, a young philosopher who preached a 'subjective materialism' of human alienation. 'Extravagant', said the anarchists, 'is the farce of the *Kakukyōdō* twisting anti-Stalinism into a dogma, suppressing the creative opinions of its members in the name of building a true and only party of the advance guard . . . and enshrining its sacred founder in the bourgeois temple.'[20]

The excitement of the early summer of 1960 had by now been

[18] *Kurohata*, 1 July 1960.
[19] *Ibid.*
[20] *Kurohata*, 1 February 1962.

replaced by a bitter feeling of frustration among the Left, which led to recrimination, confusion, and apathy, but also to some soul-searching attempts to find a new basis for fresh and possibly more successful activities. The socialists began to talk about 'vision' and (together with some communists) about 'structural reform'. The anarchists, too, launched an ambitious debate on 'the need for emancipating anarchism from the classical theories of revolution'.

Among the anarchist ranks, those who had joined the movement after the war had by now come to the forefront of its activities. Masamichi Ōsawa, one of the leading theorists of the younger generation, started questioning the validity of the revolutionary ideas that his predecessors had inherited from the 19th century. The cult of fixed principles had hampered the revolutionary movement in Japan, he declared, taking his cue from Professor Maruyama's famous analysis of the subject. In the pages of the *Jiyū-Rengō* ('*Libera Federacio*') which had succeeded the *Kurohata*, Ōsawa dealt with the new type of poverty in mass society, dehumanization or alienation. It was a novel argument, certainly among the anarchists, and from it he drew lessons for revolution: the upper, rather than the lower, strata of the proletariat would fight for the control, rather than the ownership, of the means of production; multiplication of free associations and communes rather than the seizure of political power would be the form of revolution. The change, he went on, would be gradually carried out through structural changes in various social groups, in each industry, school and university, local community and individual family; hence revolution would be social and cultural rather than political, and arts and education would play an important role in it.[21] Ōsawa's propositions were soon under attack as 'an anarchist variety of reformism' or revisionism. He was rightly criticized for his neglect of Japanese realities, the mixture of elements both new and old, the contrast of modern technology and semi-feudal social relationships; and it was indeed against this curious mixture that new revolt was soon to raise its ominous head. The lively debate that followed, however, made it clear that the anarchists agreed to differ on the vital question of how to achieve revolution.

THE VIETNAM ISSUE

The American bombing of North Vietnam which began in February

[21] *Jiyū-Rengō*, 1 June 1965.

1965, and the menace of total war thus created, provided the occasion for the left-wing forces to intensify their campaign against war. Thus they were able to recover from the effects of the years of disarray which had been worsened by the impact of the Sino-Russian dispute. As for the anarchists, however, their attitude towards the Vietnamese war was rather complex: they believed, as the *Jiyū-Rengō* put it, that struggle for national emancipation in underdeveloped countries would lead to world war rather than world revolution, and nationalism in these countries would lead to national capitalism in spite of its socialist mask. The anarchist alternative to the nation states should be village communes that would provide centres for the development of agricultural societies. Therefore, the anarchists should work for immediate cessation of hostilities, and they were prepared to join in forming an anti-war movement which would be a loose federation of various left-wing opinions.[22]

In fact, such a movement had just begun in the form of *Betonamu-ni Heiwa-wo Shimin-Rengō* (Citizens' Federation for Peace in Vietnam) soon to be known as *Beheiren*, and the anarchists, bearing the black flag, had participated in the demonstrations which led to its formation in April 1965. Its founder, Minoru Oda, who had studied in America, drafted what he called 'a Citizens' Pact between Japan and America for Peace and against War', in which he declared for 'international civil disobedience'. He distinguished between 'democracy for the people' and 'democracy of (and by) the people', and saw in the latter the principle of his own movement which was to be translated into demands for direct democracy and direct action by the citizens.[23] Indeed, Oda's views had much in common with anarchism, but the anarchist movement as such does not seem to have exerted much influence on the activities of the *Beheiren*, which sought to attract attention by publishing an advertisement for peace in the *New York Times* and by actively aiding the American soldiers who deserted while on leave in Japan.

In 1965, the anti-war movement was further accelerated by events which appeared to confirm Japan's deeper involvement in the war in Vietnam: her *rapprochement* with South Korea, including close economic co-operation, and the dispatch of the Korean 'Tiger' Division to South Vietnam. Ratification of the treaty with South

---

[22] *Jiyū-Rengō*, 1 June 1965.

[23] Oda, 'Genri-toshiteno-Minshushugi-no-Fukken (Rehabilitation of Democracy as a Principle)', *Tenbō* (*Prospect*), August 1967.

Korea was forced through the Diet in the teeth of opposition both inside and outside. It was a repetition of the 1960 struggle, another crisis in parliamentary democracy. It was said, argued Ōsawa, that the government's rash action was an 'outrage', but a bill on internal security or on foreign and military affairs had rarely been passed without such an 'outrage'. Each time an 'outrage' took place, he went on, a 'threat to parliamentary democracy' was talked about by journalists, and two camps of party politicians inveighed against each other and then contrived a truce. 'This is the scene we have tirelessly watched for the 20 years since the end of the war.' He asked whether parliamentary democracy could thrive at all in Japan, where class division was so intense and involved that mediation or moderation through parliament appeared almost impossible. Moreover, he believed, parliamentary democracy was becoming outdated, as a dominant political institution throughout the world and was sooner or later to be replaced by direct democracy and federalism. So he urged his followers to raise the voice of no confidence in political parties and the Diet.[24]

From the protest against ratification of the treaty with South Korea was born a new working-class organization called the *Hansen-seinen-i* (*Hansen-Seinen-Iinkai* or Anti-War Youth Committee), which was soon to provide young activists from the ranks of trade unionists to co-operate with the Zengakuren militants in a series of direct actions against war. It is true that the initiative in launching the *Hansenseinen-i* was taken by the Youth Section of the Socialist Party in August 1965, in conjunction with the Youth Department of the Sōhyō and the *Shaseidō* (*Shakaishugi-Seinen-Dōmei* or Socialist Youth League connected with the Socialist Party) with a view to creating a nation-wide youth movement against the war in Vietnam; and militant trade unionists played a prominent role in several demonstrations and sit-ins around the Diet during the Korean Treaty struggle. In spite of the socialists' pretence of patronage, however, the new organization developed into a movement for protest against the very existence of the Socialist Party and the Sōhyō. 'Post-war democracy', remarked one of the movement's leaders, 'has come to mean the existing political order for petit-bourgeois life ... "Democracy" has been emaciated into the petty act of voting, and trade unions, which had been highly valued as a blessing of post-war democracy, have become service organs which would secure for us sufficient wages to maintain the standard of petit-bourgeois living through

[24] *Jiyū-Rengō*, 1 December 1965.

"democratic" parleys between capital and labour.'[25] Thus the campaign of the militant unionists against war was also a form of protest against the 'false' prosperity of the workers. Moreover they were ready for direct action in the streets, but apparently not in the factories.

Direct action in the factories was left in the hands of more professional revolutionaries, the anarchists. They had, however, no following among organized labour, and consequently their 'propaganda by deed' took the daring form of a few determined men sneaking into a munitions factory and cutting off the supply of electricity for 10 or 15 minutes. This was what actually took place when twelve or thirteen anarchists raided a machine-gun factory at Tanashi, Tokyo, in October 1966. This raid, and another in Nagoya, were organized by a *Behan-i* (*Betonamu-Hansen-Chokusetsu-Kōdō-Iinkai* or Anti-Vietnam War Direct Action Committee), which consisted mostly of anarchist students. This body published details of the munitions industry in Japan under the heading of 'Group Portrait of the Merchants of Death', and called for 'factory occupation' and 'sabotage' against them.[26] Indeed, bold action earned sympathy and support for the anarchist students, but some anarchists distrusted what they called 'the prelude to terrorism' and irresponsibility.[27] In fact, the *Behan-i* soon disintegrated, with the disturbing result that the leader of a group called *Haihansha* (Revolt Society), who had taken part in the Tanashi raid, later became a police spy.[28]

THE 1967–8 CLIMAX

1967 was the year when the militant students, with the aid of activist workers of the *Hansenseinen-i*, started a series of direct actions against the war in Vietnam: a sit-in demonstration at the American air base at Tachikawa (Sunagawa) in May, and the 'Haneda Incident' in October when, in an attempt to prevent Premier Sato's visit to South Vietnam, about 2,500 students and their working-class allies clashed with the *Kidōtai* (riot police) near Haneda Airport. Direct action, which inevitably meant a battle with the well-armed police, now fashioned the style of their protest: the students armed themselves

[25] Keishi Takami, *Hansen-Seinen-Iinkai*, 1968, p. 131.
[26] Behan-i (ed.), *Shi-no-Shōnin-e-no-Chōsen* (*Challenge to the Merchants of Death*), 1967, passim.
[27] *Jiyū-Rengō*, 1 February 1967.
[28] *Asahi-Shinbun*, 7 August 1969.

with wooden staves and helmets painted with the colours and name of the sect to which they belonged.

By this time the Zengakuren had recovered from the chaos that followed the 1960 struggle and the ceaseless transmutation of its various sects now yielded temporarily to relative stability, as the sects were grouped into three Zengakurens, each with an esoteric name: the *Kakumaru-Zengakuren* dominated by the *Kakumaru* (*Kakumeiteki-Marukusushugi* or Revolutionary Marxist) faction of the Trotskyist *Marugakudō* (*Marukusushugi-Gakusei-Dōmei* or Marxist Student League); the *Sanpa-kei* (Three School Faction) *Zengakuren* which consisted of three sects – the *Chūkaku* (Central Core) faction of the same Marxist Student League, the *Shagakudō* (*Shakaishugi-Gakusei-Dōmei* or Socialist Student League), consisting primarily of those students who had been expelled from the Communist Party (formerly Communist Student League), and the *Kaihō* (Emancipation) faction of the *Shaseidō* (*Shakaishugi-Seinen-Dōmei* or Socialist Youth League), a body which had been expelled from the Socialist Party but maintained its original aim of establishing an alliance of the students and workers; and finally the Communist Zengakuren which was then called the *Heimin-Gakuren* (*Heiwa-to-Minshushugi-wo-mamoru-Zenkoku-Jichikai-Rengō* or National Federation of Student Unions for Defence of Peace and Democracy) and soon to be called the *Minsei-kei-Zengakuren*, Minsei being the communist sponsored *Minshu-Seinen-Dōmei* or Democratic Youth League. The above outline of the Zengakuren may be confusing enough for the uninitiated; it suffices to add that divisions could and did go further as differences of opinion developed as to the degree of militancy or the relative priority of each article of faith, such as anti-imperialism or anti-Stalinism, or priority in actions, such as extra-campus struggles or confrontation within each university. Indeed, the *Sanpa*, the most heterogeneous of the three, later split, and the anti-imperialist Zengakuren, a motley collection of Trotskyists and Maoists, emerged. It seems that the students were utterly incapable of stable alliance, and their intolerance was illustrated by *uchigeba* (internal violence), physical fights between the sects and factions including several cases of brutal beatings. The anti-communist Zengakuren remained a minority, and the communist students, who took a more active interest in campus democracy and student welfare, were said at the time of the Haneda incident to have controlled nearly 80% of all the student unions.[29]

[29] *Asahi-Shinbun*, 9 October 1967.

In the following year (1968) the students' extra-campus struggles 'escalated' as they fought increasingly violent battles with the *Kidōtai*: the massive demonstrations in January against the visit to Sasebo of the American nuclear submarine *Enterprise*; the raid on the Ōji US Field Hospital in Tokyo; support for the stubborn resistance of the peasants who refused to sell their land as a site for a new international airport at Narita in the spring; and the riotous demonstrations in Shinjuku (Tokyo) on 'International Anti-War Day' in October when more than a thousand students and others were arrested.

'The Opening of the Era of Direct Action' encouraged the anarchists as it coincided with the radicalization of student movements abroad, in particular the 'May Revolution' in Paris. In Japan, too, 'it is a well-known fact', remarked the *Jiyū Rengō* '... that university education is becoming a process of mass production as in the factories, and resistance to such tendency provides the mainspring of the students' revolt. . . . It is only natural that they should lead the revolt against the system because they are intellectual workers under training, soon to be sent to the key positions in the process of dehumanization now developing. From this point of view we may say that the time will soon come when the student movement will unite with the workers' movement.'[30] Yet the students did not appear anxious to co-operate with the workers. Militant students, especially those in the Trotskyist sects, began to regard themselves as the main army of revolution rather than the advance guard or even the 'detonator' of the working-class revolution.[31]

STUDENT POWER AND INTELLECTUAL TRENDS

The immediate issue within the campus was redress of such grievances as increases in fees, the internship system for medical students, the reluctance on the part of the university authorities to give full autonomy to the students in the management of their hostels and union buildings, and more generally the inevitable defects of mass education: enormous classes and overworked professors, and resulting 'alienation'.[32] When the students believed that they had dis-

[30] *Jiyū-Rengō*, 1 July 1968.

[31] Koken Koyama, 'Zengakuren-no-Senryaku-to-Senjutsu (The Strategy and Tactics of the Zengakuren)', *Rōdō-Mondai*, July 1968.

[32] It is interesting to note that the students did not complain much about the

covered the ultimate cause of their complaints in 'alienation' and combined this with theoretical 'situations' provided by Japanese 'Monopoly Capitalism', 'American Imperialism', and 'Russian Stalinism', it required little mental exercise for them to conclude that they should strive for revolution, even world revolution, total negation of all their enemies. Yet this mental process, which is in fact more nihilist than anarchist, wrought havoc in the Japanese universities. At the height of the campus disputes it was estimated that 110 out of the 489 universities in Japan were in serious trouble, nearly a half of them occupied by the students.[33]

One of the strongholds of student power was *Nichidai* or Nihon University, the largest example of 'private enterprise' in education, where irregularities in university finance incurred the wrath of a good many of its 86,000 students, who repudiated the spirit of 'money-making' in a 'mass-production university'.[34] Another, and more symbolic, battlefield was provided by *Tōdai* or Tokyo University, where a dispute over the status of graduate students in the notoriously autocratic faculty of medicine and an allegedly erroneous judgement passed by the governing board on one of the militant students led to devastation of much of the campus.

The movement for student power was led by an organization called *Zenkyōtō* (*Zengaku-Kyōtō-Kaigi* or All University Council for United Struggle). This body, a loose alliance of some of the anti-communist sects (especially the *Chūkaku*) and 'non-sect' radical students, attracted attention when the disputes at *Nichidai* and *Tōdai* took a serious turn in May–June 1968. A *Zenkyōtō* sprang up in each storm-centre and was acclaimed by its supporters as an excellent example of the activists uniting with the 'student masses'. After the dramatic battle fought between the *Zenkyōtō* students who had occupied the Yasuda Auditorium of Tokyo University, and the *Kidōtai* who attacked them from the land and the air, their influence further extended, and occupation of many other campuses followed. The National Federation of *Zenkyōtō*, which was set up at a rally held at Hibiya Park in September 1969, appeared perhaps most menacing of all the student organizations, an alliance of eight offshoots of the former *Sanpa-kei-Zengakuren*. Yet the National

---

defects of meritocracy: the intense competition for more promising schools, universities, and jobs, which distorted their adolescent life.

[33] *Asahi-Shinbun*, 4 August 1969.

[34] *Hangyaku-no-Barikeido* (*Barricade for Revolt*), 1968, passim.

Federation was a sign not of the strength but of the weakness of each sect. Yoshitaka Yamamoto, the leader of the *Tōdai-Zenkyōtō*, who came to take the chair at the rally, was arrested by the *Kidōtai* – it was reported that he 'even seemed to have come to be arrested'.[35]

Yamamoto, then a 27-year-old graduate student of physics, had played an important part as a 'non-sect' radical in co-ordinating the warring sects of the 'New Left'. The ideology of those whom he represented has been described as that of 'self-negation', 'a sub-species of anarchism'.[36] In his opinion, campus occupation with barricades signified 'negation of the university which produces men to serve capital as if in a factory, and also negation of the existence of students whose only future was to be cogs in the power machine thus created'. Occupation of professors' studies and research laboratories had to be carried out as an act of negation of scientism, which he regarded as the achievement of the 'hollow' post-war democracy and also as a prop of neo-imperialism. The university struggle was only 'a form of manifestation of social contradictions' – therefore 'there is no half-way house in the struggle before the establishment of student power', the 'power of fighting students with a clear perception of the whole social struggle'.[37] A mixture of elitism and nihilism can easily be discerned in these bold assertions. Characteristically, he took little interest in history. These peculiarities would explain the absence of reference in his writings to a theory of transition. Indeed, history meant to him and to his fellow students only the history of the ignominious post-war democracy that ought to be rejected if possible by direct action. When action seemed doomed, it appears, he surrendered himself, an act which could be construed as motivated again by the same spirit of negation.

The activist students, especially 'non-sect' radicals, sought emotional as well as theoretical justification of their action in the translations of Marcuse, Guevara, and Cohn-Bendit. Their intellectual needs were also met by some Japanese writers, such as Takaaki Yoshimoto with his doctrine of the state as a system of communal illusions, and Gorō Hani with his panegyric of autonomy in free universities as well as free cities.

Yoshimoto has been referred to as 'an anarchist intellectual', and has published *An Ode of Resistance* in support of the anarchist

---

[35] *Asahi-Shinbun*, 5 September 1969.

[36] Shingo Shibata (ed.), *Gendai-Nihon-no-Radikarizumu (Japanese Radicalism Today)*, Tokyo, 1970, pp. 342, 346.

[37] Yamamoto, *op. cit.*, pp. 86, 92, 138.

Behan-i (Anti-Vietnam War Direct Action Committee). The son of a shipwright, he was very much concerned with the indigenous ideas and attitudes, the hopes and sorrows of the silent masses. His wartime experience taught him to tackle seriously the doctrine of ultranationalism which he regarded as highly suggestive for a pure theory of the state. His studies of Marx after the war led him to conceive of the state as illusion or fantasy: the political state, as he saw it, was a 'communality reached through evolution of religious alienation'.[38] Yoshimoto was against classical Marxism of 'class' and 'proletariat', and assigned to the intellectuals the role of assimilating the unexpressed desires of the masses and standing up against the system of common illusion, the state.

The 'old' Marxist Hani exerted considerable influence on the activist students through his popular book *The Logic of the Cities* (1968), which is said to have sold 800,000 copies in one year, and through other writings and speeches. He pleaded for a federation of autonomous cities, the model of which he saw in Renaissance Italy, and which he believed would provide the foundation of future socialism. He held that the students, like the citizens of free cities, had the right to arm, and did no more than exercise their rights when they erected barricades in their universities.

Hani was only one of many apologists for the students. Under the post-war democracy which the students detested, flourished the type of publishing house which specialized in 'anti-system' intellectual commodities. Indeed, the intellectual origins of student power in Japan should be traced to the combined influence of all these and similar writings. The latest commodity in vogue was nihilism. Within the framework of nihilism and the ideology of negation, the students were eclectic enough to pick up novel ideas and slogans from whatever books and articles they happened to lay hands on: 'university commune', 'university revolution', 'the illusory state', 'the role of the intellectuals', 'direct democracy', 'direct action', and so on.

At the height of student power, Ōsawa, the anarchist writer, who was on the look-out for signs of anarchist revival, welcomed what he called 'the recrudescence of revolutionary violence'. The 'Epoch of Great Revolt', as he called it, coincided with the period of automation, and rationalization, and it is significant, as he rightly pointed out, that 'the first really rebellious violence' in post-war Japan should have occurred during the heroic struggle of the armed

[38] Yoshimoto, 'Jiritsu-no-Shisō-teki-Kyoten (Intellectual Basis of Independence', *Tenbō* (*Prospect*), March 1965, 27.

miners against the closure of the pits at Miike in 1960. This was, however, a romantic view of the desperate fight of unhappy men trapped in a declining industry, the rationalization of which, under existing arrangements, resulted in the flight of capital, leaving the men half starving by the unwanted pits. Ōsawa hoped that 'revolutionary violence' to which the students had resorted at Haneda, Ōji and Narita, would soon spread into the ranks of the workers. He felt, however, that the 'detonator theory' of students' violence had little to do with anarchism. Violence would become oppressive and reactionary rather than revolutionary, he said, 'when it is separated from the revolutionary masses and concentrated in the hands of a party of the advance guard', and also when it became excessive and constant. It is for this reason that he called the violence of the anti-communist Zengakuren 'half revolutionary'. 'Even if it succeeded, it would come to a new Stalinism; if it failed, it would be absorbed by a new Fascism.'[39]

What Ōsawa feared was already taking place: there was frequent and outrageous violence which became really oppressive; the *Zenkyōtō* began to lose the support of the 'student masses' as the campus disputes seemed stuck in the bog of impossible demands and the real danger of dissolution of universities loomed on the horizon. There were extravagances everywhere, not only among the students but also throughout the 'New Left'. Oda of the *Beheiren* nonchalantly proclaimed that he would start a citizens' movement from outside to smash Tokyo University if the *Zenkyōtō* failed to destroy it.[40] One sect of the *Shagakudō* (Socialist Student League) called the *Sekigun-ha* (Red Army faction), a body of three to four hundred extremist students, went so far out of its senses that it decided to organize an army of revolution to turn metropolitan Tokyo into a battlefield in November, 1969, the date of Sato's scheduled visit to the United States for extension of the Security Treaty. According to this plan, 'an armed rising and the assassination of the Premier would lead to the establishment of a revolutionary provisional government'.[41] Their leaders were arrested, and there were many other arrests throughout 1969, which almost crippled the fighting capacity of the militant sects, though apparently not enough to prevent the remaining Red Army students from hijacking a JAL plane to Pyongyang in the

---

[39] Osawa, 'Yomigaeru-Kakumeiteki-Bōryoku (Resuscitation of Revolutionary Violence)', *Kuro-no-Techō* (*Black Notebook*), January 1969.

[40] Oda in *Gendai-no-Me* (*Contemporary Witness*), March 1969.

[41] *Asahi-Shinbun*, 13 September 1969.

following year. The militants' strength began to collapse under the weight of their own provocations, especially under the pressure of legislation they had provoked: the University Temporary Measures Act which was rushed through in August 1969 after the already too familiar spectacle of the government simply ignoring opposition both inside and outside the Diet.

Extravagance also marked the form of their apostasy. One of the leaders of the Anti-Yoyogi *Zengakuren* at the time of the 1960 struggle is known to have received funds from right-wing sources and he later became the manager of a yacht training club. It is indeed an ominous sign that *Zenkyōtō's* 'irrationalism' was admired by a novelist of the new Fascism.[42]

The new radicalism of the 'New Left' had sprung up mainly because post-war democracy had not functioned as its critics thought it should. The militants' protests and direct action appear to have contributed to the impairment of the already weakened democratic institutions and practices. It was of no use the anarchists holding out the millenarian mirror of direct democracy, as if it were a practical alternative to parliamentary democracy. The anarchists, like many others, often had second thoughts. Some of them despaired of the 'emotional rebels', and proposed a more realistic attitude towards political democracy and Marxism. The voice of realism, however, was too weak to make much impression at the time.

As for the students' revolt in the late 1960s, it was clearly not anarchism as such but emotional anarchy of nihilism that sustained student power and its violence. Anarchism, apart from the 'pure' type which is always inclined to terrorism, has played the role of a sympathetic critic of the 'New Left', although the anarchists' sympathy with direct action, especially at an early stage of student power, seems to have somewhat blunted the edge of their criticism. In fact, they remained as critics of the political left, both new and old. In this respect, the views of Tatsumi Soejima, a doll-maker and an anarchist of 40 years' standing, expressed shortly before his death in 1963, are worth recording: 'I cannot imagine a social revolution taking place in human history. All the revolutions of the past were political revolutions, and so will those of the future be. Anarchism, which denies political revolution, will become a moral force and deal with the problem of how to live, and I believe in such anarchism. . . . I do not mean that there ought not to be a political

[42] Shibata (ed.), *op. cit.*, 40. ·

revolution; it is a necessity, and the essence of anarchism lies in how to participate in that revolution.'[43] Although the new generation of anarchists is still groping its way towards new theories of autonomy and federation, anarchism itself, it seems, has become somewhat ethical, and this is no doubt its strength as well as its weakness.

[43] *Jiyū-Rengō*, 1 February 1963.

Nicolas Walter

Anarchism in Print: Yesterday and Today

A Bibliographical note

NOTHING FAILS LIKE FAILURE; THE LESS ANARCHISTS ARE READ, THE less they write, and the less they are written about. The anarchist movement has risen and fallen in turn for more than a century, and in the trough just before the current wave there was probably less new literature concerning anarchism than ever before. My object here is to examine the situation in this country at that time, roughly between 1945 and 1960, and then to see how it has changed during the last ten years. (I have excluded articles in periodicals in order to avoid over-complication.)*

FREEDOM AND THE FIFTIES

AFTER THE SECOND WORLD WAR, MOST PEOPLE CAME INTO CONTACT with anarchism through *Freedom*. This had been founded when Kropotkin settled in England in 1886 and was therefore the oldest left-wing paper in the country (if not the world). It won considerable publicity when three of the editors were imprisoned for anti-militarist propaganda in 1945. During the following years it continued to appear every month, then every fortnight, then every week, but its circulation fell until it was seldom much more than 1,000, and the paper was little known outside the movement. But the Freedom Press always published more than just a paper, and it still produced new editions of classic pamphlets, such as Alexander Berkman's *The ABC of Anarchism* and Errico Malatesta's *Anarchy*, as well as several by Peter Kropotkin – by far the most frequently published and widely read anarchist writer in English (as in most languages).

The Freedom Press also produced new pamphlets even in the worst days – *Marxism, Freedom and the State* (1950), an anthology of Bakunin's later writings by K. J. Kenafick (who had previously

* I would like to express my gratitude to Paul Avrich and Colin Ward for their help.

written a study of Marx and Bakunin); *Workers in Stalin's Russia* (1944) by Marie Louise Berneri (a leading member of the British movement from her arrival as a refugee from Fascism in 1937 to her early death in 1949); a translation of *Peter Kropotkin: His Federalist Ideas* (1942) by Camillo Berneri (her father, who had been murdered by communists in Barcelona); *The Kronstadt Revolt* (1942) by Anton Ciliga; *The Wilhelmshaven Revolt* (1944) by 'Icarus'; *Barbarism and Sexual Freedom* (1948) and *Delinquency* (1951) by Alex Comfort; *Italy After Mussolini* (1945), *Mutual Aid and Social Evolution* (1946), *Ill-Health, Poverty and the State* (1946), and *Sexual Freedom for the Young* (1951) by John Hewetson; *Youth for Freedom* (1951), *Food Production and Population* (1952), and *Who Will Do the Dirty Work?* (1952) by Tony Gibson; *Syndicalism: The Workers' Next Step* (1951) by Philip Sansom; several other syndicalist titles by Tom Brown; and *New Life to the Land* (1942), *Railways and Society* (1943), *Homes or Hovels* (1944), *Anarchism and Morality* (1945), and *The Basis of Communal Living* (1947) by George Woodcock (then still active in the anarchist movement).

Probably the most influential Freedom Press publications were those of Herbert Read, whose support for the war in 1939 and acceptance of a knighthood in 1953 alienated him from most active anarchists, but whose intellectual attraction continued for many years. The Freedom Press republished *Poetry and Anrrchism* (1941) – originally published in 1938 – and published *The Philosophy of Anarchism* (1940), *The Education of Free Men* (1944), *Existentialism, Marxism and Anarchism* (1949), and *Art and the Evolution of Man* (1951). Most of his anarchist writings were collected by commercial publishers in such volumes as *The Politics of the Unpolitical* and *Anarchy and Order*.

The Freedom Press produced a few books as well, apart from an annual selection of articles from *Freedom* (from 1951 onwards) – an anthology of Kropotkin's writings by Herbert Read; a two-volume translation by Holley Cantine of most of Voline's libertarian history of the Russian revolution, *La révolution inconnue* (1947); a short but important analysis of the role of the anarchists in the Spanish revolution and civil war by Vernon Richards (the main figure in the Freedom Press from 1936 onwards); a memorial volume to Marie Louise Berneri, and a posthumous collection of her articles; one of E. A. Gutkind's pioneering contributions to environmental studies; and a brief but comprehensive introduction to anarchism by George Woodcock.

Thus *Freedom*, the Freedom Press, and the Freedom Bookshop – all at 27 Red Lion Street, London – constituted the main focus of anarchist propaganda in Britain; but not the only focus. There was the Syndicalist Workers Federation (the result of a split in the movement at the end of the war) which produced a paper most of the time and also its own pamphlets – including some more by Tom Brown – the best known being a statement of *Workers' Control* and a survey of *How Labour Governed, 1945–1951* (now due for a sequel – *Twenty Years After?*). Up in Glasgow, Guy Aldred maintained his idiosyncratic anti-parliamentarian agitation after half a century, his most interesting publication being not so much his final paper, *The Word*, as the second version of his memoirs, *No Traitor's Gait!*, which appeared in irregular instalments and remained unfinished at his death in 1963. And it would be wrong to forget the little publishers who produced such things as Alex Comfort's first collection of essays, *Art and Social Responsibility*, or elegant reprints of Shelley's *Defence of Poetry* and Wilde's *The Soul of Man Under Socialism*; while obscure papers like *The University Libertarian* would sell a few hundred copies for a few years before disappearing into oblivion.

From the United States came surveys of American libertarianism by Rudolf Rocker and James Martin; an account of the efforts made by Russian anarchist exiles to help their comrades in Russia, by one of the exiles, Boris Yelensky; a summary of anarchist principles by another, G. P. Maximoff; two collections of articles by the briefly libertarian journalist, Dwight Macdonald; a collection by the then obscure libertarian writer, Paul Goodman; the memoirs of two leading personalities in the Catholic Worker movement, Dorothy Day and Ammon Hennacy; one of the best of all prison books, compiled by the editors of the remarkable paper *Retort*, Holley Cantine and Dachine Rainer; and a short account of anarchism, extracted from Rudolf Rocker's book *Anarcho-Syndicalism* (1938), was included in Feliks Gross's anthology of ideologies.

All this anarchist or near-anarchist material was difficult enough to find, but it was also difficult to find new material written about rather than by anarchists, and published in commercial editions for general readers. A few classics of libertarian thought did appear across the Atlantic – a definitive edition of Godwin's *Enquiry concerning Political Justice*; a new edition of Kropotkin's *Mutual Aid* by Ashley Montagu (the Pelican edition by H. L. Beales still used to turn up in secondhand bookshops); a new edition of T. E. Hulme's translation of Sorel's *Reflections on Violence* (though it must be noted that this has almost nothing to do with anarchism as most anarchists understand it). At the same time many of Tolstoy's anarchistic writings were kept in print in the 'World's Classics' series, and separate translations of his last political essay, *The Law of Love and the Law of Violence*, appeared on each side of the Atlantic.

NEW WORK

Some good new work was done – George Woodcock, as he moved away from the movement, produced valuable biographies of Godwin, Proudhon, and (with Ivan Avakumović) Kropotkin, as well as a collection of literary essays; Henri de Lubac's Catholic study of Proudhon was translated; G. P. Maximoff compiled a sympathetic digest of Bakunin's writings, while Eugene Pyziur wrote an unsympathetic but equally valuable analysis of Bakunin's ideas; the sections of Rudolf Rocker's memoirs covering his activity in the Jewish anarcho-syndicalist movement in Britain from 1895 to 1918 were translated from Yiddish; Augustus John's fragmentary autobiography also gave a glimpse of the anarchist movement of the past; and before she died Marie Louise Berneri completed a survey of utopian thought from the libertarian point of view.

The standard textbooks and political thought and history scarcely mentioned anarchism, but there were historical and biographical works which did touch on various aspects of libertarian theory and activity – Sir Alexander Gray's witty survey of the socialist tradition scampered through Proudhon, Bakunin and Kropotkin, as well as Sorel and, even more perversely, Bertrand Russell; Lane Lancaster's volume in the *Masters of Political Thought* series contained a typically superficial chapter on Kropotkin; Norman Cohn's *The Pursuit of the Millennium* uncovered some of the medieval roots of the anarchist ideology; David Fleisher and D. H. Monro produced useful theses on Godwin; J. Hampden Jackson's volume in the 'Teach Yourself History' series gave a quick survey of anarchist history; Martin Buber's *Paths in Utopia* had some original things to say about Proudhon, Kropotkin, and Gustav Landauer; James Joll's history of the Second International mentioned the attempts by the anarchists to take part; the first (and still the only) volume of Richard Hostetter's history of Italian socialism gave some information about the early anarchists; Gopinath Dhawan and Joan Bondurant related Gandhi's ideas to the anarchist tradition; E. J. Hobsbawm's analysis of primitive rebels included a fascinating chapter on the Andalusian anarchists and a few extracts from Makhno's memoirs; Richard Hare, Avrahm Yarmolinsky, and Eugene Lampert covered various aspects of anarchism in their studies of the Russian revolutionary movement; Leonard Schapiro's detailed account of the establishment of the communist dictatorship in Russia included a good description of the anarchist movement before its destruction; Max Nomad added another instalment to his idiosyncratic surveys of revolutionary thought; E. P. Thompson's magnificent biography of William Morris included much important material on the early British anarchist movement; and Henry Pelling's volume on socialism in the 'British Political Tradition' series included a few relevant documents; above all, G. D. H. Cole's history of socialist thought devoted several chapters of the first two volumes to anarchist writers.

The situation in the social sciences was confusing. Many works which anarchists found relevant were not consciously connected with anarchism at all. Thus the writings of Ashley Montagu may certainly be seen as a continuation of Kropotkin's work on mutual aid, but this should not be stressed. Such writers as Lewis Mumford and Leopold Kohr could be seen as working in the tradition of Proudhon, Bakunin, Kropotkin and other anarchist theorists towards political decentralization and economic integration, but this would be a narrow way of looking at them. So anarchists drew valuable ideas from sociologists such as Seymour Melman and Michael Young, psychologists such as Wilhelm Reich and Erich Fromm, philosophers such as Bertrand Russell and Martin Buber, cyberneticians and neurologists such as Norbert Wiener and Grey Walter, political scientists such as C. Wright Mills and Milovan Djilas, and similar writers in many other fields.

Particularly interesting books were those relating to such questions as whether any human societies managed to do without government, whether industry could be run with some form of workers' control, whether the education of children and the treatment of criminals could dispense with authority and compulsion, whether local health and welfare could be organized on libertarian rather than on bureaucratic lines. Thus there were some anthropological studies, of which the most relevant single one was John Middleton's and David Tait's *Tribes without Rulers*; industrial studies such as James Gillespie's *Free Expression in Industry* and Gordon Rattray Taylor's *Are Workers Human?*; educational writings as near as anarchism as it is possible to get without actually being anarchist, especially by David Wills and, above all, A. S. Neill, and criminological work by Paul Reiwald;

and good accounts of the Peckham experiment, an inside view by Innis Pearse and Lucy Crocker and an outside one by John Comerford.

More explicitly anarchist was the work of Alex Comfort. *Authority and Delinquency in the Modern State* was a serious scholarly book, but its subtitle – 'A Criminological Approach to the Problems of Power' – reveals its subversive implications and it is full of subversive ideas. In the same way *Sexual Behaviour in Society* looked like a textbook for social scientists and social workers but was also (like his pamphlet) an early call for what came to be known as the 'new morality' or the 'permissive society', and it must have exploded in the minds of many unsuspecting readers. And *The Pattern of the Future*, which was a collection of innocuous seeming broadcasts, was in fact an unequivocal call to (or rather, from) arms. Perhaps the situation in the period before 1960 can be best described as that in which Alex Comfort was little known and rather frightening.

CHANGE IN THE SIXTIES

The change in that situation came on both sides of the Atlantic during the 1960s, counting from the entry at the beginning of the decade of the anarchists into the anti-war movement (which future anarchologists may consider to be as important, on a much smaller scale, as Sorel considered the entry of the anarchists into the syndicalist movement) to the participation of the anarchists in the student rebellion at the end of the decade. But this change took time to come about, and it is really only now that anarchism can be favourably treated by serious writers and that anarchism at last means money – for publishers, that is, not for anarchists.

Freedom continued, its circulation sometimes rising to its old wartime level above 4,000 at times of particular upheaval, when anarchists became involved in popular movements. In 1961 the Freedom Press also began a monthly paper, *Anarchy*, which has been edited ever since by Colin Ward and has held a pretty steady circulation between 2,000 and 3,000. There have been some more pamphlets – new editions of Berkman and Malatesta; *The First Person* (1963), a collection of reprinted articles by George Barrett (an anarchist writer who died in 1917); *Towards a Free Society* (1960), a survey of socialism by Charles Martin; a new translation by Vernon Richards of Kropotkin's *The State: Its Historic Role* (1969). There have also been some more books – new editions of Paul Eltzbacher's survey of 19th-century anarchist thought and of Max Stirner's *The Ego and His Own*, and Vernon Richards's digest of Malatesta's life and ideas.

But the Freedom Press – though still active for a decade in Fulham and now in new premises at 84B Whitechapel High Street, London – was unable to keep up with the rising interest in anarchism, and many other foci appeared, all lively but mostly transient. Not only in London but in many other places (especially university towns) anarchist papers and pamphlets have been and are being produced, mostly in duplicated form, but they seldom penetrate beyond their immediate environment. The Syndicalist Workers Federation continued to produce a paper and some more pamphlets. The anarchist wing of the nuclear disarmament movement produced little literature of its own, though such Committee of 100 papers as *Resistance* were anarchist in all but name, and a group called Nonviolence 63 issued a couple of anarchist pamphlets in 1963. An individualist group has produced a paper called *Minus One* and interesting brief statements of their interpretation of anarchism by S. E. Parker, Jean-Pierre Schweitzer, and Jeff Robinson. Alfred Reynolds, the main figure in a libertarian group called the Bridge Circle, published a short collection of his articles in its paper *The London Letter* called *Pilate's Question* (1964). In 1966 a group of anarchists produced an English number of the American paper *The Rebel Worker* and followed it with two numbers of *Heatwave*, leaning towards the surrealists, provos, situationists and hippies. The Libertarian Teachers Association has brought out a valuable bulletin growing from a single sheet to a forty-page paper called *The Libertarian Teacher*. The Christian anarchists have an occasional paper, *Logos*; the radical Christian paper, *The Catonsville Roadrunner*, is very near to anarchism; and it is significant that the Peace Pledge Union has published Ronald Sampson's pamphlet, *The Anarchist Basis of Pacifism* (1970).

Perhaps the most interesting of the anarchist foci is the protean group which from 1965 to 1967 produced the paper called *Cuddon's Cosmopolitan Review* (after a paper published a century earlier), in 1965 published a pamphlet by several London anarchists called *Anarchism*, in 1966 produced a few issues of a syndicalist broadsheet called *Ludd* for the seamen's strike, from 1965 to 1967 ran the Wooden Shoe bookshop in central London (which gave its name to one issue of a paper in 1967), from 1967 to 1968 published a series of mainly historical pamphlets culminating in a rather eccentric statement of *The Aims and Principles of Anarchism*, and from 1968 has published the *Bulletin of the Anarchist Black Cross* (an international welfare organization); a more permanent paper called *Black Flag* has been in the offing for some time – indeed it was prematurely included in a recent Communist Party pamphlet attacking anarchists and other 'ultra-leftists' – and the recent book *The Floodgates of Anarchy* is by two members of the group, Stuart Christie and Albert Meltzer.

Finally the Solidarity Group, which emerged from the Trotskyist movement in the late 1950s, has produced a stimulating paper and series of pamphlets, maintaining a strong libertarian syndicalist line often approaching pure anarchism. Its large output includes the first (abridged) English edition of Ida Mett's *The Kronstadt Commune* (1967) and an important new exposure by Maurice Brinton of the bolshevik attitude to the workers' control movement in the Russian revolution.

CLASSICS AND OTHER WORK

At the same time as all this activity, commercial publishers began to produce books in some quantity dealing with various aspects of anarchism and sometimes even taking anarchism as a main subject. There have not been many new editions of classic texts other than those of the Freedom Press (nothing like the massive rescue work on Bakunin being undertaken in French by the International Institute for Social History in Amsterdam), but there are a few – Max Stirner's *False Principles of Our Education* translated by Robert Beebe and edited by James Martin; Lysander Spooner's *No Treason: The Constitution of No Authority*; *Russian Philosophy*, a three-volume anthology edited by James Edie and others, containing some valuable pieces of Bakunin and Tolstoy; a badly edited but still useful collection of *Tolstoy's Writings on Civil Disobedience and Non-Violence*; Stewart Edward's short anthology of Proudhon (the first in English, following several in French) and Alan Ritter's study of Proudhon's political thought (in which connection one may mention Nicholas Riasanovsky's study of Fourier's thought). A lot of Kropotkin may be expected next year, when he comes out of copyright; several of his books in English have already been reprinted – *Memoirs of a Revolutionist* in three editions – but there is no prospect of a proper collection of his writings, any more than for Bakunin, Proudhon, or any other libertarian author.

In the area of modern classics, Herbert Read continued to produce anarchist essays up to his death in 1968, as may be seen from his collections *To Hell With Culture* and *The Cult of Sincerity*; a useful survey of his anarchist career is given by George Woodcock in Robin Skelton's memorial symposium. Alex Comfort's latest collection of essays, *Darwin and the Naked Lady*, summed up the themes of his recent books on the social application of biology (one being a more explicit edition of his book on sex), in which he has been particularly successful in putting modern libertarian ideas on a scientific basis. Across the Atlantic Paul Goodman has produced a stream of books containing some of his enormous output of articles and speeches over a decade during which his paradoxical contribution has been that what he once put forward as utopian suggestions now seem to be obvious solutions. And an even more condensed version of Rudolf Rocker's old account of anarchism has been included in Priscilla Long's anthology of New Left writings.

Then there have been some American anthologies, of socialist thought in general or of anarchist thought on its own – *Socialist Thought* by Albert Fried and Ronald Sanders includes Proudhon, Bakunin, Kropotkin, and Sorel; *Modern Socialism* by Massimo Salvadori includes Proudhon, Bakunin, and Sorel; *The Anarchists* by Irving Louis Horowitz contains some long extracts from classic anarchist writers, but much irrelevant and inferior material as well; *Patterns of Anarchy* by Leonard I. Krimerman and Lewis Perry gives a more faithful impression of anarchist ideas but is still unsatisfactory: indeed no anthology in English has yet approached the standard of *Ni dieu ni maître* by Daniel Guérin and others, a massive and magnificent compilation first published in Paris in 1965 and now in its third (paperback) edition.

There have been several biographical works – Madeleine Stern's life of the American Stephen Pearl Andrews, Martin Malia's definitive account of Herzen's early career (illuminating the origins of Russian anarchism), Michael Prawdin's study of Nechayev (showing just how far he was from anarchism), Peter Sedgwick's translation of Victor Serge's memoirs (unfortunately abridged), I. L. Horowitz's study of Sorel, Philip Foner's edition of the autobiographies of the Chicago Martyrs, Richard Drinnon's fine life of Emma Goldman, James Hulse's study of Kropotkin in *Revolutionists in London*, Dorothy Day's inside account of the Catholic Worker movement, and another autobiographical volume from Ammon Hennacy.

There have been many historical works – a new edition of Cohn's

The Pursuit of the Millennium has been expanded, and George Hunston Williams's analysis of the 'radical reformation' gives more information on the religious origins of the anarchist ideology; a symposium on the Internationals by Milorad Drachkovitch contains a chapter on anarchist internationalism by Max Nomad; Barbara Tuchman's impressionistic picture of the world before the first world war contains a sadly inaccurate account of the anarchist movement. Among the many books on Russia, two good histories of Russian political thought have come from Thornton Anderson and S. V. Utechin; Eugene Lampert produced another survey of revolutionary ideas; Franco Venturi's vast exposition of populism up to 1881 throws much light on early Russian anarchism; Frederick Kaplan has written a detailed analysis of the bolshevik attitude to workers' control; Alexander Rabinowitch has written a detailed account of the July Days in 1917; David Footman's study of Makhno, which appeared in a symposium in 1959, was incorporated into his history of the Russian civil war; and Paul Avrich finally produced a full account of the whole Russian anarchist movement, following it with the first scholarly history of the Kronstadt rising in English. Among books on Spain, Burnett Bolloten's authoritative exposure of the communist destruction of the Spanish revolution incidentally gives a detailed account of the revolution itself; and E. J. Hobsbawm's semi-popular survey of bandits culminates with a sympathetic portrait of Francisco Sabaté. But there is still no proper account of Spanish anarchism in English. Victor Alba's study of the Latin American Labour movement took the role of the anarchists and anarcho-syndicalists into account, but again there is no proper history of Latin American anarchism. France fares even worse – Eugenia Herbert has sketched the artistic connections of anarchism, Rayner Heppenstall has touched clumsily on criminal aspects of anarchism, and J. C. Longoni's *Four Patients of Dr. Deibler* gives a narrative of four anarchist terrorists of the 1890s. But there is no good book on French anarchism in English, above all no translation of Jean Maitron's classic *Histoire du mouvement anarchiste en France*, which was published as long ago as 1951. But for that matter there are not even any acceptable accounts of anarchism in Britain or America, though the current movements in both Britain and the United States have been superficially described by George Thayer, and Corinne Jacker has attempted a history of the American movement.

Farther East, Adi Doctor has produced a study of Indian anarchism (concentrating rather unexpectedly on Gandhi and Bhave), and Robert Scalapino and George Yu have produced one of Chinese anarchism (up to the 1920s); Olga Lang followed with a fine biography of the Chinese anarchist writer Pa Chin, and the symposia on 20th-century politics in China by Jack Gray and Mary Wright include valuable essays by Martin Bernal. Of the many centennial studies of Gandhi, those by Bandyopadhyaya and Bhattacharyya took particular account of his anarchist tendencies. Tatsuo Arima's study of Japanese intellectuals in the Taishō period includes the anarchist Ōsugi Sakae; but again there is no proper study of the earlier episode of Kōtoku Shūsui in English (though there is much relevant information in Hyman Kublin's life of Sen Katayama).

On a more general level, George Lichtheim's standard book on Marxism includes a good short chapter on the relations of Marxism with anarchism and syndicalism; and the first volume of his history of socialism includes a stimulating chapter on Proudhon (the second volume is unfortunately less interesting). Robert Tucker's latest book on Marx has a useful discussion of the anarchist aspect of Marxism; a more interesting discussion of the same subject by Hal Draper is included in the latest *Socialist Register*. Max Nomad has added yet another instalment to his series of surveys, as well as a typically idiosyncratic autobiography (*Dreamers, Dynamiters and Demagogues*). Julius Braunthal's two-volume history of the Internationals is mainly concerned with communists and social democrats, but the first volume has a brief account of anarchist internationalism. The closing passage of the final volume of Cole's history of socialist thought – rejecting both communism and social democracy – was widely noted by anarchists. A particularly interesting contribution is Maurice Cranston's imaginary dialogue between Marx and Bakunin, broadcast in 1962 and printed in his collection of such dialogues. Lyman T. Sargent's survey of contemporary ideologies contains a brief and inaccurate but fair and up-to-date summary of anarchism.

Then there have been some new general histories of anarchism, at last replacing the old ones by Zenker, Eltzbacher, Vizetelly and Rocker – the best known, most widely sold, and probably the most generally useful being that by George Woodcock, then that by James Joll, and a long way behind a poor synthesis by Atindranath Bose – and no doubt there will soon be plenty more; but again no work in English yet matches Daniel Guérin's short but penetrating book *L'Anarchisme*, first published in Paris in 1965 and only recently available in translation. The anarchists themselves have tried to do this sort of thing in pamphlet form, in America and Australia as well as in Britain, but as I know from my own experience of producing such a study – *About Anarchism* (published by the Freedom Press in 1969) – it is a difficult and unsatisfactory task.

There has not been much proper documentation outside the anarchist press of anarchist participation in popular struggles (as usual: the anarchist role in even the Russian and Spanish revolutions is still widely ignored because it is so erratically recorded). The nuclear disarmament movement, for example, has been described badly by Herb Greer, fairly well by Christopher Driver, and briefly by Norman Moss, but none of these have taken much notice of the part played by the anarchists; and this is scarcely mentioned in Frank Parkin's disappointing sociological study. Even less attention has been given to anarchist activity in the general anti-war movement before 1945, and when it has the results have often been unfortunate – the worst instance perhaps being a startlingly ignorant passage in David Martin's general study of pacifism.

Before the squatters campaign has fallen into oblivion one of its main figures, Ron Bailey, has luckily produced a Penguin Special; he previously brought out a couple of pamphlets at earlier stages in the homeless campaign of the 1960s, and in this connection one should also mention the valuable Solidarity pamphlet on the King Hill campaign in Kent – *K.C.C. versus the Homeless* (1966).

The uneven literature on the confusing student movement has so far had little to say about its libertarian aspects, perhaps the best book here being the Penguin Special on the Hornsey affair; another relevant Penguin Special in the field of education is of course Leila Berg's eloquent threnody for Risinghill school. Even the French 'events' of 1968, which have been exhaustively (and exhaustingly) described in French, have been only thinly covered on this side of the Channel, though there is a translation of the Cohn–Bendits' own account, and the British half of *The Beginning of the End* by Angelo Quattrocchi and Tom Nairn is one of the best things written on the subject. Some of the documentation of the Chinese cultural revolution hints at the anarchic tendency which occasionally emerged, but this has not yet been properly established. Similarly the current situation in the United States has not been fixed firmly enough to view clearly. And there are also Germany and Italy, and Russia and Czechoslovakia, and so on.

The situation in the social sciences has remained confusing; the main difference now is that more writers seem willing to consider anarchy as a social, political and philosophical idea worth seriously discussing rather than simply dismissing. Further figures have been added to those found relevant by anarchists – such as Russell Barton and Erving Goffmann in psychology, R. D. Laing and David Cooper in psychiatry, Herbert Marcuse in political science, Lewis Herber in environmental studies, Theodore Roszak in educational and cultural studies, Ronald V. Sampson in the social aspects of literary criticism – and especially interesting books include Lucy Mair's *Primitive Government* and Lawrence Krader's *Formation of the State* in anthropology, and the anthology edited by Ken Coates and Tony Topham on workers' control. But the full integration of the anarchist contribution to the social sciences is still to come, as the old orthodoxies of Marxism and liberalism on either side are relaxed.

One significant phenomenon has been the appearance of several good old (as well as new) books in paperback editions – Goldsworthy Lowes Dickinson's *A Modern Symposium*, Bertrand Russell's *Roads to Freedom*, Max Nomad's *Rebels and Renegades* and *Apostles of Revolution*, Geoffrey Gorer's *The Life and Ideas of the Marquis de Sade*, Karl Mannheim's *Ideology and Utopia*, E. H. Carr's *Michael Bakunin*, Franz Borkenau's *The Spanish Cockpit*, Gerald Brenan's *The Spanish Labyrinth*, W. H. Chamberlain's *The Russian Revolution*, Lewis Mumford's *The Culture of Cities*, A. S. Neill's *Summerhill* – and this will presumably continue as part of the wider paperback revolution. An analogous phenomenon has been the appearance (especially in the United States) of some expensive facsimile reprints of important classics – most of Kropotkin's books in English, for example, and such crucial texts as Max Nettlau's *Bibliographie de l'anarchie* (from Burt Franklin of New York) and Josef Stammhammer's *Bibliographie des Sozialismus und Kommunismus* (from Otto Zeller of Aalen) – and this will certainly continue and involve periodicals as well as books. Dover Publications (together with Constable in London) have just launched a venture which combines both these phenomena – a series of paperback editions of anarchist classics, with facsimile texts and new introductions, beginning with Emma Goldman's *Anarchism and Other Essays* – and this too will no doubt spread.

In general, it looks as if during the 1970s we may expect further historical and biographical description of anarchism as a phantom of the past; we should also hope for the more important (and more difficult) social and political analysis of anarchism as a spectre haunting the present; we may then look forward to a fresh expression of anarchism as a vision of the future: this will probably take the form of imaginative literature above all – a category which has been excluded from this survey because it is too variable and complicated to treat briefly, but which is perhaps the most intense and influential form of anarchism in print.

NEW BOOKS MENTIONED

(Only the place and date of first publication are given; starred titles are also available in cheap paperback editions)

Victor Alba: *Politics and the Labor Movement in Latin America*, Stanford, 1968.

Guy Aldred: *No Traiter's Gait!*, Glasgow, 1955–63.

Thornton Anderson: *Russian Political Thought*, Ithaca, N.Y., 1967.

Tatsuo Arima: *The Failure of Freedom*, Cambridge, Mass., 1969.

Paul Avrich: *Kronstadt, 1921*, Princeton, 1970.

Paul Avrich: *The Russian Anarchists*, Princeton, 1967.

Ron Bailey: *Squatting and the Homeless*, Harmondsworth, 1971.

Jayantanuja Bandyopadhyaya: *Social and Political Thought of Gandhi*, Bombay, 1969.

Leila Berg: *Risinghill*, Harmondsworth, 1968.

Marie Louise Berneri: A Tribute, London, 1949.

Marie Louise Berneri: *Journey Through Utopia*, London, 1950.

Marie Louise Berneri: *Neither East Nor West*, London, 1952.

Buddhadeva Bhattacharyya: *Evolution of the Political Philosophy of Gandhi*, Calcutta, 1969.

Burnett Bolloten: *The Grand Camouflage*, New York, 1961.

*Joan Bondurant: *Conquest of Violence*, Princeton, 1958.

Atindranath Bose: *A History of Anarchism*, Calcutta, 1967.

Julius Braunthal: *History of the International, 1864–1914*. Translated by Henry Collins and Kenneth Mitchell, London, 1966.

Maurice Brinton: *The Bolsheviks and Workers' Control*, London, 1970.

*Martin Buber: *Paths in Utopia*. Translated by R. F. C. Hull, London, 1949.

Holley Cantine and Dachine Rainer (editors): *Prison Etiquette*, Bearsville, N.Y., 1950.

Stuart Christie and Albert Meltzer: *The Floodgates of Anarchy*, London, 1970.

*Ken Coates and Tony Topham (editors): *Industrial Democracy in Great Britain*, London, 1968.

*Norman Cohn: *The Pursuit of the Millennium*, London, 1957.

*Daniel and Gabriel Cohn-Bendit: *Obsolete Communism: The Left-Wing Alternative*. Translated by Arnold Pomerans, London, 1968.

G. D. H. Cole: *A History of Socialist Thought*, London, 1953–60.

John Comerford: *Health the Unknown*, London, 1947.

Alex Comfort: *Art and Social Responsibility*, London, 1946.

Alex Comfort: *Authority and Delinquency in the Modern State*, London, 1950.

Alex Comfort: *Darwin and the Naked Lady*, London, 1961.

*Alex Comfort: *Nature and Human Nature*, London, 1966.

Alex Comfort: *The Pattern of the Future*, London, 1949.

*Alex Comfort: *Sex in Society*, London, 1963.

Alex Comfort: *Sexual Behaviour in Society*, London, 1950.

Maurice Cranston: *Political Dialogues*, London, 1968.

Dorothy Day: *Loaves and Fishes*, New York, 1963.

Dorothy Day: *The Long Loneliness*, New York, 1952.

Gopinath Dhawan: *The Political Philosophy of Mahatma Gandhi*, Ahmedabad, 1946.

Adi H. Doctor: *Anarchist Thought in India*, Bombay, 1964.

*Milorad M. Drachkovitch (editor): *The Revolutionary Internationals*, Stanford, 1966.

*Richard Drinnon: *Rebel in Paradise*, Chicago, 1961.

Christopher Driver: *The Disarmers*, London, 1964.

*James M. Edie, James P. Scanlan, and Mary-Barbara Zeldin (editors): *Russian Philosophy*, Chicago, 1965.

*Stewart Edwards (editor): *Selected Writings of Pierre-Joseph Proudhon*, Translated by Elizabeth Fraser, Garden City, N.Y., 1969.

David Fleisher: *William Godwin: A Study in Liberalism*, London, 1951.

Philip S. Foner (editor): *The Autobiographies of the Haymarket Martyrs*, New York, 1969.

David Footman: *Civil War in Russia*, London, 1961.

Albert Fried and Ronald Sanders (editors): *Socialist Thought*, Garden City, N.Y., 1964.

James Gillespie: *Free Expression in Industry*, London, 1948.

Paul Goodman: *Art and Social Nature*, New York, 1946.

*Paul Goodman: *Compulsory Miseducation*, New York, 1962.

*Paul Goodman: *The Community of Scholars*, New York, 1962.

Paul Goodman: *Drawing the Line*, New York, 1962.

*Paul Goodman: *Growing Up Absurd*, New York, 1960.

*Paul Goodman: *Like a Conquered Province*, New York, 1967.

Paul Goodman: *The New Reformation*, New York, 1970.

*Paul Goodman: *People or Personnel*, New York, 1965.

Paul Goodman: *The Society I Live in is Mine*, New York, 1963.

*Paul Goodman: *Utopian Essays and Practical Proposals*, New York, 1962.

*Alexander Gray: *The Socialist Tradition*, London, 1946.

Jack Gray (editor): *Modern China's Search for a Political Form*, London, 1969.

*Herb Greer: *Mud Pie*, London, 1964.

Feliks Gross (editor): *European Ideologies*, New York, 1948.

Daniel Guérin: *Anarchism*, Translated by Mary Klopper, New York, 1970.

Erwin Anton Gutkind: *The Expanding Environment*, London, 1953.

Richard Hare: *Portraits of Russian Personalities between Reform and Revolution*, London, 1959.

Ammon Hennacy: *The Autobiography of a Catholic Anarchist*, New York, 1954.

*Ammon Hennacy: *The Book of Ammon*, New York, 1965.

Rayner Heppenstall: *A Little Pattern of French Crime*, London, 1969.

Eugenia W. Herbert: *The Artist and Social Reform*, New Haven, 1961.

Eric J. Hobsbawm: *Bandits*, London, 1969.

Eric J. Hobsbawm: *Primitive Rebels*, Manchester, 1959.

The Hornsey Affair. By Students and Staff of Hornsey College of Art, Harmondsworth, 1969.

*Irving Louis Horowitz: *Radicalism and the Revolt against Reason*. Carbondale, 1961.

Irving Louis Horowitz (editor): *The Anarchists*, New York, 1964.

Richard Hostetter: *The Italian Socialist Movement*, Princeton, 1958.

James W. Hulse: *Revolutionists in London*, Oxford, 1970.

Corinne Jacker: *The Black Flag of Anarchy*, New York, 1968.

J. Hampden Jackson: *Marx, Proudhon and European Socialism*, London, 1958.

*Augustus John: *Chiaroscuro*, London, 1952.

*James Joll: *The Anarchists*, London, 1964.

*James Joll: *The Second International*, London, 1955.

Frederick I. Kaplan: *Bolshevik Ideology and the Ethics of Soviet Labor*, New York, 1968.

K. J. Kenafick: *Michael Bakunin and Karl Marx*, Melbourne, 1948.

Lawrence Krader: *Formation of the State*, New York, 1968.

Leonard I. Krimerman and Lewis Perry (editors): *Patterns of Anarchy*, Garden City, N.Y., 1966.

Hyman Kublin: *Asian Revolutionary*, Princeton, 1964.

Eugene Lampert: *Sons against Fathers*, Oxford, 1965.

Eugene Lampert: *Studies in Rebellion*, London, 1957.

Lane W. Lancaster: *Masters of Political Thought*, Vol. 3: *Hegel to Dewey*, Boston, 1959.

Olga Lang: *Pa Chin and His Writings*, Cambridge, Mass., 1967.

*George Lichtheim: *Marxism*, London, 1961.

*George Lichtheim: *The Origins of Socialism*, New York, 1968.

*George Lichtheim *A Short History of Socialism*, New York, 1970.

Priscilla Long (editor): *The New Left*, Boston, 1968.

J. C. Longoni: *Four Patients of Dr. Deibler*, London, 1970.

Henri de Lubac: *The Un-Marxian Socialist*. Translated by R. E. Scantlebury, London, 1948.

Dwight Macdonald: *The Responsibility of Peoples*, London, 1957.

Dwight Macdonald: *The Root is Man*, Alhambra, Calif., 1953.

Lucy Mair: *Primitive Government*, Harmondsworth, 1962.

*Martin Malia: *Alexander Herzen and the Birth of Russian Socialism*, Cambridge, Mass., 1961.

David A. Martin: *Pacifism*, London, 1965.

*James J. Martin: *Men Against the State*, De Kalb, Ill., 1953.

G. P. Maximoff: *Constructive Anarchism*. Translated by H. Frank and Ada Siegel, Chicago, 1952.

*G. P. Maximoff (editor): *The Political Philosophy of Bakunin*, Glencoe, 1953.

*John Middleton and David Tait (editors): *Tribes Without Rulers*, London, 1958.

D. H. Monro: *Godwin's Moral Philosophy*, Oxford, 1953.

*Norman Moss: *Men Who Play God*, London, 1968.

*Max Nomad: *Aspects of Revolt*, New York, 1959.

Max Nomad: *Dreamers, Dynamiters and Demagogues*, New York, 1964.

*Max Nomad: *Political Heretics*, Ann Arbor, 1963.

Frank Parkin: *Middle Class Radicalism*, Manchester, 1968.

Innes H. Pearse and Lucy R. Crocker: *The Peckham Experiment*, London, 1943.

*Henry Pelling (editor): *The Challenge of Socialism*, London, 1954.

Michael Prawdin: *The Unmentionable Nechaev*, London, 1961.

Eugene Pyziur: *The Doctrine of Anarchism of M. A. Bakunin*, Milwaukee, 1955.

Angelo Quattrocchi and Tom Nairn: *The Beginning of the End*, London, 1968.

Alexander Rabinowitch: *Prelude to Revolution*, Bloomington, 1968.

Herbert Read: *Anarchy and Order*, London, 1954.

Herbert Read: *The Cult of Sincerity*, London, 1969.

Herbert Read: *The Politics of the Unpolitical*, London, 1946.

Herbert Read: *To Hell With Culture*, London, 1963.

Herbert Read (editor): *Kropotkin: Selections From His Writings*, London, 1942.

Paul Reiwald: *Society and Its Criminals*. Translated by T. E. James, London, 1949.

Nicholas V. Riasanovsky: *The Teaching of Charles Fourier*, Berkeley, 1969.

Vernon Richards: *Lessons of the Spanish Revolution*, London, 1953.

*Vernon Richards (editor): *Errico Malatesta: His Life and Ideas*, London, 1965.

Alan Ritter: *The Political Thought of Pierre-Joseph Proudhon*, Princeton, 1969.

Rudolf Rocker: *The London Years*. Translated by Joseph Leftwich, London, 1956.

Rudolf Rocker: *Pioneers of American Freedom*, Los Angeles, 1949.

*Massimo Salvadori (editor): *Modern Socialism*, New York, 1968.

Lyman T. Sargent: *Contemporary Political Ideologies*, Homewood, Ill., 1969.

*John Saville and Ralph Miliband (editors): *The Socialist Register 1970*, London, 1970.

Robert A. Scalapino and George T. Yu: *The Chinese Anarchist Movement*, Berkeley, 1961.

*Leonard Schapiro: *The Origin of the Communist Autocracy*, London, 1955.

*Victor Serge: *Memoirs of a Revolutionary*. Translated by Peter Sedgwick, London, 1963.

Robin Skelton (editor): *Herbert Read: A Memorial Symposium*, London, 1970.

Madeleine B. Stern: *The Pantarch*, Austin, Texas, 1968.

Max Stirner: *The False Principle of Our Education*. Translated by Robert H. Beebe. Colorado Springs, 1967.

Gordon Rattray Taylor: *Are Workers Human?*, London, 1950.

George Thayer: *The British Political Fringe*, London, 1965.

George Thayer: *The Farther Shores of Politics*, New York, 1967.

E. P. Thompson: *William Morris: Romantic to Revolutionary*, London, 1955.

Tolstoy's Writings on Civil Disobedience and Non-Violence, New York, 1967.

Leo Tolstoy: *The Law of Love and the Law of Violence*. Translated by Mary Tolstoy, New York, 1948.

Leo Tolstoy: *The Law of Violence and the Law of Love*. Translated by L. Perno, London, 1959.

Barbara Tuchman: *The Proud Tower*, New York, 1966.

*Robert C. Tucker: *The Marxian Revolutionary Idea*, New York, 1969.

*S. V. Utechin: *Russian Political Thought*, New York, 1963.

*Franco Venturi: *Roots of Revolution*. Translated by Francis Haskell, London, 1960.

Voline: *Nineteen-Seventeen*. Translated by Holley Cantine, London, 1954.

Voline: *The Unknown Revolution*. Translated by Holley Cantine, London, 1955.

George Hunston Williams: *The Radical Reformation*, Philadelphia, 1962.

George Woodcock: *Anarchism*, Cleveland, 1962.

George Woodcock: *Anarchy or Chaos*, London, 1944.

George Woodcock: *Pierre-Joseph Proudhon*, London, 1956.

George Woodcock: *William Godwin*, London, 1946.

*George Woodcock: *The Writer and Politics*, London, 1948.

George Woodcock and Ivan Avakumović: *The Anarchist Prince*, London, 1950.

Mary C. Wright (editor): *China in Revolution*, New Haven, 1968.

Avrahm Yarmolinsky: *Road to Revolution*, London, 1957.

Boris Yelensky: *In the Struggle for Equality*, Chicago, 1958.

Geoffrey Ostergaard

Indian Anarchism:
The Sarvodaya Movement*

To PIN THE LABEL 'ANARCHIST' TO THE CONTEMPORARY SARVODAYA movement in India might seem at first sight to be either the act of a hostile critic, anxious to expose its follies, or, at best, an act which invites misunderstanding. The label is certainly not one which the Sarvodayites themselves use. In India, as in the West, anarchism is popularly associated with violence, and, like Tolstoy before them, the Indian apostles of non-violent anarchism prefer a label which bears no traces of dynamite. However, one purpose of this article is to show that the social and political doctrines of Sarvodaya do in fact constitute a species of the anarchist genus. This purpose may be achieved most easily by comparing and contrasting Sarvodaya doctrines with what may be termed mainstream Western anarchism – the tradition of thought stemming from Proudhon through Bakunin and Kropotkin to Malatesta. But, before proceeding to this exercise, it may be helpful to outline the origins of the contemporary Sarvodaya movement.

REVOLUTIONARY GANDHISM

Its founding father is, of course, Gandhi, and the term 'Sarvodaya', meaning 'the welfare of all', was first used by him as the title of his translation of Ruskin's *Unto This Last*. But the Gandhi who inspires those who are now committed to achieving 'the Sarvodaya society' by non-violent revolution is not the Gandhi of the popular Western image. In this image Gandhi is seen primarily as a nationalist leader whose main objective was to win independence for India by

* This article incorporates material from the introductory chapters of the forthcoming study by G. Ostergaard and M. Currell, *The Gentle Anarchists*, Clarendon Press, Oxford. The permission of the publishers to use the material is gratefully acknowledged.

the novel technique of non-violent resistance. Such a truncated figure bears little resemblance to the real Gandhi who was as much concerned with moral and social as with political change, and who saw *swaraj* (self-government) as only the first step towards a radical reconstruction of the whole social order leading to the establishment of *Ram Raj*, the kingdom of God. The Gandhi who is the founding father of the Sarvodaya movement is the Gandhi who, early in his career, acknowledged himself a disciple of Tolstoy, who developed an integral philosophy based on the twin principles of truth and non-violence, and who insisted that *satyagraha*, literally 'holding fast to truth', is not simply a technique. Above all, it is the Gandhi who emphasized the *positive* character of non-violence and who underlined the importance of *constructive* work.

Although there is abundant evidence that this was always the real Gandhi, it was the side of Gandhi which became most apparent in the last years of his life. Speaking of his 'Constructive Programme'[1] in 1944, he told his followers: 'Through it you can make the villagers feel self-reliant, self-sufficient and free so that they can stand up for their rights. If you can make a real success of the constructive programme, you will win Swaraj for India *without civil disobedience*.'[2] And in the last year of his life, the year of independence, he confessed: '*In placing civil disobedience before constructive work I was wrong*. . . . I feared that I should estrange co-workers and so carried on with imperfect Ahimsa.'[3] It was this same Gandhi who, after independence, opposed the suggestion that the constructive workers should enter politics in an attempt to further the goal of a non-violent social order. The moment non-violence assumed political power, he argued, it contradicted itself and became contaminated. The role of the constructive workers, rather, was to guide political power and to mould the politics of the country without taking power themselves. And it was this Gandhi who, on the day before his assassination, in the document known as his 'Last Will and Testament', proposed that Congress should disband as a political party and flower again in the form of a *Lok Sevak Sangh* or Association of Servants of the People.

[1] Gandhi's 'Constructive Programme' was developed piecemeal. In its final form it embraced eighteen items of social work, the best known being the promotion of *khadi* – hand-spun, hand-woven cloth. See M. K. Gandhi, *The Constructive Programme*, Navajivan, Ahmedabad, 1945.

[2] Pyarelal, *Mahatma Gandhi: The Last Phase*, Navajivan, Ahmedabad, 1956, I, p. 44 (emphasis added).

[3] *Ibid.*, I, p. 314 (emphasis added).

This proposal, as we know, was rejected by Congress, but at a conference of constructive workers held in March 1948 the decisions were taken to form a loosely structured fellowship of *Lok Sevaks*, to be known as the Sarvodaya Samaj, and to pursue the idea, mooted earlier by Gandhi, of uniting in one umbrella-type organization the specific associations, such as the Spinners' Association and the Village Industries Association, which Gandhi had founded to carry out the various items of his Constructive Programme. Out of the latter decision emerged in the following year the *Akhil Bharat Sarva Seva Sangh*, the All India Association for the Service of All.[4] It is this body which constitutes the core organization of what may be called 'revolutionary Gandhism'.

'Revolutionary Gandhism' may be distinguished from two other types of Gandhism to be found in contemporary India: 'political Gandhism' and 'institutional Gandhism'. 'Political Gandhism' finds expression in the policies of those, mainly but not only in Congress, who have sought to realize at least some of Gandhi's goals by conventional political action. In concrete terms it is represented by the Khadi and Village Industries Commission and the official programmes of Community Development and *Panchayati Raj* (local self-government). 'Institutional Gandhism' finds expression in a number of independent and voluntary organizations, such as the Kasturba Memorial Trust and the *Harijan Sevak Sangh*, which are concerned to promote particular aspects of the Constructive Programme and which decided not to unite with the *Sarva Seva Sangh*.[5]

Although the three types of Gandhism are not sharply separable in the field of social action, 'revolutionary Gandhism' differs from the other types in both its spirit and its objectives. In their general approach to the problems of social reconstruction and political action, those associated with *Sarva Seva Sangh* come closest to carrying on Gandhi's work along the lines envisaged in the last years of his life.

The leader and inspirer of *Sarva Seva Sangh* is Vinoba Bhave, the person now widely acclaimed as Gandhi's 'spiritual heir'. It was Vinoba who discovered the talisman which was to give new shape

[4] In 1963 *Akhil Bharat* was dropped from the name of the organization as a symbolic recognition of its universalistic objectives.

[5] The Kasturba Memorial Trust, founded in 1944 in memory of Gandhi's wife, is devoted to the welfare of women and children in the rural areas. The *Harijan Sevak Sangh* is the association concerned with the uplift of the 'untouchables' whom Gandhi had renamed *Harijans* or Children of God.

and impetus to the Gandhian constructive movement. This was the first land-gift made on 18 April 1951 which marked the beginning of the campaign for *Bhoodan*. The immediate object of this campaign was to abolish landlessness among the Indian peasantry by persuading landowners voluntarily to donate a proportion of their lands for redistribution to the landless labourers who constitute the poorest fifth of India's rural population. Out of *Bhoodan* emerged in the mid-1950s the present campaign for *Gramdan* (gift of the village) which seeks the complete surrender of property rights in land in favour of the village community – 'villagization' as distinct from nationalization of the land.[6]

The movement inspired by Vinoba is often referred to as the *Bhoodan–Gramdan* movement. But this description is in fact misleading. *Bhoodan* was, and *Gramdan* now is, only part of the *immediate* programme of a movement which aims at a 'total revolution', a complete revaluation of values, leading to the establishment of the Sarvodaya society not only in India but also, ultimately, throughout the world. *Gramdan* is properly to be seen as the symbol of this non-violent revolution. In concrete terms, it constitutes the first practical step towards establishing in India a social order in which the virtues of truth, love, and compassion reign supreme.

Three further observations may be made about 'revolutionary Gandhism'. First, it is a *creative* Gandhism which has produced new insights into the potentialities of non-violence. It is the Gandhism of those who have taken to heart Gandhi's own statement: 'There is no such thing as "Gandhism" and I do not want to leave any sect after me.'[7] The Sarvodayites see themselves as *continuing* Gandhi's 'experiments with truth', *developing* an experiential doctrine which is far from being complete, if indeed it can ever be thought capable of completion. From this perspective, the texts of the founding father are always worthy of respect, but they are not sacred: his successors stand on his shoulders and may well see further than he did. Thus, while Gandhi's central principles remain unchallenged, the application of these principles in action is a matter of continual adaptation in the light of changing conditions, fresh experience, and new insights.

[6] For a recent discussion of *Gramdan* and a select bibliography of works in English on the movement, see the pamphlet, edited by Devi Prasad, *Gramdan, the Land Revolution in India*, War Resisters' International, 1969.

[7] This statement is used as an epigraph by *Gandhi Marg*, the quarterly journal of Gandhian thought, published by the Gandhi Peace Foundation, New Delhi.

Related to this is the undoubted fact that Gandhi's successors, notably Vinoba, have stressed and developed the revolutionary implications of the founder's ideas. Thus, Gandhi's ideal society, a condition of enlightened anarchy in which social life has become so perfect as to be self-regulated and 'there is no political power because there is no state',[8] has been brought nearer to the centre of the picture. And the important Gandhian social concept of 'trusteeship', which during Gandhi's lifetime proved capable of widely divergent interpretations, has been given its most radical interpretation so that it can be used to justify the policy of common ownership of land.[9]

The third observation concerns the relation of Sarvodaya ideology to traditional elements in Indian culture. Sarvodaya presents itself as an indigenous creed, a specifically Indian approach to socialism. This view has been challenged by a recent critic, Adi Doctor, who argues that the Sarvodaya ideal of a stateless society has no basis in ancient Indian political thought.[10] Doctor is undoubtedly correct in his main contention, but his argument misses a central point about Sarvodaya ideology: that it represents, in part at least, an attempt to reconstitute an ancient tradition of Indian *religious* thought in which the divine nature of man is suggested. Among the key concepts that Gandhi drew and reinterpreted from this tradition were those of *satya*, *ahimsa*, *karmayoga*, and *varnasramdharma*.[11] Of these the most important for the anarchist aspects of Sarvodaya was the second. The anarchism of Sarvodaya is, in fact, arrived at largely, if not wholly, by spelling out the social and political implications of Gandhi's reinterpretation of the concept of *ahimsa*. The apparent paradox of an emphasis on non-violence combined with the absence of a philosophy of anarchism in ancient Indian political

[8] *Young India*, 2 July 1931. The full statement is quoted in G. Dhawan, *The Political Philosophy of Mahatma Gandhi*, Navajivan, Ahmedabad, 3rd ed., 1957, p. 282.

[9] On the ambiguity of the trusteeship concept and its role in holding support for the independence movement of groups with apparently diverse interests, see P. J. Rolnick, 'Charity, Trusteeship and Social Change in India', *World Politics* XIV, 3, 1962.

[10] A. Doctor, *Anarchist Thought in India*, Asia Publishing House, Bombay, 1964.

[11] *Satya*, truth; *ahimsa*, non-injury, non-violence; *karmayoga*, the doctrine of self-realization through disinterested action; *varnasramdharma*, the law of right conduct relating to the fourfold division of Hindu society and the four stages of life.

thought is explained by the fact that, until Gandhi, *ahimsa* was seen simply as an ethical principle for the self-realization of the *individual*. *Ahimsa* was not a principle to be applied to politics and the organization of social life. It was Gandhi's great contribution to make it a principle of *social* ethics and to insist on its application, as far as possible, to all social relations.

The central value of non-violence provides the main link between Sarvodaya ideology and traditional Indian culture. But related to it are other traditional values of a less ultimate kind, notably those of village life, the joint family, and decisions by consensus. At the same time, there is a clear rejection of certain ancient values, particularly those associated with the caste system. The short answer to whether Sarvodaya ideology is traditional or modern is that it is neither: it is a synthesis of both, with non-violence providing the criterion for the acceptance or rejection of either traditional or modern values.[12] Using the terms in their technical rather than popular senses, Sarvodaya doctrine combines both 'revolutionary' and 'reactionary' elements. This unusual, though not unique, combination helps to account for the strength of its appeal in a developing society such as India.

SARVODAYA AND ANARCHISM

Considered as ideologies, the extent of the common ground between Sarvodaya and mainstream Western anarchism is considerable. Both see the modern state with its claim to a monopoly of the legal instruments of coercion as a great obstacle to a free, co-operative social order in which men really practise *self*-government. Echoing the familiar anarchist critique of what now passes as self-government, Vinoba asks: 'If I am under some other person's command, where is my self-government? Self-government means ruling your own self. It is one mark of *swaraj* not to allow any outside power in the world to exercise control over oneself. And the second mark of *swaraj* is not to exercise power over any other. These two things together make *swaraj* – no submission and no exploitation.'[13] For both the anarchist and the Sarvodayite, the duty of the individual

[12] For a discussion of how Gandhi used traditional symbolism for modern purposes, see R. I. and S. H. Rudolph, *The Modernity of Tradition*, Chicago University Press, 1967.

[13] Vinoba Bhave, *Democratic Values*, Sarva Seva Sangh Prakashan, Kashi (Benares or Varanasi), 1962, pp. 13–14.

to obey his own conscience is the supreme norm, taking precedence over the state's claim to obedience. Neither envisages a society without some restraints on the individual, but both demand that the restraints necessary to maintain an ordered society be submitted to voluntarily. Both emphasize the factor of moral authority in maintaining social control and cohesion, and believe that, given the appropriate social institutions, it could entirely replace political and legal authority.

In their conceptions of the conditions for the realization and maintenance of a society of free, self-governing individuals, again there is close agreement. First and foremost is the abrogation of private property in the means of production. As in the family, so in society, property is to be held in common, each contributing according to his capacity and receiving according to his needs. For the Sarvodayites in contemporary India, this implies pooling the ownership of village land through *Gramdan* and, for those outside the village, a full acceptance of Gandhi's principle of trusteeship – the idea that any property one may possess, including one's talents, is held on behalf of, and is to be used in the interest of, society. With the abrogation of private property goes, it is believed, the inequalities it engenders. Both Sarvodayites and anarchists envisage a society in which individuals are at the same time free *and* equal. An important point stressed by both is the need to recognize the equal value of the various kinds of work performed by individuals. Echoing Kropotkin's plea for integrated work and Tolstoy's insistence on Bread Labour, Gandhi and Vinoba call for the abolition of the distinction between mental and manual labour and for the recognition of the dignity of work done with the hands.

A further important condition of a free society, stressed by Sarvodayites and anarchists alike, is decentralization: social power must be widely dispersed if tyranny and exploitation are to be avoided. For the 19th-century anarchist-communists this condition could be achieved if the local commune were regarded as the basic unit of social organization. Enjoying complete autonomy with regard to its internal affairs, it would be linked on a federal basis with other communes at the regional, national, and supranational levels for the administration of business involving relations with other communes. For the Sarvodayites, the village would be the basic unit. Each village would constitute a miniature republic and be linked with other villages, as Gandhi put it, not in a pyramidal fashion 'with the apex sustained by the bottom'. Rather, the structure would be that of 'an oceanic circle' in which 'the outermost circumference will not wield power to crush the inner circle but will give strength to all within and derive its strength from it'.[14]

Such a decentralized polity implies a decentralized economy. Large-scale industry and its concentration in vast megapolitan centres is to be avoided or reduced to the absolute minimum. Industries are to be brought to the villages so that it will be possible for a village, or a group of villages, to constitute an agro-industrial community practically self-sufficient in respect of the basic needs of its inhabitants. The present generation of Sarvodayites, like most 19th-century anarchists, do not see economic decentralization as an attempt to put back the clock. Less ambiguously than Gandhi, Vinoba does not reject modern technology as such. On the contrary, like Kropotkin, he welcomes it: he insists only that technology be humanized and applied for the welfare of all instead of being used to bolster a system of social exploitation.[15]

In working for their goals, the Sarvodayites join with the classical anarchists in condemning orthodox political action. No good service can be rendered by the state. 'My voice', says Vinoba, 'is raised in opposition to good government . . . What seems to me to be wrong is that we should allow ourselves to be governed at all, even by a good government.'[16] Those who seek political power, even for beneficent ends, will inevitably be corrupted. The seat of power, argues Vinoba, casts a magic spell over those who occupy it. 'If instead of those at present occupying it, we were to occupy it, we would do things very similar to what they are doing.'[17]

Parliamentary democracy stands condemned for several reasons. Despite the institution of popular elections, it does not really result in state policy being guided by public opinion. It involves also the principle of majority rule which in practice may mean the tyranny of the majority over the minority, not the welfare of all. For the Sarvodayites, decisions consistent with the latter can be reached only by adherence to the principle of unanimity which compels the search for a consensus. Again, parliamentary democracy involves political parties which are divisive forces and which seek power by hook or by crook, by vilification of their opponents, and by bribes and threats.

[14] M. K. Gandhi, *Sarvodaya*, Navajivan, Ahmedabad, 1954, pp. 70-1.

[15] Vinoba thus envisages atomic power being used in decentralized village industries.

[16] Vinoba, *op. cit.*, pp. 12-13.

[17] Quoted in Doctor, *op. cit.*, pp. 57-8.

In place of orthodox political action, the Sarvodayites, like the anarchists, advocate direct action by the people themselves. The politics of the power-state, *Raj-niti*, must be replaced by the politics of the people, *Lok-niti*. The former involves conflict and competition, the jostling and struggling of elites, the conciliation and containing of sectional interests, the striking of bargains, and playing the well-worn party game. *Lok-niti*, in contrast, involves an attempt to make the people aware of their own inner strength and encouraging them to solve problems for themselves. Explaining the distinction, Vinoba points out: 'It is just this strengthening of society that is the object of the *Bhoodan* movement. It is therefore a political movement, but one that is opposed to current political methods. Our aim is to build up a new kind of politics, and in order to do so we keep ourselves aloof from the old kind.'[18]

The strategy of 'the new politics' is based on the belief that 'revolutions are never achieved by power or party politics'.[19] The Sarvodaya revolution, like the anarchist revolution, can be made only from below, not from above. The Sarvodaya workers do not constitute a revolutionary party appealing to the people for support and promising to usher in the millennium. They exist only to give help and advice: the people themselves must take the initiative and work out their own salvation.

If, thus, Sarvodaya echoes some of the familiar doctrines of Western anarchism, there are nevertheless important differences. For an understanding of the movement, the contrasts are perhaps more illuminating and serve to underline that Sarvodaya is a distinctive species of the anarchist genus.

THE DIFFERENCES

The most obvious difference is the Sarvodaya attitude to religion. Of the great anarchist thinkers of the West, only Leo Tolstoy based his anarchism on religious foundations. Most anarchists in the mainstream tradition have followed Bakunin in coupling God and the state, and rejecting both for the same reason: their denial of the sovereignty of the individual. In the West, atheism and anarchism appear as natural bed-fellows, the twin offspring of Protestantism when taken to its logical conclusion. Sarvodaya anarchism, however, is fundamentally religious. An unshakable faith in God and the

[18] Vinoba, *op. cit.*, p. 56.
[19] *Ibid.*, p. 86.

primacy of spirit constitute the core of the philosophy of most, though not quite all, Sarvodayites. However, it is necessary to add that their religious opinions are decidedly catholic in character. No special status is accorded to Hinduism, and all religions, and even sincere atheism, are seen as deserving equal respect.[20] All religions are merely different ways of seeking God, truth, the ultimate reality.

For Sarvodayites the importance of religion lies in its buttressing of the belief in an objective moral order. Belief in God they see as ruling out ethical relativism; and moral injunctions, therefore, take on the character of absolutes. This ethical absolutism provides another contrast with most Western anarchists who, like Kropotkin, have attempted to provide rational and naturalistic foundations for their ethical codes. The consequences of this different approach to ethics are vividly apparent in respect of the central moral principle of Sarvodaya, non-violence. To Sarvodayites non-violence presents itself as a categorical imperative, not as a rule to be adopted on rational utilitarian grounds. In this connection, we may note Gandhi's distinction between passive resistance and *satyagraha*. The former is a technique which may be, and often has been, used by those who do not exclude the use of violence in certain circumstances. This kind of non-violence Gandhi regarded as the non-violence of the weak. *Satyagraha*, in contrast, is the non-violence of the strong, adopted because it is believed to be the only morally right course of action and which would be used even when the resisters had superior physical force on their side. Most Western anarchists, of course, have not been pacifists, but even when they have been, they have usually tried to justify non-violence on pragmatic grounds.

To complicate the matter still further, the Sarvodayites combine an absolute commitment to non-violence with a flexibility which on occasions appears to be outrageously inconsistent. In part, this flexibility stems from Gandhi's insistence that absolute truth cannot be known to the as yet unfulfilled human mind. A human being, however good, can arrive only at relative truth. Since non-violence is deemed to be *the* way to truth, it follows that no human being can ever achieve perfect non-violence. Combined with the premise that there is an evolutionary tendency towards non-violence which is unevenly distributed among mankind, this leads to the conclusion that non-violent resistance is not always possible as a practical collective policy. It was not possible, for example, so many Sarvodayites believed, in the Sino-Indian border war of 1962 because the

[20] Cf. Gora, *An Atheist with Gandhi*, Navajivan, Ahmedabad, 1951.

Indian people, for all Gandhi's and Vinoba's efforts, were not strong enough to adopt *ahimsa*. And, since *ahimsa* is a doctrine of the strong and even violence is preferable to non-violence adopted for cowardly reasons, military resistance was justifiable, although the Sarvodayites themselves could not participate in it.

This kind of reasoning leads to a further difference between Sarvodaya and mainstream Western anarchism. The latter is predicated on the assumption not only that it is possible for men to live an ordered existence without the state but that it is possible for them to do so *now*. In its extreme form, this assumption finds expression in the Bakuninist theory of spontaneous revolution according to which the masses, inspired by the efforts of dedicated revolutionaries, would shortly rise to throw off, once and for all, the artificial chains of the state. The Sarvodayites, however, are convinced 'gradualists': they see the anarchist goal in much the same way as Godwin did, as something to be reached only after men have become more perfect than they now are. Vinoba's gradualism is apparent in his visualization of three distinct stages of political development: first, a free (i.e. independent) central government; second, the decentralized self-governing state; and third, pure anarchy or freedom from all government. With political independence, India entered the first stage; and with the introduction of *Panchayati Raj* institutions, it is proceeding into the second stage. Sarvodaya political proposals, including the furtherance of party-less democracy, are conceived as contributing to the development of this second stage.

In the Sarvodaya view, therefore, the third stage, the stateless society, will develop to the extent that the people become more self-reliant and create new self-governing institutions. There is thus to be no direct frontal attack on the state, but a progression from free central government through the decentralized self-governing state to the condition of pure anarchy. This view is different from that of both classical anarchism and Marxism. Like the Marxists and unlike the anarchists, the Sarvodayites believe that the state will 'wither away' rather than be abolished; but like the anarchists and unlike the Marxists, they believe that action must be taken *now* to dispense with the institution of ultimate and organized violence.

At a deeper level, however, the suggestion of stages of development disappears in the Sarvodaya theory of social action. This is a consequence of the Gandhian rejection of the means–end dichotomy which underlies most Western patterns of thought. For the Gandhian, means are never merely instrumental: they are always end-creating.[21] What is regarded as the objective is conceptually only a starting-point: the end can never be predicted and must necessarily be left open. All that is certain is that from immoral or even amoral 'means' no moral 'end' can result. Applying this philosophy of action to the point under discussion – the ultimate goal of the stateless society – the fusion of ends and means implies that there is no transition period or, what amounts to the same thing, every period is one of transition. With truth and non-violence as both the means and the end, the Gandhian acts *now* according to these principles, and thereby achieves the 'goal' he is striving for. For him as for Bernstein and Sorel, although in a different sense, the movement is everything; the final goal is nothing.

Commitment to such a philosophy of action accounts for a further difference between Sarvodaya and Western anarchism. It would be incorrect to say that Western anarchists have shown no interest in constructive activity. But, in the main, Western anarchism has been content to echo Bakunin's famous dictum: 'Destruction is itself a form of creation!' In historical retrospect, anarchism in the West appears essentially as a movement of protest: a protest against the whole social and political structure of modern industrial society. The Sarvodayites, in contrast, have never been content with mere protest. With their emphasis on constructive work, 'Be ye also doers of the word!' has always been their text.

One particular item in Gandhi's Constructive Programme, prohibition, points to another difference between Sarvodaya and Western anarchism: the former's severely ascetic character. Western anarchism has its intellectual roots in the puritan tradition and has always had its 'simple-lifers'. Indeed, from one perspective, all anarchism may be seen as a plea for the radical simplification of life – a plea symbolized in a bureaucratic world by the passionate slogan 'Incinerate the documents!' But the asceticism of Indian anarchism extends far beyond anything found in the West. The loin-clad figure, carrying all his worldly possessions in a small bundle and without a penny in his purse, is the Indian ideal. The ascetic, puritanical character of Sarvodaya anarchism is manifest in the ethical principles enunciated by Gandhi as necessary for a *satyagrahi*: truth, non-violence, poverty, non-possession, and *brahmacharya* – the latter involving not merely

[21] For an illuminating discussion of Gandhi's views on the means–end question and its importance for social theory, see Joan Bondurant, *Conquest of Violence*, Oxford University Press, 1959.

celibacy or sexual restraint but complete control over the senses. In particular, in Indian anarchism one finds no echo of the Western anarchist plea for sexual freedom: quite the reverse.

Finally, in their strategies of revolution there are significant differences.[22] The Sarvodayites see the revolution as in essence a revaluation of values. The first step in this revolution is to convert individuals, if possible on a mass scale, by appealing to both their intellect and their emotions. The new values chosen for emphasis are those which have a direct bearing on some major social problem, such as the plight of the landless labourers, so that their acceptance and practice are likely to lead to radical social change. Since the new values are difficult to practise, a phased programme is contrived so that ordinary men are able to advance by relatively easy steps towards the new society. Gradually, through co-operative effort, the people proceed to create new institutions and new forms of social life.

In seeking the conversion of individuals to the new values, the Sarvodayites direct their appeal to all men and women, without discrimination by sex, caste, creed, or class. In comparison with classical anarchism (and, of course, with Marxism), it is the absence of any appeal to class which most distinguishes the Sarvodaya strategy of revolution. Anarchists, other than syndicalists, have not assigned to the industrial proletariat the central role assigned to it by (Western) Marxists, but they have not expected to enlist the oppressors, the powerful, and the privileged in the cause of revolution.

The Sarvodaya rejection of class appeal and any form of class struggle rests on the explicit belief that the 'real' interests of any individual, or groups of individuals, are never in conflict with those of the rest of mankind.[23] In this respect, Sarvodaya anarchism is more akin to the 'utopian socialism' of the Owenite co-operators. Sarvodaya, like Owenism, sees itself as essentially a universalistic movement. In its activities, it finds itself concerned to improve the lot of particular social groups – especially 'the low, the lost, the last, and

---

[22] See Jayaprakash Narayan, *Socialism, Sarvodaya and Democracy*, Asia Publishing House, Bombay, 1964, pp. 165–70, and V. Tandon, *The Social and Political Philosophy of Sarvodaya after Gandhiji*, Sarva Seva Sangh Prakashan, Varanasi, 1965, chap. V.

[23] 'Sarvodaya means that the good of all resides in the good of one. That there could be interests of one person, which are against the interests of another, is inconceivable. Similarly, there could be no interests of any one community, class, or country which would be against the interests of any other community, class or country. The idea of opposition of interests is itself wrong.' Vinoba Bhave, *Revolutionary Sarvodaya*, Bharatiya Vidya Bhavan, Bombay, 1964, p. 2.

the least' – but, in principle, it espouses no interest less than that of the whole of mankind. Put in another way, Sarvodaya sees itself as the true philosophy of humanity, and the Sarvodaya society will be achieved as and when all men begin to practise this philosophy in their daily lives. The success of its non-violent revolution is to be measured by the extent to which Sarvodaya ceases to be a separate movement and liquidates itself in such a way that 'movement' and 'society' are no longer distinguishable.

A LEGITIMATE ANARCHISM

Sarvodaya ideology, we may conclude, constitutes a very distinctive variety of anarchism. But, considered as a social movement, it is equally distinctive: it is unique in being a *legitimate* anarchist movement. In the West anarchist movements have been both suppressed and tolerated, depending largely on whether or not the public authorities have regarded them as a threat to the existing social order. But, even when tolerated, none of them has been endowed with legitimacy. This attribute the Sarvodaya movement enjoys in full measure. Successive Indian prime ministers have paid tribute to Vinoba, the movement's programme of *Gramdan* has been endorsed by the government, and – as in 1969 – the annual conference of Sarvodaya workers has been inaugurated by the President of the Republic.

The paradoxical characteristic of being a legitimate anarchist movement is the resultant of several factors. One, of course, is its association with Gandhi, 'the Father of the Indian Nation', a national symbol of still considerable efficacy. Closely related to this is the movement's commitment to non-violence. This commitment inhibits the power-holders in Indian society from defining the movement as an overt threat to the established order. This inhibition, it should be added, has been aided by Vinoba's interpretation of non-violence. To date, he has *not* sanctioned attempts to achieve the movement's main objectives by the use of non-violent resistance on the lines made familiar in Gandhi's *satyagraha* campaigns.[24] By

[24] Although 'negative' *satyagraha* has not been used to promote *Bhoodan* or *Gramdan*, *local* Sarvodaya organizations have used it on occasions for limited objectives, such as preventing eviction of tenants. Vinoba's view is that the successful and moral use of non-violent resistance presupposes that a consensus already exists in favour of one's objective: no such consensus yet exists with regard to common ownership of land. 'Negative' *satyagraha* remains a tactical option open to the movement once it has succeeded in winning widespread acceptance of the *Gramdan* idea, and there is a strong body of opinion within the movement favouring this option.

eschewing 'negative' *satyagraha* and emphasizing instead 'positive' *satyagraha* (in Vinoba's phrase, non-violent *assistance* rather than non-violent *resistance*), the movement has avoided a *direct* confrontation with existing power-holders.[25]

Three other factors contributing to the movement's legitimacy may be noted. The first is the movement's concentration on its immediate programme of *Gramdan*, the promotion of *khadi* and other village industries, and the development of the *Shanti Sena* or Peace Army.[26] This programme is consistent with the existing value system and may be seen as supplementary or complementary to the programme of Congress governments. The second is its nativistic character. As we have already seen, the movement presents itself, and is interpreted by others, as an essentially indigenous movement seeking to preserve and to rehabilitate peculiarly Indian values that have been lost or are in danger of subversion as a result of the process of modernization. Finally, there is the religious character of the movement. Its leadership is largely in the hands of religious men whose convictions are consistent with the universalistic values of Hinduism. The movement's espousal of universalistic religious values makes it difficult for opponents to attack it without at the same time appearing to question these values.

The factors which have contributed to making the movement legitimate and, hence, respectable help to account for whatever success it may be thought to have achieved. At the same time, these very factors may also help to account for its lack of success. The movement, in other words, has had to pay a price for its respectability. This price includes a failure to fashion for itself a distinctive public image. It is seen by some as an offshoot of Congress and, as such, becomes associated with the failures of that party to realize Congress policies. Its apparent unwillingness to challenge directly the existing power-holders and the government has led it to adopt what even some of its own supporters see as compromising stands on

[25] Vinoba argues that the hallmark of genuine *satyagraha* is the direction in which it moves – from 'gentle to gentler to gentlest' – in contrast to the direction taken when violence is used in conflict situations. It should be noted that *satyagraha* differs from other forms of non-violent action in seeking only the conversion and not the coercion of the opponent. See Joan Bondurant, 'Satyagraha versus Duragraha', in G. Ramchandran and T. K. Mahadevan (eds.), *Gandhi – His Relevance for Our Times*, Bharatiya Vidya Bhavan, Bombay, 1964.

[26] These three items constitute what the movement calls its 'Triple Programme'. The *Shanti Sena* was established in 1957 as primarily a non-violent police (rather than defence) force, and now numbers about 12,000 members.

important issues, such as the Sino-Indian and Indo-Pakistan conflicts. Further, while its universalistic appeal encourages wide support, such an appeal is inevitably shallow: the movement, so far, has failed to elicit the enthusiasm of any important segment of Indian society. Again, while the emphasis of the movement on religious and nativistic values has contributed to its support among the more traditional elements of Indian society, it has militated against attracting sustained support among the sections of the intellectual strata who are most sympathetic towards modern and secular values.

Nevertheless, compared with Western anarchist movements, the Sarvodaya movement does have significant successes to its credit. Although the number of full-time workers involved in it is relatively small – perhaps no more than 10,000 at the present time[27] – the movement's activities have touched millions of Indians. Over four million acres of land were donated in *Bhoodan* by more than half-a-million landowners. A large proportion of this land proved to be uncultivable or legally disputed, but as a result of the campaign nearly half-a-million landless peasants received between them a total of more than one million acres. The movement clearly failed to abolish landlessness and it underestimated the difficulties involved in the distribution of the land-gifts, but in many states of the Union more land has been distributed as a result of *Bhoodan* than, so far, by state governments as a result of land-ceiling legislation.

The movement's achievements in respect of *Gramdan* are more difficult to assess.[28] Because of its more radical character, *Gramdan* proved harder to promote than *Bhoodan*. Under the original concept of *Gramdan*, the object was to pool all village land and distribute it on an equitable basis for the purposes of cultivation, either by individual families or co-operatively, or both. By the early 1960s some 6,000 of India's 550,000 villages had accepted this concept, but most of these

[27] No accurate figures are available of the numbers of workers involved in the movement. In 1965 the number of *Lok Sevaks* registered with *Sarva Seva Sangh* was 8,621. For particular campaigns, thousands of others may be drawn into full-time or part-time work for limited periods.

[28] Very little empirical research on *Gramdan* villages has been undertaken by scholars unconnected with the movement. The most systematic analysis to date is that of Dr T. K. Oommen, 'Charismatic Movements and Social Change', unpublished Ph.D. thesis, University of Poona, 1967, based on the study of a small number of *Gramdan* villages in Rajasthan. See also his 'Problems of Gramdan', *Economic Weekly*, 26 June 1965, and 'Myth and Reality in India's Communitarian Villages', *Journal of Commonwealth Political Studies*, IV, 2, 1966. Oommen is highly critical of the claims made by the movement.

villages were small, very poor – even by Indian standards – and confined to low-caste and trival areas. In this situation, the movement made a tactical retreat in order to recover the momentum it was in danger of losing. This retreat took the form of revising the concept of *Gramdan* in such a way as to make important concessions to the principles of private ownership. Under the new concept of *Sulabh* or modified *Gramdan,* adopted in 1963, the idea of village ownership of land is retained, but a distinction is drawn between ownership and possession. A village may now be declared *Gramdan* if 75 per cent of the adults consent and if 75 per cent of the landowners, owning at least 51 per cent of the land, agree to make over their titles to the village assembly consisting of all adults in the village. The donors must further agree to set aside 5 per cent of their land for cultivation by the landless of the village, and also to contribute $2\frac{1}{2}$ per cent of their income to a village fund to be used for community and development purposes. This done, the donor retains possession of the remaining 95 per cent of the land donated. By joining *Gramdan* he loses certain rights of ownership, such as the right to transfer land by sale to persons who have not joined the *Gramdan,* or to mortgage it to private individuals; but he retains the right of cultivation which, moreover, he may pass on to his heirs.

Armed with this modified concept, the movement launched a whirlwind campaign for it in the autumn of 1965. The campaign proved highly successful, and by October 1969 over 140,000 villages had declared for *Gramdan.* As a result, *Gramdans* are no longer confined to marginal villages, and large contiguous areas of the country have become involved in the movement. This development greatly increases the *potential* of the movement's influence on the politics of the country. With the multiplication of *Gramdam* declarations, the movement raised its sights from *Gramdan* through *Blockdan* and *Districtdan* to *Statedan.*[29] The campaign was focused on one state in particular, Bihar, and although the objective of *Bihardan* was not achieved by the time set – Gandhi's birth centenary – Bihar with over 60,000 *Gramdans* is now virtually a *Gramdan* state.

[29] A 'block' is a group of about 100 villages in the government's Community Development Programme. *Blockdan* is defined as a block in which 85 per cent of the revenue villages or 75 per cent of the population (excluding that of the towns) have declared for *Gramdan.* A 'district' is one of the 300 or so main administrative units of the country. *Districtdan* is achieved when all blocks in a district have met the condition of *Blockdan. Statedan* refers to a state in the Indian Union in which all districts have met the condition of *Districtdan.*

In evaluating this achievement, however, it must be noted that the figure of 140,000 villages relates to *Gramdan declarations*. As a process, *Gramdan* involves three distinct stages: (1) *prapti* in which the required proportion of villagers declare in favour of *Gramdan* and sign a document to this effect; (2) *pushti* in which the basic conditions of *Gramdan* – the setting-up of a village assembly, the vesting of land titles in it, and the distribution of a portion of the land to the landless – are fulfilled; and (3) *nirman* in which development and social reconstruction of the village proceeds under the aegis of the village assembly. In the overwhelming majority of the villages concerned, to date only the first stage has been reached; no more than a few thousand have entered the second stage; and in fewer still are there as yet, in early 1970, any visible signs of development work. In other words, most *Gramdan* declarations are as yet only 'declarations of intent': it remains to be seen whether the intentions will be followed by actions indicative of a revolutionary transformation of social relationships.[30]

Perhaps the fairest comment to make at the time of writing is that the movement has some substantial achievements to its credit, mainly at the propaganda level, but that it has not yet fulfilled the expectations it has aroused. No more than a few bricks have been laid in the foundations of a non-violent social order. And only a rash observer would confidently predict that the building which eventually arises in the new India will conform, even approximately, to the canons of Sarvodaya social architecture. For the movement the next few years are likely to prove crucial. Much of the initial public interest in the *Bhoodan* campaign stemmed from the fact that it appeared to offer a non-violent alternative to a communist-directed revolution. In the politically confused, crisis-ridden situation that India finds herself as she enters the 1970s, the forces of communism appear stronger than they have been at any time since 1951. Bitterly divided among themselves though these forces are, they have gained substantial ground in recent years, especially

---

[30] At the Sarvodaya annual conference of 1969, Vinoba called for a super-whirlwind campaign to consolidate *Gramdans*, if necessary on a *de facto*, as distinct from a *de jure*, basis. An important tactical issue within the movement has been whether it should concentrate on developing existing *Gramdans* or seek to spread the *Gramdan* idea more widely. Vinoba has always favoured the latter, arguing that development work should be left to the government agencies and to the villagers themselves. The movement lacks the resources of both finance and trained personnel to undertake development work itself on a large scale.

among the poor and landless peasants of West Bengal, Kerala, Andhra Pradesh, and Tamilnad. The forcible seizure of land and the temporary establishment of a 'red base' in the Naxalbari district of West Bengal in 1967 have inspired similar attempts elsewhere to promote a Maoist-type revolution. The recent breakthrough in Indian farming – the so-called 'Green Revolution' – has brought greater prosperity to the upper strata of the peasantry, but it has also created new social tensions which nurture the 'Naxalite' movement. In this situation, the Sarvodayites find themselves faced with the need to demonstrate with some urgency that a non-violent revolution through *Gramdan* is indeed a realizable concept. If they fail to do this, their historical role may turn out to have been no more than to act as a John the Baptist to a violent Messiah in the shape of the long-predicted communist revolution in India.

Rudolf de Jong

Provos and Kabouters

'THE FUNDAMENTAL TROUBLE WITH THE ANARCHIST IS THAT, though he may be highly intelligent, he has no sense.' With this remark Alexander Gray begins his conclusions on anarchism in his book *The Socialist Tradition*.[1] But this statement is not a conclusion, it merely begs the question. Because what is 'sense' in a world of war, hunger, militarism and repression? What is the meaning of 'sense' to people who reject – as anarchists do – the realities of the foundations of our society?

'*Ich weiss, dass du mich für einen ziemlich schlechten Politiker hältst. Halte es nicht für Eigenliebe von meiner Seite, wenn ich dir sage, dass du dich irrst. Nämlich du schätztest und schätztest mich nach meinen Handlungen in der zivilisierten Gesellschaft, der Welt der Bourgeois; hier benehme ich mich in der Tat ohne alle Berechnung und ohne das geringste Zeremoniell, mit scheltender, rücksichtloser Aufrichtigkeit.*'[2] This passage, from a letter by Michael Bakunin to Alexander Herzen, already expresses the no-sense of the anarchist. Perhaps it may be a key to the understanding of his theories and practices. Can method be found behind their no-sense?

The fundamental characteristic of anarchism is its attack on authority.[3] Not a special authority – church, state or property – but

[1] Alexander Gray, *The Socialist Tradition: Moses to Lenin*, London, 1948, p. 380.

[2] Letter of Michael Bakunin to Alexander Herzen, 28 October 1869, published (with a wrong date) in *Kursbuch*, 19, 1969.

[3] 'Der historische Anarchismus des 19. Jahrhundert, . . . hat zum erstenmal in der Geistesgeschichte nicht nur den Staat oder die Herrschaft einer bestimmten Klasse oder eines bestimmten Standes, sondern die Herrschaft als solche grundsätzlich in Frage gestellt und dieses Problem zum Mittelpunkt seines Denkens und Handelns gemacht.' Peter Heintz, *Anarchismus und Gegenwart. Versuch einer anarchistischer Deutung der modernen Welt*, Zürich, 1951, p. 9.

authority as such. Here lies the fundamental difference with the other socialists – with Marxists, social-democrats and communists. 'You are creating a new authority of the so-called scientific socialism, and the bearers of your scientific socialism will become a new class of rulers and bureaucrats, more intolerant even than the capitalist class ... ' was the prophetic warning of Bakunin to Marx and his authoritarian followers, repeated again and again in anarchist propaganda. Indeed nearly all Marxist schools had, and still have, one thing in common in their theories and practical policies: they hope to change the world by using a power structure and authority. So they are always fighting – either in a revolutionary or in a reformist way, as parliamentary democrats or totalitarians – for power. Their appeal to the masses has always been: give *us* the power to do things, to change things. (When they do have the political power they ask the masses: trust *us*.)

THE COUNTER-SOCIETY

The answer of anarchism to the problem of how to change the structure of society without creating new authorities and without struggling for power inside the existing society is to be found in the concept of the *counter-society*. Already P.-J. Proudhon, with his exchange bank, tried to create the nucleus of another, a free society. The anarcho-syndicalist movements already wanted to build a structure for a new society – based on federalism and solidarity – during the struggle against capitalist society. According to this conception, revolution was not the take-over of the state by a socialist party in order to *start* a socialist reconstruction of society, but revolution should be the victory of socialism in the factories and workshops.

The concept of the counter-society – the people, not power – is particularly useful if we look at popular and rural anarchism in Russia and Spain. In the eyes of the workers and peasants the counter-society was the *real* society. The official society – state, police, clergy, aristocracy and middle classes – was not only the people's enemy, but a strange and alien body, imposed upon their natural society, and consisting of violence, oppression, injustice and sin. If only this unnatural oppression – state, church, property – could be destroyed, the real society, consisting of free people, working together in free communes and in solidarity with each other, would re-emerge in new forms. This idea recurs again and again among anarchists. The Russian anarchist Emma Goldman wrote about the (original) soviet: 'it is the old Russian *mir* in an advanced and more revolutionary form. It is so deeply rooted in the people that it sprang naturally from the Russian soil as flowers do in the fields.'[4] A writer on the Spanish anarchists exclaims: 'There it is again, this constantly recurring Spanish theme of philosophical anarchism, this practical experience that if nobody interfered all went well.'[5]

Indeed, this picture of the actual society and the anarchists' idea of the free society was more realistic and had more sense than many liberal and socialist scholars of Spanish history and society cared to admit. The Spanish revolution of 1936 proved that libertarian communism at least had many practical possibilities and brought more socialism than fifty years of communist rule in Russia.

In the industrial countries of Western Europe and North America with their liberal and constitutional revolutions, 'people' and 'power' never became so fundamentally and dramatically opposed to each other as, for instance, in Spain. The concept of a counter-society – the existence of a revolutionary and anti-authoritarian working class, completely alien to the bourgeois world and its state – became increasingly unrealistic as state and society became intermingled. Underestimation of the flexibility of capitalist societies is a weak point in all revolutionary theories. With the onset of political democracy, economic planning and social security, the world of the workers was more or less integrated with the bourgeois world; national industrial societies emerged and anarchist movements faded into the background. Orthodox anarchists continued to argue that *fundamentally* nothing had changed in capitalist societies, but their emphasis on 'fundamentally' showed that in fact many things had changed in the daily lives of the ordinary people and in their attitude towards the state.

Now, since the 1960s, a new kind of opposition has been growing in Western industrial societies and libertarian and anarchistic ideas have been re-emerging too. The new opposition is partly formed by minorities who are not yet part of the national society. But

[4] Paul Avrich, *The Russian Anarchists*, Princeton, 1967, p. 252.
[5] J. Langdon Davies, *Behind the Spanish Barricades*, cited by Gerald Brenan, *The Spanish Labyrinth: An Account of the Social and Political Background of the Civil War*, Cambridge, 1943, pp. 195–6.

there is also a revolt by young people, who are not born in 'another country' but 'inside the whale', rebels by choice, not by their position in – or outside – society. These are the sons rejecting the affluent warfare society of their liberal fathers. They do not have 'by nature' a counter-society, they have to create one. Sociologically, they have very little in common with the workers and peasants who formed the historical anarchist movements. However, if we look at the old anarchists we see among them many aristocrats, intellectuals and artists, who rejected their societies on the same grounds as do the young rebels of today. Already in the middle 1960s a lot was written about the similarities between the American New Left (SNIC) and the Russian revolutionary students and nihilists of the 19th century. And two years before the black flag of anarchism reappeared in the streets of Paris during the May revolution of 1968, the movement of a little group of new anarchists reached the headlines of the world press and an international television public: the Provos of Amsterdam.

If there was any movement to which the verdict 'no-sense' seemed applicable, it was 'Provo'. There were fifteen issues of an often poorly printed periodical, inviting its readers to blow up a new traffic tunnel; the reprinting of an old leaflet, *The Practical Anarchist*, which included very unpractical recipes for making sea-mines, which were to be placed in the holy-water fonts of churches; magic happenings around a little boy's statue – 'Lieverdje' – with shouts of 'No happy-smoker is a riot-stoker'; the provocation of the police and the authorities to the point of authentic panic, with the terrifying battle-cry 'The police is our dearest friend'; a strong attack on royalty with the formation of an Orange committee, 'the pearl of the Jordaan', and smoke-bombs thrown against a royal wedding procession. Completely innocent people were beaten up by the police and even thrown into prison. Dutch justice was completely discredited in the eyes of thousands of people. An atmosphere of tension prevailed in Amsterdam with an eruption of violence such as Holland had not witnessed in peace-time since 1934. There was propaganda for a white-bicycle plan, a white-chicken plan, a white-chimney plan, a white-woman plan. A young girl student was arrested and searched to the skin at the police station by policemen, for giving raisins to passers-by in the street. The chief of police and the burgomaster of Amsterdam lost their jobs. Over 13,000 votes were cast for the Provo movement at the election for the municipal council of Amsterdam and one seat in this council was won. And suddenly there occurred a Provo happening, proclaiming 'the death of Provo', on 13 May 1967 (twenty months and one day after the appearance of the first issue of *Provo*). However, a new movement was started in early 1970 with the proclamation of *Oranje Vrijstaat* (Orange Free State) by the *Kabouters* (Goblins). In the municipal elections on 3 June, the Kabouters obtained almost 38,000 votes in Amsterdam (11 per cent of the total votes) and 5 seats in the 45-member council.[6]

THE DUTCH BACKGROUND

Before trying to make sense out of the Provos and the Kabouters and to relate them to anarchism, let us first have a short look at Dutch society as it is today and at Dutch anarchism.

Dutch society and Dutch politics have always been characterized by a high degree of stability, typical of the burghers who founded and led the state. Law and order are held in high esteem, mitigated by a middle-of-the road philosophy and a sense of liberal tolerance. Extremism is rare. After the struggle against Spain in the 16th and 17th centuries, the Dutch never again attempted a revolution, but eagerly accepted the fruits of other people's revolutions (1789, 1848, 1917, 1918).

Religion and religious fragmentation have affected society and politics to a very high degree. The result is a great variety of political parties (governments are always made up of coalitions), a strange moralism in politics and society and a very particular phenomenon, which is a source of amusement to foreign observers: the *zuilen-system*. ' . . . *verzuiling*, which means literally "columnization" or "pillarization", the idea being that the various blocs of the population represent separate "pillars" (*Zuilen*), each valuable in its own right, and together indispensable in supporting the national structure; the phenomenon of *verzuiling* is by no means confined to politics. Each denominational bloc has set up a whole array of organizations encompassing practically every sphere of social life.

[6] The Kabouter Party took part in the elections in 12 municipalities, and received 54,324 votes and 12 seats in six municipal councils. At the time of the Provo movement, independent movements and periodicals emerged in several towns. The most original review was perhaps *Ontbijt op Bed* ('Breakfast in Bed') in Maastricht.

Schools and universities, radio and television corporations, trade unions, health and welfare agencies, sport associations, and so on, all fit into the *zuilensystem*. [. . .] the usual division is fourfold, between a Calvinist, a Roman Catholic, a "general" and a socialist bloc."[7]

The *zuilensystem* has played a very important role in the emancipation of the Calvinist 'little men', the Catholics, and the socialist workers, contributing also to the stability of Dutch society in the emancipation and modernization process towards national integration.

The great depression and the German occupation had both a deep and a lasting influence on people's minds. The reaction was a strengthening of national unity and cohesion. After the liberation in 1945 Dutch life was for many years dominated by a mixture of political restoration (even reaction), economic social security and economic control. The socialists – who had first entered the government just before the war – became as conformist as any other *zuil*; they saw in the social peace of Holland a model for the world, forgetting that the alienation of the people from the trade unions, from the political parties and from the decision-making process was almost complete. The only real issue of world importance – the liberation of Indonesia from its colonial status – was treated in a colonial and provincial manner. And the outcome did not disturb the position of the responsible politicians or parties. The communists, who had fought bravely in the resistance, formed the only opposition (they got about 12 per cent of the votes just after the war), but they spoilt everything by their Stalinism.

At the end of the 1950s and in the early 1960s things began to change slowly. Economic prosperity was growing. Workers fought – outside the trade unions – for higher wages. Television brought new communication between the *zuilen*. Journalism, influenced by the student weekly *Propria Cures*, became more independent. A new opposition against the cold-war policy – and Dutch moralism made the cold war very cold indeed – and its national conformist consequences was growing. A student trade union was founded and changed the image of the Dutch student within a few years. In the churches, especially the Roman Catholic, a stormy development had begun. Teenager consumption, beat and beatniks, pop and happenings, protest songs entered the scene, especially in Amsterdam.

[7] Johan Goudsblom, *Dutch Society*, New York, 1968, p. 32, a very good introduction to Dutch society.

Hitweek (today *Aloha*), a new youth-weekly, distributed information in a new form, at first only about music, but soon about every item of interest to the young generation. Activists, influenced by the English Committee of 100, organized ban-the-bomb groups and sit-downs. One of them, Roel van Duyn, puzzled by the problem 'What is to be done?', was impressed by Dada and tried to link it to anarchism. He saw the 'happenings' of the anti-smoking magician Jasper Grootveld around 'Het Lieverdje' (the 'Lieverdje' was a gift to the city of Amsterdam by a cigarette manufacturer) as an apolitical phenomenon but nevertheless directed at the enslaved consumer. Among the 'happeners' he saw 'the outsiders, the kids that don't belong to the proletariat – which had sold itself to its leaders and its television – or to the bourgeoisie or the squares, but who do belong to a big rebel group'.[8] He called them the provotariat. And, together with a few others, among them Rob Stolk, a very good-humoured and imaginative young worker, he founded a monthly and a movement. The Provo movement was born.

THE PROVO MOVEMENT

The Dutch anarchist movement arose at the end of the 19th century. In those days the social-democratic parties in Northern Europe – following the example of the German mother party – turned to parliamentarism. The opposition by revolutionary minorities inside the parties was often defeated at the congresses in a less democratic way, through manipulation of the party machines. The origins of several anarchist movements are to be found in these oppositions (the Jungen in Germany and Sweden). In Holland, however, it was the leader of the Social-Democratic Party, Ferdinand Domela Nieuwenhuis (1846–1919),[9] who turned his back on the reformist German model. In 1898 he started an anarchist paper *De Vrije Socialist* ('The Free Socialist'). A minority of socialists – several young intellectuals and some old militants of Domela's Social-Democratic League – had founded a new Social-Democratic Party (SDAP) in 1894. Most socialist workers followed the old and beloved leader. The SDAP had a hard fight to establish its position.

[8] Roel van Duyn, interview, *Delta*, Provo issue, autumn 1967, p. 28.
[9] See my article on Domela Nieuwenhuis in *Delta*, 1971.

Domela was both an asset and a liability to the anarchist movement. His personal reputation among the workers was tremendous and lasted till long after his death. The anarchism of many of his followers was poor, however, consisting mainly in an uncritical admiration of the great man and hate of the 'treacherous' social-democrats. After Domela's death *De Vrije Socialist* degenerated without losing its public of true believers and old admirers. More interesting forms of anarchism can be found outside the genuine Domela movement: in syndicalism (C. Cornelissen), anti-militarism (the IAMV), the extremely revolutionary youth movement, the *Moker* ('sledge'), in the 1920s, the monthly *Bevrijding* ('Liberation') of Bart de Ligt in the 1930s, etc.

As in other countries apart from Spain, the movement had been in decay since the early 1930s. There was no organized anarchist resistance under the occupation. After 1945 two publications reappeared but the movement was not resuscitated. Reprinting old and out-of-date arguments, these two periodicals had no influence and no readers outside their own circles of several hundred elderly anarchists. In the 1960s, when young people entered the editorial boards, their contents became a little more interesting. One more publication must be mentioned, *Buiten de Perken* ('Beyond the Limits') (1961–5), a monthly with an anarchist-syndicalist background. It tried to be 'inside reality but beyond its limits' and welcomed contributors, and, in its last year, editors with other backgrounds. Its circulation never exceeded a thousand but it was well received and read by students and other young people, including several of the founders of the Provo movement.[10] So let us now return to them.

Many anarchists – and I do not exclude myself – have been excited by the actions of the Provo movement and, at the same time, puzzled about its anarchism. Foreign anarchists, who visited the Provos, were often in despair about their lack of theoretical interest and knowledge.

A first generalization about the Provo is provided by the slogan of the French May revolution in its first stage: '*l'imagination au pouvoir!*' About 'Provo' we can say that it was imagination against power, and also the imagination at work. In spite of all the differences, the group that started the Provo movement had this in common: imagination, which they could neither express in their

---

[10] I should warn my readers that I was one of the editors of *Buiten de Perken*.

171

daily lives and work in the factory, nor in their jobs, nor at the university, nor in traditional politics and opposition movements.

'What makes us really mad is the individual's lack of influence on events. A happening is an attempt to seize at least the little part in things that you ought to have and that the authorities try to take away from you. A happening is therefore a demonstration of the power you would like to have – influence on events.'[11] 'Provo' was a way of life, a way to be happy. Here 'Provo' is already on common ground with Bakunin's appeal to the spontaneous forces of life against the abstractions of science and scientific socialism. (The Provos' appeal to the 'provotariat' – the riff-raff, the *lumpenproletariat* of modern big cities – is, of course, another element it shared with Bakuninism.)

Imagination there was, in the word-play and slogans of the Provos. *Lieve revolutie – liever evolutie* ('Dear revolution – better evolution');' a bicycle is something but almost nothing', etc. There was imagination behind the white plans, in the provocations and activities, even in the clashes with the police and in the dealings of the Provos with publicity.

The first idea behind the Provo movement was the provocation of the whole of society, without any illusions about the results. The opening page of the journal *Provo* contains the following declaration of principles:

> PROVO is a monthly sheet for anarchists, provos, beatniks, pleiners, scissor-grinders, jailbirds, Simple Simon stylites, magicians, pacifists, potato-chip chaps, charlatans, philosophers, germ-carriers, grand masters of the queen's horse, happeners, vegetarians, syndicalists, Santa Clauses, kindergarten teachers, agitators, pyromaniacs, assistant assistants, scratchers and syphilitics, secret police, and other riff-raff.
>
> PROVO has something against capitalism, communism, fascism, bureaucracy, militarism, professionalism, dogmatism, and authoritarianism.
>
> PROVO has to choose between desperate resistance and submissive extinction.
>
> PROVO calls for resistance wherever possible.
>
> PROVO realizes that it will lose in the end, but it cannot pass up the chance to make at least one more heartfelt attempt to provoke society.

[11] Roel van Duyn, interview, *op. cit.*, p. 30.

PROVO regards anarchism as the inspirational source of resistance.

PROVO wants to revive anarchism and teach it to the young.[12]

When they achieved their surprising success and found a lot of sympathizers among groups who certainly could not be classified as 'anarchists, provos, beatniks, . . . and other riff-raff', the Provos very soon lost their pessimistic outlook and realized that perhaps they could win something in the end. Provocation of society as such turned into the provocation of the establishment, of authorities and of the police, but most of all, of the false values and feelings of the establishment (which came clearly to the surface on the occasion of Princess Beatrix's wedding).

THE ESCALATION

In fact it was not the non-violent actions and provocations by the Provos that provoked the escalation in Amsterdam in 1965 and 1966, but the violent and intolerant reaction by the police and the authorities. Already in the thirties many civil rights had been curtailed in Holland, especially the right to express a dissenting opinion at demonstrations, etc. After 1945 the situation did not change. Political freedom in the streets – the right to demonstrate, to hawk in the streets, to yell – was extremely limited, almost non-existent. For everything – a demonstration, its route, the content of its banners – one needed special permission from the police. The 'Ban the Bomb' groups had already broken these bounds. The Provos automatically confronted public opinion with the fact that young people were arrested, held in jail and condemned for peacefully distributing the paper *Provo* in the streets, for peaceful happenings and for shouting 'Image, image'. At the same time, there was no persecution of policemen who had used violence without any reason; complaints concerning maltreatment were nearly always suspended. A lot of decent people were shocked by the behaviour of the police and still more by that of the judges and prosecutors in the courts and by the sentences pronounced. A painful reappraisal of the Dutch administration of justice took place. An advertisement, signed by approximately 1,200 citizens, appeared on 18 June 1966.

[12] *Delta*, Provo issue, published this statement with the note: 'from Provo 12' (p. 42). In fact the statement appeared in *Provo*, 1 and 2.

The text began with the words: 'Our sense of justice is being affronted.' It ended: 'We desire of all police officials, burgomasters, members of municipal councils, officers of justice, magistrates, members of parliament, the government, and all other authorities that they do everything in their power to restore reason and fairness to the administration of justice. This reason and fairness are not to be found at present.'[13]

Important dates in the process of escalation were the royal wedding (10 March 1966); police violence at the opening of an exhibition of photographs showing the police in action on 10 March (19 March); the sudden death from a heart attack of a worker after the police had attacked a demonstration of construction workers, dissatisfied with an administrative decision by trade union bureaucrats regarding their holiday allowance (the evening of 13 June); and an attack, the next morning, by a group of striking construction workers and sympathisers on the building of the reactionary newspaper *De Telegraaf*, resulting in serious disturbance in the inner city.

The sympathy aroused by the Provos was not so much the result of the confrontation with the police as of the peaceful and imaginative methods the Provos utilized against law and order. This sympathy for the Provos was further stimulated by the white plans and other unorthodox contributions to social well-being, their rejection of manipulation, their open-mindedness, anti-dogmatism and sense of freedom. In an article I wrote on the Provos, I mentioned the expression 'quiet anarchist revolution' used by Peter Heintz in his book *Anarchismus und Gegenwart*.[14] Heintz, writing in 1951, noticed the death of the traditional anarchist movement. But he also noticed the development of a quiet anarchist revolution inside modern societies. He found forms of anti-authoritarian life and experiences emerging in art and literature, in education and science, especially in the social sciences. In fact to most of the anarchist thinkers anarchism was always much more than the movement and the ideas behind it. They saw anarchism as a driving force in mankind and its history, a driving force towards more freedom, self-expression and self-realization.

In Dutch society a quiet revolution, stressing real democratic values and trying to escape from authoritarian and bureaucratic ties, had been well under way since the 1950s. This development took place in all social groups and all *zuilen*, breaking down the *zuilen-*

13 *Delta*, Provo issue, p. 105.
14 See note 3 above.

system and in a sense remaking alliances – not of political parties but of groups of people – when certain practical issues regarding tolerance and dissent were at stake. In almost every party, among many newspaper staff, television staff and in many official organizations and institutions there was a kind of guerrilla war between progressive and open-minded people against the more conservative elements. A lot of people did not want to get involved in politics, not because they had no interest, but precisely because they had political and social interests but became sick and tired of the 'regents'[15] mentality of the parties and in the political process. In the Provo movement they recognized some of their own criticisms, dreams and ideas. It was interesting to observe that the positive response to the Provos came from people of all sections of society and certainly not only from the old Left. The negative response to the Provos came from leftist authoritarians – including, of course, the communists and 'regents' from the Labour Party – as well as from rightist defenders of law and order. The overwhelming majority of the population rejected the Provo movement completely, and there was a serious effort at witch-hunting against the Provos by the newspaper *De Telegraaf*, appealing to all kinds of prejudices (long hair, drugs, laziness, asocial, etc.). An investigation concerning the municipal council elections of 1966 revealed that 'among Provo voters, 32 per cent came from the two highest socio-economic levels, outdistancing all other political parties in this respect. The level of education among Provo voters was remarkably high; considerably more of them (24 per cent) had secondary school or university education than had the voters of other political parties; only 7 per cent of the total electorate had this much academic training.'[16]

The death of the Provo movement had several causes. The authorities had adopted a more intelligent policy concerning happenings and demonstrations. Provos realized that their actions lost their meaning after they had lost their originality. Provos never had a common general conception; 'We agree to disagree', they said. They did not see any possibility of realizing their white plans. The most important was Luud Schimmelpennick's white-bicycle plan: a project aimed at ending motorized traffic in the inner city of Amsterdam and replacing it by more public transport and the free use of several thousand white bicycles, thus at once attacking the real

[15] 'Regents', the great patrician families which dominated Dutch politics in the days of the Republic.

[16] Constance E. van der Maesen, in *Acta Politica*; a summary is given in *Delta*, Provo issue, pp. 110–11.

problem of urban transport in a social way and the anti-social idol of the enslaved consumer, his car. The Provo movement attracted a lot of people who were only egotists or interested in the tension of police violence. Among the Provos there were several with a complete lack of responsibility for their own deeds. A kind of open commune in a Provo boat ended in complete failure. Of the original group – perhaps 25–30 people – some went away, some turned to drugs, the first Provo council member became a film actor in Italy, many remained active in some way.

FROM PROVO TO KABOUTER

The influence of the Provos survived, however. Perhaps we may compare the Provos with certain new groups, schools and reviews in art and literature: expressionism, cubism, the Stijl group and Cobra, for instance. They all lived for very short but very intense periods, but they changed art and had a lasting influence. The Provo movement did not want to become a structure, but Dutch society and politics after the Provos was not exactly the same as before. The Provo movement was a catalyst in the quiet revolution. There is much more freedom in the streets now. Amsterdam became a centre of underground culture and sexual freedom. Opposition inside parties and organizations expresses itself more freely. Television makers have more possibilities than elsewhere. The Labour Party has turned to the left. A new party was founded, 'Democrats 66', which tried to avoid an inner power structure. Student revolts have erupted, a few faculties have been democratized. Alternative schools and universities have been tried but failed. Actions against the destruction of old neighbourhoods and against air pollution followed the patterns set by the Provos.

The concentration of capital and the closing of several factories and firms caused unrest among the working people and brought forward the question of workers' control and participation. In the Catholic church non-authoritarian alternatives are growing and gradually replacing the old hierarchical structure. The 'imagination' of the Provos was used again by young women in their campaign against sex discrimination. 'Provo' was sleeping, not dead.

But especially among the students, there also developed an almost orthodox Marxism with an old-fashioned worshipping of the workers' struggle.

Roel van Duyn, who had published an interesting book about Kropotkin's ideas, linking these ideas to modern cybernetics and opposing cybernetics to Marxist dialectics, took over the Provo seat in the municipal council at the end of 1969. With him, imagination entered too. Roel van Duyn wrote a memorandum about sabotage as an alternative form of defence. The burgomaster refused to have it printed and discussed in the council.

About the same time, a movement to occupy empty houses in old neighbourhoods that had started in 1968 drew attention to the fact that house proprietors and the authorities often let houses go to ruin, because there was more interest in commercial building and in easy sanitation than in the well-being of the people involved.

As with the Provos, several persons and actions came together and formed the *Oranje Vrijstaat* of the Kabouters. Roel van Duyn, as member of the municipal council, became its first ambassador, accredited by the 'foreign' – but not alien – state, the Kingdom of the Netherlands. In the proclamation of *Oranje Vrijstaat* (5 February 1970) we read: 'Out of the subculture of the existing order an alternative society is growing. The underground society grows out of the ground now and it begins – independent of the still ruling authorities – to live its own life and to rule itself. This revolution takes place now. It is the end of the underground, of protest, of demonstrations; from this moment we spend our energy on the construction of an anti-authoritarian society.'

If we compare the Kabouters with the Provos we see several differences. 'Kabouter' has more 'flower-power' and 'love'; it expresses friendly Kropotkinism instead of Bakuninism. The Kabouters are optimistic about their possibilities. They do not attack society with provocations, but through the confrontation of everybody, including the authorities, with real problems and the possibility of alternative non-authoritarian solutions for them. The proclamation of *Oranje Vrijstaat* ends with a summing-up of all kinds of alternative openings, and solutions: an alternative solution of the housing problem (a Provo white plan had already suggested the weekly publication of a list of empty houses); an alternative solution for the slums. There are alternative shops, selling fruit and vegetables cultivated without insecticides; an alternative service for elderly people; and all kinds of direct actions (planting trees in the streets of Amsterdam, removing stones from dangerous spots in children's playgrounds, the opening of swimming pools on Sundays.

The Kabouters share the most important characteristic of the Provos: imagination. 'Provo' was, in the first place, imagination against power; the Kabouter mentality emphasizes imagination at work. But, of course, the power structure often attacks and destroys the results of the Kabouter imagination.

The following points can now be made about the relation between 'Provo–Kabouter' and the old anarchist movements.

1. Instead of the old conception of a 'natural' counter-society, needing only to be liberated from the authoritarian wolves, state and property, the Kabouters put forward the concept of an alternative society, yet to be constructed. (But the construction of an alternative society already lay behind the idea of 'modern schools', etc., and was present in many aspects of anarcho-syndicalism.)

2. The elderly anarchist movements had lost all real contact with society and the daily life of ordinary people. The anarchists became outsiders, sometimes soaring away in revolutionary dreams. The Provos and the Kabouters do not soar, they want to base themselves completely on reality, paying attention to the daily needs of ordinary people. As a result their actions and behaviour have found a real response in Dutch society, a response that anarchist movements had failed to obtain since the great depression in the early 1930s.

3. While acting within society and reality, Kabouters refuse, however, to become the *prisoners* of the standards and limits of reality.

4. Conclusion: Kabouters do not want to wait and to watch until things change for the better; they act in order to change things now; and they act according to their own standards and value system, neglecting the values of an authoritarian society and creating an alternative society. By doing so they hope also to influence developments in the old society.

But are their actions really changing the power and class structure of modern capitalist society? And will the actual authoritarian society die as the Kabouter movement spreads without fighting back and using violence?

'Kabouter' is – and 'Provo' has been – attacked by both old and new leftists. Several critics see the successes of the two movements as typical examples of repressive tolerance. They argue – as do others in Western Europe and the USA – that the class struggle, the confrontation of and the polarization between the 'oppressed masses' and the oppressors, are the only real things that count in our world. The Kabouter movement, in their eyes, is a dangerous phenomenon, opium for an elite pseudo-revolutionary group. In Kabouter activity they see only escapism and no-sense.[17]

So we come back again to Alexander Gray. It all depends on our view of society. If we accept the concept of a quiet anarchist revolution, the Kabouter movement certainly makes sense. And it is interesting to note that the idea of a quiet revolution is different from the conviction – common to all older anarchist and Marxist movements – that it is the class struggle which decides in the end. In the anarchist tradition, however, we find a more ambivalent approach to the existing society. Reclus, Kropotkin, Nettlau and most other anarchist thinkers did not oppose revolution and evolution, but saw them as complementary social processes and favoured each evolutionary step in the right direction. *'In diesem Sinn glaubt [Nettlau] an die Reihe: von liberal zu libertär, sowie er an gute Erde für eine gesunde Pflanze glaubt und erwartet nichts von einer klasse, sei sie noch so proletarisch, in der stets bessere und schlechtere Elementen sich bekampfen und paralysieren.'*[18]

Alas, the quiet anarchist revolution is certainly not the only characteristic of our times. We see also developments in another direction, towards more militarism, oppression and exploitation of men by men, towards bigger and bigger decision-making power in fewer and fewer hands. A quiet authoritarian revolution is just as real as the anarchist one. But if we are aware of the fact that both revolutions are going on at the same time – and perhaps *Like a Conquered Province* by Paul Goodman is the best example of a libertarian seeing both tendencies at work – does it make any difference? There seems no greater and more bitter alienation in neo-capitalist society than between the leftist circles crying for confrontation, calling for unity between students and masses, etc., and the ordinary workers who form the majority of their 'masses'. In our societies we have to reckon with welfare states and non-revolutionary majorities (even people who belong to the revolutionary minorities, at the same time but in other social roles, often belong to the majorities). Polariza-

---

[17] An unfair attack, full of nonsense about Provo's no-sense, was published in *Kursbuch*, 19: Konrad Boehmer and Ton Regtien, 'Provo – Model oder Anekdote?'

[18] Max Nettlau, 'Biographische und Bibliographische Daten,' *International Review of Social History*, 1969, p. 459. Peter Heintz writes 'Der konsequente "politische" Anarchismus muss die für den Marxismus zentrale klassenkampftheorie verwerfen,' . . . (p. 62). The only useful publication in the English language is the special Provo issue of *Delta*, 'A Review of Arts, Life and Thought in the Netherlands', autumn 1967.

tion against silent majorities in the end results in more authoritarianism. To make these majorities more conscious of the world they are living in, Kabouter imagination seems the more libertarian *and* the more realistic approach.

Will the Kabouters have a future? The dangers and problems that caused the death of 'Provo' are still there. Perhaps 'Kabouter' will become a reform movement, as any other reformist organization. But, in any case, the future needs the anti-authoritarian imagination of the Kabouters.

Eduardo Colombo

Anarchism in Argentina and Uruguay

ARGENTINA AND URUGUAY ARE THE TWO MOST DEVELOPED LATIN American countries, with the largest middle classes and the greatest degree of urbanization. Argentina covers 2,700,000 sq. km. and has a population of 23 million, of whom 8 million live in what is known as Greater Buenos Aires (the capital and its suburbs). Uruguay covers 187,000 sq. km. and has a population of 2,600,000, more than a third of whom live in the capital, Montevideo (1,173,000 inhabitants). In both countries the city dominates over the countryside. Argentina's urban population stands at 66 per cent and Uruguay's at 78 per cent.[1]

This urban preponderance and the massive external and internal immigrations have led to idiosyncratic modes of political participation. By mid-19th century the land had been taken from the Indians in Argentina and vast landed estates were concentrated in the hands of a few families of the land-owning bourgeoisie. The latifundia system based on extensive exploitation continues almost unchanged up to the present day. This helps to preserve certain traditional forms of stratification and gives a special character to internal migrations. The persistence of latifundia has certain known repercussions: low productivity and monoculture; the existence of a traditional 'aristocracy' and its corresponding political hegemony; the persistence of a two-level society with different styles of life for the high and low strata: in the aristocracy the *señorial* style, with little or no inclination towards activities or investments favourable to development; in the lower classes the maintenance of the *patrón–peón* relationship, paternalism and highly personalized primary-type

[1] Gino Germani, *Política y Sociedad*, Ed. Paidós, Buenos Aires, 1962, p. 17.

relations, 'apathy, low levels of aspiration, and insurmountable barriers between the two levels'.[2] All this is important for the understanding of the politico-social phenomenon known as 'Peronism' which created so many difficulties for anarchism in particular and the Left in general.

In 1885, in the epoch of *El Perseguido* ('an anarchist paper – it comes out when it can – published by voluntary subscription'), Argentina had a population of 4 million of whom 37 per cent lived in towns of over two thousand inhabitants. The process of urbanization 'developed in two long phases: the first – between 1869 and 1914 – caused by mass immigration from Europe; the second, approximately from 1930–5 to 1950–5, was the result of internal migrations and was also on a large scale'.

At the beginning of the first mass immigration most of the land had already been concentrated in the hands of a few owners; after fifty years of immigration, in 1914, foreigners formed half the active population but only 10 per cent of the landed property owners. 'The traditional families had managed to maintain and substantially to increase the latifundia system and in 1947 three-quarters of the land was still divided into little more than 20,000 agricultural holdings, less than 6 per cent of the total holdings. Leasing the land was and still is the method most used – that or other more unfair procedures . . . .'[3]

While the upper class – the traditional families – maintained extensive control of the agropecuarian sector, the middle class was at first composed of small and medium businesses. 'Later, particularly from 1910 onwards, the growth of the middle class was due primarily to the expansion of the "employee" sector: white-collar workers, employees and officials, professionals and technicians of the public and private bureaucracies . . . .'[4] In Argentina the proportion of the middle strata tripled in the eighty years from 1870 to 1950.

Social stratification in Uruguay is similar. Uruguay received a large share of immigrants: between 1830 and 1930 one million Europeans came into the country. In 1908, 18 per cent of the people living in Uruguay had been born abroad. In Montevideo this figure rises to 31 per cent.[5]

[2] *Ibid.*, p. 222.
[3] *Ibid.*, p. 221.
[4] *Ibid.*, p. 223.
[5] Data on Uruguay are taken from Carlos M. Rama, *Sociología Uruguaya*, Buenos Aires, 1965.

These general aspects of the social structure of the countries of the River Plate clearly have important implications for the development of the anarchist movement:

(1) Anarchism was, from the beginning and up to the 1930s, a predominantly workers' movement, based on the urban proletariat — even though at its peak it occasionally had some organization among and response from the peasants.

(2) A high proportion of this proletariat were European immigrants; that is to say, they came from countries where the process of industrialization had begun long before and this implied that their way of life, attitudes and ideology were those of a *secular* society.[6]

THE EARLY ANARCHIST MOVEMENT
IN ARGENTINA

The origins of the first socialist organizations in Buenos Aires are rather obscure. Max Nettlau dates the foundation of the Buenos Aires section of the International in 1872; he describes this as ideologically 'good socialism, rather general, neither anarchist, nor [. . .] political nor authoritarian'.[7] José Ingenieros, in an article published in the *Almanaque Socialista de la Vanguardia* of 1899, says that the first group appeared in 1871; this was apparently a French group, and later a Spanish and an Italian group were founded. Generally speaking they were either socialists who believed in government by a workers' party, or republicans or internationalists. One group was started in Córdoba in 1874. In 1876 the Bakuninist *Centro de Propaganda Obrera* (Centre for Workers' Propaganda) was

[6] '[. . .] In the undifferentiated institutional complex which characterizes the pre-industrial social structure, the "sacred" predominates. Sacred here does not only mean religious in the strict sense of the word, but also a-temporal, untouched by change, unchangeable by succeeding generations, reaffirming the stability of unalterable *traditional* values. Industrial society has, on the other hand, been called *secular*, no longer based on unchangeable traditional values but on rational attitudes, on readiness to change following the dictates of free analysis and above all the use of reason.' Gino Germani, *op. cit.*, p. 72.

[7] Max Nettlau, *Contribución a la Bibliografía Anarquista en América Latina hasta 1914*, Ed. La Protesta, Buenos Aires.

founded. An anarchist paper, *El Descamisado*, was published from 1876 onwards. Before the end of the 19th century several newspapers were published from Buenos Aires with varying degrees of success. On 13 June 1897 *La Protesta Humana* first appeared. Originally it came out weekly but in 1903 it changed its name to *La Protesta* and appeared daily from April 1904. Despite various set-backs – embargoes, closures, destruction of machinery, attacks by patriotic groups and so on – it continued to survive and, appearing intermittently, it has now reached issue no. 8,115.

The first militant workers' union – the Bakers' Union[8] – was founded in 1887 with the aid of Malatesta who was in Argentina between 1885 and 1889. Perhaps Malatesta's presence and tact helped to minimize rivalries and to eliminate the controversy between communist and collectivist anarchists. Debate remained on a more practical level, between those who favoured organizing and those who opposed it – though these latter should not be confused with the individualists who never had much influence in Argentina. The organizers stressed the workers' organization as the natural weapon for the struggle. The *sociedades de resistencia* (resistance groups), as the FORA's organizations are now and have always been called, were in their view the principal instrument for strikes, direct action, or 'revolutionary gymnastics'. This line almost completely dominated Argentine anarchism for many years. The anti-organizers, also anarcho-communists, and the individualists claimed that within the *sociedades de resistencia* the anarchists were no longer revolutionaries since they became totally involved in reformist activities. Their pressure was very important since it 'obliged the organizers in the workers' unions to hold to their anarchist allegiance and beliefs'.[9]

The social-democratic workers took the first steps towards a confederation. A commission was first created to carry out the wishes of the Paris Socialist Conference (June 1889) and from it derived the *Centro Internacional Obrero* (International Workers' Centre) which convened a meeting for 1 May 1890. The foundations were then laid for the *Federación Obrera* (Workers' Federation) which was created in 1891 with half a dozen unions. Its mouthpiece was the Marxist *El Obrero* ('The Worker'), which harshly attacked anarchism. The *Federación Argentina de Trabajadores* (FAO, Argentine Workers' Federation) was formed in 1901, and in 1902,

[8] Diego Abad de Santillán, *La FORA*, Ed. Nervio, Buenos Aires, 1933.

[9] Eduardo G. Gilimon, *Hechos y Comentarios*. No printing or publishing dates.

at its second congress, a socialist minority broke off (the groups which stayed within the Federation had 7,630 members, those which left 1,780).[10] The dissident unions formed themselves into the legalistic and reformist *Union General de Trabajadores* (UGT, General Workers' Union) in 1903.

In 1902 there were lengthy strikes by the bakers, dockers and others. 15,000 men belonging to the Cart and Coach-drivers' Federation joined the FAO. The following figures give some idea of the development of the workers' revolutionary organization: 'From 15 April to 15 July 1903, the 42 associate societies received 15,212 subscriptions and over the same period in the following year the figure rose to 32,893 subscriptions and the number of societies to 66', according to a report of the Administrative Commission of the fourth congress held in 1904. At this congress the Federation changed its name to the *Federación Obrera Regional Argentina* (Argentinian Regional Workers' Federation) or FORA, as it is still known today, and the *Pacto de Solidaridad* (Solidarity Pact) was agreed. At the following congress – the fifth – the 'finalist' declaration was approved. 'The fifth Argentine Workers' Regional Conference, in accordance with the philosophical principles which provide the reason for the existence of the organization of workers' federations, declares: "That it advises and recommends the widest possible study and propaganda to all its adherents with the object of teaching the workers the economic and philosophical principles of anarchist communism. This education, by preventing them from concentrating merely on achieving the eight-hour day, will emancipate them completely and consequently lead to the hoped-for social evolution." '

This fifth congress declaration became the basic policy for many years, and the movement, orientated as it was towards anarchist ends, opposed any other concept of trade unionism. Revolutionary syndicalism was criticized for wanting to maintain the class structure beyond the revolution. 'We must not forget that a union is merely an economic by-product of the capitalist system, born from the needs of this epoch. To preserve it after the revolution would imply preserving the system which gave rise to it. The so-called doctrine of revolutionary syndicalism is a fiction. We, as anarchists, accept the unions as weapons in the struggle and we try to ensure that they should approximate as closely as possible to our revolutionary ideals. [. . .] That is to say, we do not intend to be mentally dominated

[10] D. A. de Santillán, *op. cit.*, p. 102.

by the unions; we intend to dominate them. In other words, to make the unions serve the propagation, the defence and the affirmation of our ideas among the proletariat.'[11]

Most of the Argentine anarchist movement was similarly opposed to a specific organization of anarchism on a national scale, that is to say, to an anarchist federation. They accepted 'affinity' groups, *ateneos*, working with the unions or in the districts, and peoples' libraries, but they felt that a stable party type of organization would lead to the degeneration of anarchism into authoritarianism. Internationally, this 'forist' conception of anarchism was attacked by Malatesta among others. Nevertheless it lasted as long as anarchism remained the principal mass movement among the proletariat.

From the beginning the FORA organized itself outside any sort of legal legitimization, and in any work conflicts it demanded direct negotiations with the owners. It used the strike, the boycott, sabotage and the general strike. The fifth congress advised the workers 'not to let themselves be taken prisoner without justification' and urged them to defend themselves with any kind of violence.

In February 1905 martial law was imposed after an abortive military *coup*, and was used as an excuse to shut down *La Protesta*, ransack workers' centres and send various militants to Ushuaia.[12]

Towards the end of the first decade of the century a certain Colonel Falcón was appointed Chief of Police and distinguished himself in the persecution of anarchists and the workers' movement. At the 1909 First of May demonstration organized by the FORA in the Plaza Loren in the centre of Buenos Aires, the police opened fire on the demonstrators, several of whom were killed. A general strike was declared; the workers' centres were shut down and there were some 2,000 arrests. The strike lasted nine days and was one of the most spontaneously unanimous movements. The Chief of Police was widely blamed, and on 13 November of the same year a young anarchist, Simon Radowitsky, threw a bomb at his car and killed him and his secretary outright. 'After the initial general confusion an unprecedented repression set in: *La Protesta* was raided, its machinery destroyed, workers' centres underwent the same fate; within 48 hours thousands had been arrested; many were sent to Tierra del Fuego; others, the foreigners, were deported after many

[11] Emilio López Arango and D. A. de Santillán, *El Anarquismo en el Movimiento Obrero*, Ed. Cosmos, Barcelona, 1925, p. 57.

[12] Ushuaia, in Tierra del Fuego at the southern tip of the Republic, is the site of a prison renowned for the harshness of the climate and the cruel treatment of the prisoners.

tortures.'[13] Martial law was declared and lasted until January 1910.

The repression seemed, however, to rejuvenate the anarchist movement. *La Protesta* reappeared in January, as soon as martial law had been lifted and its editorial and administrative group had been freed from their painful imprisonment on board the warship *Guardia Nacional*. In March a new anarchist daily evening paper, *La Batalla*, began to appear.

Next came the violent *Centenario* repression. A few months after *La Batalla* began to come out, the centenary of the revolution of May 1810 was celebrated – the anniversary of the colonies' independence from Spain. Since worker and anarchist agitation was on the increase, martial law was reimposed and a new, extremely vicious repression began, followed by another general strike, arrests, deportations, closures, assassinations and tortures. And so it went on. Simon Radowitsky could not be condemned to death since he was a minor, but he was sentenced to life in Ushuaia jail. Constant agitation was kept up on his behalf, since he was always regarded as one of the anarchist heroes, and eventually, after several failures, he was rescued in the 1930s with help from outside.

Anarchist activity was very intensive in the two decades between the 'centenary' repression and the *coup d'état* of General Uriburu. It had a powerful workers' centre, and often a majority following in spite of the efforts of the parliamentary socialists to fuse with or control the workers' movement; and it also had an extensive press: two dailies and dozens of union papers; *La Antorcha*, which took a violent incendiary line; the 'supplement' of *La Protesta* which appeared weekly for several years and later fortnightly, and in which Malatesta, Fabbri, Nettlau, etc., all wrote and which took an inquiring and receptive intellectual line.

In 1919 there occurred the 'tragic week' in which the police killed a number of workers during a strike; a general strike was proclaimed and fiercely suppressed. In 1920–1 strikers in Patagonia were 'pacified' by forces under Colonel Varela. When, however, details of Varela's methods became known, *La Antorcha* and *La Protesta* launched a campaign against the 'killer of Patagonia' which culminated in the assassination of Varela by an anarchist worker, Kurt Wilckens, on 27 January 1923.[14]

[13] E. Lopez Arango and D. A. de Santillán, *op. cit.*, p. 23.

[14] For the Patagonia strike, consult *La Protesta* and its supplement, and also papers such as *La Antorcha* and Osvaldo Bayer's recent piece published in the review *Todo es Historia*, no. 14, June 1968.

On 6 September 1931 the era of military governments began in Argentina. It was accompanied by the most unveiled repression, which was a great blow to the anarchists: persecutions, closures, deportations, executions. On 11 September, Penina, a distributor of *La Protesta*, was shot in Rosario; shortly afterwards Di Giovanni and Scarfo met the same fate. All three died shouting 'Long live anarchy!' The FORA went underground. Three working-class drivers, arrested while distributing *La Protesta* and *La Voz del Chauffeur* ('The Driver's Voice'), were condemned to death by a military court, though the sentence was later commuted to life imprisonment. Since it had become impossible to distribute *La Protesta*, the editorial group decided to bring out an underground paper called *Rebelión*. Martial law was lifted in 1932 and the weekly, *La Antorcha*, and the daily, *La Protesta*, in collaboration with *Ideas*, *Rebelión*, FORA and the local workers' unions of Santa Fé and Rosario, brought out a joint manifesto called 'Eighteen Months of Military Terror' informing the people about the politico-social situation.

At the end of September 1930, two workers' organizations amalgamated; these were the USA (*Unión Sindical Argentina*, Argentine Trades Union) representing a syndicalist trend, and the COA (*Confederación Obrera Argentina*, Argentine Workers' Confederation) which was socialist. From these derived the present CGT (*Confederación General de Trabaio*, General Labour Confederation). In its first public announcement the CGT declared: 'The CGT, a body which represents the healthy elements of the workers' groups in this country, believes in the administrative renewal undertaken by the provisional government and is ready to support it. ... This confederation is also convinced that the provisional government only maintains martial law in order to ensure public tranquillity. ...' [15]

In 1932 the second Regional Anarchist Conference was held in Rosario. (The first was held in 1922, at Avellaneda, in the province of Buenos Aires.) It was the outcome of agreements and understandings reached in the Villa Devoto prison by the anarchist militants imprisoned there during the Uriburu repressions. At this second congress a majority agreed on the necessity of setting up a specifically anarchist organization on a national scale, and a regional committee for anarchist co-ordination (CRRA) was created to this end. The efforts of this committee led to the foundation of the Argentine Anarcho-Communist Federation (FACA) in 1935, which

[15] Data from 'Bosquejo histórico de La Protesta', *La Protesta*, 1957, no. 8,033.

changed its name at its fourth congress in 1955 to the present one of Argentine Libertarian Federation (FLA).

FACA carried out an intense campaign on behalf of political prisoners. Anarchist activity also intensified during the Spanish civil war. FACA brought out special editions of its newspaper, *Acción Libertaria*, and the SIA (*Solidaridad Internacional Anti-Fascista*) was started. This movement spread all over the country and provided efficient aid. Various militants were sent to Spain. FORA and its associate unions organized strikes and public meetings and continued their normal programme. But now the organization was clearly weaker and its impact diminished.

In 1943 another military *coup* led to more closures and repressions and opened the way for General Perón's seizure of power.

While Peronism lasted, the whole anarchist movement went completely underground. All trade union premises, whether autonomous or associated with FORA, were closed: *La Protesta* was banned and began to come out secretly whenever it could, as did the other newspapers of the movement. In 1952, after the imprisonment and torture of several FORA dockers, and despite the ideological differences which have always split the anarchist movement, an intense information campaign was jointly carried out by all sections of the libertarian movement. A newspaper, *Agitación*, was published and commissions were set up in the capital and the inland towns.

On the fall of Perón, several FORA unions which had been operating clandestinely were reformed, as autonomous entities; these included the unions of the plumbers, bakers, drivers, dockers and the Shipbuilding Workers' Federation. The latter organized a prolonged strike for a six-hour day -- a long-standing FORA demand. But the strike failed owing to managerial intransigence and the complete lack of solidarity on the part of the reformist workers' movement centred around the CGT. (This was one organization, but it comprised many factions rivalling with each other for control.) A number of papers began to reappear openly: *Acción Libertaria*, *La Protesta* (fortnightly), the old organ of FORA, *Organización Obrera*, and, intermittently, different union papers. In the post-Perón era *La Protesta* was closed down again and its executive editor imprisoned.

On various occasions anarchists formed groups within the student movement. Generally these were short-lived, and after the 1918 university reform they usually operated through the University Federation.

Gradually the once dynamic anarchist movement dwindled to inward-looking small groups of old militants with a sprinkling of young people who pass through the groups and leave without a trace. In the last ten years activities have been reduced to meetings and conferences in the groups' premises, public meetings of the FLA in commemoration of the Spanish civil war, or of the FORA for the First of May, or of the FORA committee for prisoners and deportees on the anniversary of Sacco and Vanzetti.

THE EARLY URUGUAYAN ANARCHIST MOVEMENT

As in Argentina, anarchism developed in the first quarter of the 20th century in Uruguay with outstanding success and left a profound mark on the country and the period. In the last decades of the 19th century Montevideo contained an incipient proletariat which existed in the conditions of brutal exploitation typical of the first stages of capitalism. The city had a population of 110,000 inhabitants, and almost all the workers (17,024) lived in 589 settlements with 8,050 communal units in all.[16]

On 25 July 1875 the Regional Federation of the Eastern Republic of Uruguay was founded as a branch of the AIT (International Workers' Association), siding with the Bakuninist anti-authoritarian AIT which emerged from the split at the Hague Conference.[17] A leaflet published in 1878 setting out its statutes, rules and subscription centres was written by Renaud-Reynaud, a typographer and later journalist, an 'ex-communard' who left France after the failure of the Commune in 1871. Following the founding of the AIT in 1875 anarchist predominance in worker and revolutionary circles continued uninterrupted until the end of the 1920s. In 1885 the *Federación de Trabajadores del Uruguay* (Uruguayan Federation of Workers) took over the old Uruguayan section of the AIT, and its

[16] For the origins of the Uruguayan anarchist movement, data have been taken from the following publications: *Obreros y Anarquistas*, Carlos M. Rama, Enciclopedia Uruguaya: no. 32; *Cuadernos de Marcha*, no. 22, Montevideo, 1969; Max Nettlau, 'A Contribution to the Bibliography of Latin American Anarchism', in *Certamen Internacional*, La Protesta, 1927; *La Protesta Humana* (a contemporary collection).

[17] The Montevideo section sent a letter to the Berne Congress of the International (October 1876). It was accepted by the International at the Verviers Congress (August 1877). Max Nettlau, *op. cit.*

newspaper *Federación de Trabajadores* ('Workers' Federation') replaced the previous *El Internacional*[18] but took a similar ideological line. The new federation carried out important organizational work, creating *sociedades de resistencia* which functioned as craft unions.

Despite repressions and set-backs this movement continued to expand. In 1905 the Dock Workers' Federation set about organizing a congress of all the unions (*sociedades de resistencia*) which took place in March of that same year; from it there developed the FORU (Uruguayan Workers' Regional Federation) which was based on the same type of union support as the federations of 1875 to 1885. The socialists did not take part.

At this first congress emphasis was laid on the eight-hour day and the abolition of piece-work. Simultaneously the FORA was holding its fifth congress in Buenos Aires. There, with the support of the delegates of the FORU, the famous anarcho-communist 'finalist' declaration was passed. The line laid down at the fifth congress of the FORA was completely accepted and reiterated at following congresses in Uruguay. The FORU declared: 'Our organization is purely economic and is unlike and opposed to all bourgeois and worker political parties in that they are organized to take over political power while our aim is to reduce the existing legal and political state forms to purely economic functions and to replace them with a free federation of free associations of free producers.'

From the beginning the FORU adopted a Bakuninist-collectivist line which, with little ideological trouble, moved towards anarcho-communism, partly under the influence of Malatesta who had organized the first Bakers' Union in Buenos Aires, in spite of the fact that the forist line on workers' organization differed somewhat from Malatesta's. FORU thus became the only workers' organization and it maintained trade union unity and anarchist hegemony among the workers until the split of 1921-3.

The following congresses discussed, besides labour problems, issues of the widest social implication, such as the struggle against alcoholism and the creation of rationalist schools and workers' libraries, though co-operatives were opposed for ideological reasons. 'Solidarity strikes' and the occupation of factories were adopted as means of struggle. The permanent action of the proletariat was seen as the 'revolutionary gymnastics' which would prepare the ground

[18] On 5 May 1878 *El Internacional* came out in Montevideo. The first issue of *Federación de los Trabajadores* is dated 5 September 1885. Max Nettlau, *op. cit.*

for the 'final struggle'. It was argued that direct action was the only means of struggle, and that it should include the boycott, sabotage and the general strike.

In 1919 the Co-ordinating Committee for Anarchist Groups was formed by twenty regular groups, which was the forerunner of the FAU (Uruguayan Anarchist Federation) of 1926. As in Argentina the difference between finalists and those with immediate aims was never settled.

The centre around which anarchist intellectuals gravitated during these years was the *Centro Internacional de Estudios Sociales*, founded by a group of tailors in 1898. Here libertarian debates on subversive and anarchist ideas were carried on, artistic theories discussed. The centre provided the dynamism required to mobilize public opinion and strengthen the unions. Among the more outstanding members were Florencio Sánchez, innovatory dramatist, playwright and founder of the River Plate theatre (he was director of *La Protesta* in Buenos Aires); Roberto de las Carreras, the first South American anti-hero (*maldito*) writer; Rafael Barrett; and the poets Falcó and Leoncio Lasso de la Vega, etc. Besides all these there were also those who founded, directed and wrote in the extensive subversive press. The number and diversity of anarchist publications published in Uruguay is astounding. Most of the unions had their own propaganda sheets after 1895 when *El Obrero Panadero* ('The Baker') came out. The official organ of FORU, *Emancipación*, appeared monthly; in 1911 it changed its name to *La Federación* and the following year to *Solidaridad*. An even wider public was reached by the publications of the *Centro Internacional de Estudios Sociales*. Each of the ideologically differing anarchist groups had their own bulletin; some came out with relative regularity, others when they could. All were subject to the unpredictability of police repression. In 1915, during the war, María Collazo founded *La Batalla*, which was to be the most important of the Uruguayan anarchist papers. Antonio Marzovillo was to keep it going for fifteen years.

During the first quarter of the 20th century there was some debate with the individualist anarchists, but this trend gained little support in the Plata region. Similarly the early collectivist and Proudhonian tendencies were rapidly engulfed by anarcho-communism which predominated on both banks of the River Plate. The crucial debate was between 'finalists' and those who pursued immediate aims, but while anarchism remained strong, the first trend dominated in the workers' movement.

The creed of this *fin de siècle* anarchism was a flaming belief in universal brotherhood, in a world of comrades liberated from the curse of the weekly wage, where work could 'dignify' man. It believed in education and science and brought positivism, rationalism and secularism together. To us, exposed to world wars, atomic explosions, industrialization and ostentatious consumption, its world-view seems rather simplistic. Our way out may lie rather in another of their central values – rebellion, the refusal to accept the status quo: 'Our aim is to develop the spirit of rebellion latent in every individual and help the worker to free himself from all false patriotic, religious or "boss" concepts and to lose all respect for law and institutions', declared *El Surco* (25 June 1919).

Of the first strikes the most important were the tram strike in 1895 and the dockers' strike in 1896. The waves of strikes in 1905 (21 in Montevideo and 6 inland) were of particular importance, especially the first general railway strike and that of the Montevideo dock workers. In November 1906 when the President, Batlle y Ordoñez, promulgated the law on the eight-hour day, he declared: 'The eight-hour day has actually already been achieved by many of the unions', thus underlining the positive gains of the previous ten years of intense union activity.

The Mexican revolution of 1910–17 must be mentioned in passing. This was 'supported by the unions and the revolutionaries. The anarchists had contacts with the *Partido Liberal Mexicano* of the brothers Flores Magon prior to 1910. Volunteers went out from La Plata, collections were taken, [. . .] endless discussions went on as to whether the tactic of revolutionary violence that the Mexicans were using was or was not the most appropriate, etc. The socialists [. . .] criticized the Mexican revolutionaries, since in their view "the advent of socialism can only be achieved by a slow evolution and self-awareness on the part of the proletariat". However, the anarchists and the non-reformist socialists of the extreme Left supported the Mexicans warmly.'[19]

The Russian revolution forms a chapter apart, since it rapidly won the support of the whole Uruguayan workers' revolutionary movement, and led to violent arguments among anarchists and finally to a split in the FORU. The anarchists were now declining but they made considerable efforts during the 1936 Spanish revolution. A movement to help the CNT-FAI was started from the

[19] Carlos Rama, 'La cuestión social', in *Cuadernos de Marcha*, no. 22.

Casa de los Libertarios. In 1936 a magazine, *Esfuerzo*, appeared of which fourteen numbers were published until 1938.

20TH-CENTURY ANARCHISM

In Argentina

Anarchism as a modern revolutionary ideology is, in the theoretical field, a pointed criticism of the established system with special reference to the system of political *domination*.

We are not concerned here with the Utopian aspects of the revolutionary ideal,[20] but with the fundamental anarchist political theory (as illustrated in the refusal to legislate on the future society) that the essence of the *revolutionary system* is its incompatibility with the *established system*[21] and therefore: 'If the revolutionary project *is* what the society is *not*, if its essence is critical thought, the total negation of established society, it is clear that both the established system and the revolutionary idea form part of the same *historical continuity*.'[22]

Revolution breaks this historical continuity, revolution is insurrectional action, only action can create new social conditions.[23] This is important because anarchism's fundamental stand is a total opposition to established society; it cannot accept any form of integration into the system.

This total confrontation with the established system was, as they

[20] Perhaps it is worth re-reading Sorel and his theory of the myth here. '[. . .] no attempt should be made to analyse these image systems like things which can be divided into their elements. These historical forces should be taken as a whole, and great care must be taken not to compare what has been achieved with the ideas accepted before action.' Georges Sorel, *Reflexions on Violence*, Ed. Francisco Boltrán, Madrid, 1915, p. 27.

See also the relation between modern revolutionary movements and the 'millenarianism' which they contain, as a positive force for change; e.g. in Eric Hobsbawn, *Primitive Rebels*, Ed. Ariel, Barcelona, 1968.

[21] See André Decouflé, *Sociologie des révolutions*, P.U.F., Paris, 1968. This contains a theory of revolution in modern, sociological language basically similar to that of G. Landauer in *Die Revolution*, Spanish translation, Ed. Proyección, Buenos Aires, 1961; and Herbert Marcuse, *One-Dimensional Man*, Ed. J. Mortiz, Mexico, 1968.

[22] *La Protesta*, no. 8,113, June 1969.

[23] Proudhon expresses this idea ('The idea and its categories spring from action and must return to action or be degraded by its agent') and it is taken up again in Marx, and also in Bakunin. For Proudhon, see also Pierre Ansart, *Marx et l'anarquisme*, P.U.F., Paris, 1969.

were well aware, the real situation of the urban proletariat in Buenos Aires and Montevideo at the beginning of the century. Faced with the traditional mentality of the ruling class and the appalling economic exploitation, the only legal means for change was the suffrage. But in the first quarter of the 20th century 50–70 per cent of the key politically significant electoral age-group (adult males over twenty years old) resident in the central areas (the capital and coastal provinces) were foreign-born. In electoral terms this meant that between 50 and 70 per cent of the population were disenfranchised just where voting potentially had the maximum importance.[24]

During this period of the take-off of industrialization the embryonic capitalist system excluded the proletarian masses from any real participation in law and in fact in the management and running of the system. Various institutions existed to ensure and control their exclusion, such as social services run with the object of keeping the poor well segregated; the police; laws, such as the 1909 law against 'unhealthy' immigration, i.e. prostitutes, syphilitics and anarchists, or law no. 4,114,[25] the electoral law, etc.

Gradually, however, channels of integration emerged, as the economic situation improved in the next stage of economic development. The middle class increased in numbers, composed mainly of second-generation immigrants with university degrees – the university was a major route upwards for many years – and, most important, the development of a reformist trade union movement which was prepared to negotiate on the class struggle. This stage saw a great deal of labour legislation.

But winning rights does not necessarily mean any actual gain. During the French revolution Brissot said: 'The enormous harm that the anarchist doctrine has caused our armies is now obvious. Under the cover of equality of rights it seeks to establish actual universal equality; whereas the one sustains society, the other only injures it. Anarchism wants to level out talent and stupidity, virtues and vice, positions, salaries, services.'[26]

The objective reality of economic exploitation and political domination did not change, but the influence of increased material well-being and consumption changed subjective reality. Anarchism

[24] Gino Germani, *op. cit.*, p. 225.

[25] The so-called 'Residence' law, no. 4,144 – recently brought back into operation by the present Argentine military government – allows the deportation of foreigners.

[26] Quoted by P. Kropotkin, *La Gran Revolución*, Ed. Tupac, Buenos Aires, 1940, p. 304.

no longer expressed the revolutionary aspirations of the new proletariat. While anarchism still called for revolution, the social situation had become increasingly conformist; while it demanded direct action, the paternalistic state was dicussing labour problems with union leaders.

The change in the international ideological climate must also be taken into account. The 1914 war put an end to internationalist ideas; then came the triumph of the Russian revolution and the constitution of the Soviet state, the failure of revolution in Central Europe, the advent of fascism, and the tragic end of the Spanish revolution. The second wave of immigration began at a time when the anarchist movement was clearly declining. 'These internal migrations were very considerable; from 1936 to 1947 the proportion of Argentines born in the provinces who moved to the metropolitan area of Buenos Aires amounted to almost 40 per cent of the natural increase of the population of these same provinces. This mass exodus brought vast numbers of people from the underdeveloped areas – people previously completely outside the country's political life – into the big cities and in particular into Buenos Aires.'[27] This internally migrating proletariat had been suddenly uprooted from a *traditional* way of life and deposited in the big city. It was not as the previous influx of the European proletariat, fleeing from highly developed industrial areas. It was the industrial revolution which brought this proletariat into the cities.

In Argentina, limited participatory democracy was already in a state of crisis. The 'revolution' of 6 September 1930 marked the beginning of the period of military *coups* and the 'patriotic fraud' of the conservative backlash. From then on the army has, either openly or covertly, controlled the state apparatus – no institutional structure existed which could integrate large masses into the system. These masses demanded some kind of participation but were bemused by the violent impact of the *secular* society. Charismatic leadership provided the answer: it adapted itself to mass demands for participation and granted the masses a series of actual gains which changed the traditional structure of the country. This movement, commonly known as 'Peronism', was bitterly opposed by the ruling classes (the bourgeoisie and the traditional upper classes) because it led to an increase in popular participation. On the other hand the Left generally failed to understand the process, and when it did not gain the support of this new proletariat – unattracted by its

[27] G. Germani, *op. cit.*, p. 230.

secular ideology – it attacked Peronism as a whole and in return was violently repressed by the state's special forces.

Anarchism – like the other groups of the traditional Left, the Communist and Socialist Parties – saw only one side of the problem: the military fascist origins of the ruling group (Perón himself, and his political origins in military freemasonry and his early contacts with Nazism and fascism), and the suppression of oppositional political liberties, the persecutions, closings down of newspapers, imprisonments, police tortures, deaths, permanent states of emergency, etc. They were unable to perceive the increased participation which Peronism provided for the great masses of the people. They themselves remained isolated, unable to fulfil their promises. Their criticisms became increasingly abstract and removed from attainable reality. Peronism reinforced the drift of anarchism towards marginalism, and strengthened reformist trade unionism and the paternalist state, which reached its maximum under the charismatic leadership of Perón. Thus anarchism is suffering from what one can call a decay in 'praxis'. It became virtually impossible for anarchist groups to keep to their ideas and their practice when faced with popular withdrawal from direct-action organizations. Maintaining their ideological 'purity' now meant withdrawing increasingly from reality; but giving up 'purity' meant moving towards reformism. How could electoral abstention be advocated if only a small number of militants abstained and no one even noticed? Some of the older anarchists became conformists, abandoned the revolution, disowned insurrection, the people, and the possibility of change and withdrew into an anarchist liberalism which pined for democratic liberties. Others secluded themselves in 'sects', ritualized their ideology and periodically brought out the liturgy of the revolutionary martyrs, the Chicago martyrs or Sacco and Vanzetti.

In Uruguay

Uruguayan anarchism acquired its present form when it lost the support of the workers' movement. A statement by the 1956 anarchist conference, which we shall discuss later, tells us that 'The deportation of foreign comrades in the Terra epoch[28] was a harsh

---

[28] The Terra dictatorship followed a *coup* by the then president of the Republic, Gabriel Terra, on 31 March 1933. This was supported by the reactionary political sectors, the *latifundistas* and by foreign capital. It was virtually the only suspension of public liberties in Uruguay from the beginning of this century to the present day.

blow for the finalist libertarian movement. But the crisis had set in long before; it dates from the period of confusion following the bolshevik dictatorship's strangulation of the Russian revolution. This split the workers' movement into the FORU and the USU (*Unión Sindical Uruguaya*) which, as in Argentina, fought each other mercilessly. This facilitated the disastrous propagation of the Soviet myth among the Uruguayan workers, first by the *Bloque de Unidad Obrero* and then by the present UGT (*Unión General de Trabajadores*).' From then onwards revolutionary direct-action trade unionism declined and mass syndicalism, legalistic and subservient to external political dictates, was on the increase. The UGT was formed in 1942 and the CSU (*Confederación Sindical del Uruguay*) in 1952. The UGT acted in close relationship with Russian foreign policy and with the Uruguayan Communist Party line. The CSU collaborated with US imperialism and its unions, the AFL, CIO, ORIT, CIOSL.[29]

In the last few years, since 1958, political ideas throughout the country have become increasingly radical as the social, political and economic crises deepened. In 1964 the CNT (*Convención Nacional de Trabajadores*) was formed. This brought together almost all the organized Uruguayan workers' movements, and specified that unions should be independent of the state, political parties, ideologies and religious trends. The FAU, which I shall be returning to, works through its militants in this organization.

In the period following FORU's organizational and ideological decline until the formation of the present movement, which can be said (despite splits, set-backs and convergences) to date from the 1956 conference, several groups of the FORU and other autonomous advocates of direct action kept going, and maintained their newspapers, among these the editorial group of *Voluntad*, an anarchist paper founded in 1938.

In 1955 *Voluntad* proposed the calling of a national congress of dispersed anarchist militants with the intention of forming an Anarchist Federation. The congress was held in April 1956, and provided the basis for a specifically anarchist national organization; it brought forward new methods of action for the workers' movement which from then on acquired a certain support in Uruguay – something which did not happen in Argentina. Ideologically the congress took the classic anarchist line: internationalism and active opposition to all forms of imperialism; support for the struggle of

[29] Raúl I. Acuña, *A donde va el Sindicalismo Uruguayo?*, Ed. Arca, Montevideo, p. 12. Printed in the printing works of the Comunidad del Sur.

the colonialized peoples against the imperialist powers and also for the constructive ideas which have developed in some of these countries. It also declared that 'all rebellion and effort towards social renovation runs the risk of destroying itself in the suicidal pitfalls of nationalism and/or bolshevism, resulting in the exaltation of new exploiters and bureaucrats', and that 'our action should aim in a revolutionary way at the causes of these phenomena: social organization based on authority and exploitation, etc.' With regard to the workers the congress stated: 'We are voluntarist revolutionaries and we intend to be logical. These new and difficult times demand appropriate tactical formulations from our generation. Anarchism cannot hope that the errant unions will return. Militant anarchism should go to the workers and their unions, wherever and whatever state they are in, and breathe new life into them.' The Congress then resolved that 'Libertarian militants should act with full responsibility in the guilds or unions to which they belong, and should not refuse to take up official posts, as long as they exercise discretion as to the nature of the group and behave according to the norms of the libertarian ethic.'

Here, as in Argentina, the finalist revolutionary workers' movement – forism – was faced with a serious problem. It was difficult for old-time militants to give up the 'pure' line of the anarchist workers' movement: that is, direct confrontation with ownership, no state interference, no legal agreements. They considered that office-holding in the reformist unions or taking up paid posts amounted to a compromise with their beliefs and would inevitably lead to bureaucratic degeneration.

Finally, the 1956 congress decided to form the FAU – Uruguayan Anarchist Federation. A constitutional congress was organized and met in October and November of the same year. *Voluntad* became the mouthpiece for the FAU and changed its name to *Lucha Libertaria*. The FAU was organized into area, job and affinity groups. Ideologically speaking, says *La Protesta*, it took its place within the framework of international anarchism. At first FAU received the firm support of the Argentine Libertarian Federation, but this has now turned to complete confrontation.

The anarchists have also been operating systematically within the student movement in the schools and in the University of the Republic. The Medical Libertarian Group and the Fine Arts Group were both affiliated to the FAU during this period; both have a long tradition of struggle and are still militant.

The CAP (*Centro de Acción Popular*), which functioned for several years, roughly from 1963, was an attempt to extend action more widely among the people. Even though anarchists took part in its foundation and always worked in it, CAP was not anarchist by definition. It supported a wide anti-authoritarian socialism and was opposed to electoral politics. A CAP pamphlet states: 'The CAP is an attempt to provide a plausible alternative to closed group squabbles. The aim is to offer an alternative [. . .] so that the Left [. . .] can discuss its different ideas and methods openly and frankly. In place of hypocritical "unity" we provide an open arena for everyone to do what they feel is necessary [. . .] let positions be defined and each work his own way [. . .] we hope that two positions will emerge: one, which we hope will be ours; and a second one which will continue to fall into the errors of authoritarianism.' CAP published several information bulletins and a review, *Tarea*, which lasted for three issues.

Around this time the FAU split over disagreements as to the structure and control of the organization and over theoretical issues, arising from the Cuban revolution, on the revolutionary seizure of power. The Medical Libertarian Group, with the Fine Arts and the South groups, broke off from the FAU and formed the Groups of Libertarian Action (GAL) working within the CAP. Later, at the end of 1964, this became the *Alianza Libertaria del Uruguay*.

CONTEMPORARY ANARCHISM

In Argentina

One military government has succeeded another since 1955. The so-called 'Argentine revolution' put an end to this in June 1966 when the three commanders-in-chief of the armed forces formed a military junta. All political parties were banned and the constitution was subordinated to a so-called 'Statute of the Argentine Revolution'. Yet, contrary to past tradition, there was no systematic persecution of the anarchists, which is an indication of their reduced energies. At present the FORA still has several centres in Buenos Aires and a few small groups of militants inland. It has no unions, but groups of anarchists keep forist groups going within the different unions. The FORA committee for prisoners and deportees still looks after prisoners and keeps on with its other duties. FORA publishes leaflets, manifestos and its newspaper, *Organización Obrera*. For the last few years the traditional First of May rallies have been banned, and this has led to some arrests. Sporadic organizational work goes on within the unions, but up to now this has had no great effect or continuity. The ideology remains classic forist finalism.

The *Federación Libertaria Argentina* has premises in Buenos Aires and some groups inland; conferences and meetings are held and *Acción Libertaria* is still published. The last issue to come out was in March 1970. The publishing house *Reconstruir* and the review of the same name tie in ideologically with the FLA. The FLA has reacted strongly against the Cuban revolution, Castro-Communism and Marxism in general. The leading article of the last issue of *Acción Libertaria* declared: 'Marxist-Leninism led to Stalin's insane dictatorship – which is once again being defended in the USSR – to the esoteric cult of Mao's thought, and to Fidel Castro's tropical and homicidal arbitrariness. These are all forms of dictatorship implanted in the followers of Marxism-Leninism which try to impose their domination in the name of the socialist revolution. In the circumstances it would be ridiculous to try and work out a synthesis between Marxism as we see it in operation and libertarian socialism. . . . '

The review *Reconstruir* supports a wide-ranging libertarian socialism with articles which are more philosophical and literary than political and with historical themes from classical anarchism. Some of the articles are so liberal that they cannot be fitted into even the widest definition of anarchism. It is perhaps interesting to look at a few paragraphs from two articles by D. A. de Santillán as an example of this:[30] 'Capitalism too can transform itself, socialize itself in a certain sense, fulfil a more social function, conciliate more interests. Capitalism *per se* does not oppose direct participation and joint management of the whole economic life of the country; all one needs is organizational capacity, initiative, audacity and enough skill to compete.'[31] 'We should not try to destroy the apparatus

[30] Diego Abad de Santillán was an active anarchist militant. He defended the 'finalist' revolutionary workers' movement in *La Protesta* but left the editorial group in 1932 after ideological differences. Later he was a minister in the Spanish government during the civil war.

[31] *Reconstruir*, no. 42, May–June 1966, 'La idea y el hecho de la dictadura' by D. A. de Santillán.

capitalism has created in order to make profits; instead we should apply, widen and improve its dynamic in a social direction, for the benefit of all, since now it needs and can no longer do without the support of the entire community. [. . .] Reform is today's great revolution; the barricades have fulfilled their mission, that is if they ever had a mission. . . . '[32]

The editorial group of *La Protesta*, which is periodically elected by militants, continues to publish the paper, but sporadically, because since 1966 it comes out semi-clandestinely with no editor's or printer's name. Apart from printing difficulties its publication has not been impeded. Within the anarcho-communist line its main themes have derived from Malatesta and Bakunin, and its defence of the revolutionary movement has recently centred on student and workers insurrectional activity following the increase in international student agitation and the 1969 popular risings in Córdoba and Rosario. Other groups also exist which carry on various types of activity outside Buenos Aires, and also other publishers, collateral to the movement, who publish the anarchist classics and contemporary works.

But a new anarchist generation has now emerged apart from the above-named 'traditional' anarchist organizations. The young maintain contacts with the old but have formed their own organizations. The relations between the two groups are flexible and changing; both seek a common language. There is, it seems, a gap in the movement, a distance to be bridged. The advent of the new groups was signalled by two events: the Paris revolution of May 1968 and the Argentine popular rebellion in Rosario and Córdoba in May–June 1969. The former generated enthusiasm and small groups of militant students and workers were formed, courses were given on the basic ideas of anarchism in the premises of the Shipbuilding Workers' Federation, leaflets were distributed in the university and contacts sought with other groups inland. In May 1969 the prestige of the military government and its liberal façade of social peace was badly shaken when, following the assassination of a student by the police, student demonstrations began in the north. Workers' demonstrations followed. A new group broke away from the reformist CGT and, calling itself *CGT de los Argentinos*, confronted the government. The murder of two more students by the police of Rosario led to a spontaneous popular mobilization, barricades were erected,

[32] *Ibid.*, no. 65, March–April 1970, 'La organización profesional de la sociedad, una estructura representativa' by D. A. de Santillán.

stones overcame police bullets and after several hours of struggle the army occupied the city and declared martial law. In Córdoba the struggle began with an active strike by the workers in the area's key factories. Workers and students trooped into the city, the police tried to break them up and when they failed resorted to shooting. Troops occupied the city, and sporadic shooting continued. Army units set up councils of war, curfews were imposed, etc. Agitation extended to all the universities and to several other cities. The bourgeois press blamed Havana and, as always, an international conspiracy. Their editorials stressed the damage to private property more than the workers' lives lost. Martial law once again became a normal feature of the country's life, and a new law was passed providing for the expulsion of foreigners, 'following the example', according to the executive, 'of law no. 4144 which was in operation for more than half a century'.

That vital component of the workers' revolutionary organization, direct action, had fallen out of use during the last few decades. But it was no longer a question of the six-hour day, once demanded by the FORA; the eight-hour day itself, won with such great effort, has ceased to be respected and in some places people now worked ten- or twelve-hour days.

It must not be forgotten that Argentina is a developing country, and this conditions a series of structural factors which facilitate spontaneous popular risings; but there is one serious impediment to the creation of a revolutionary movement. Though there was extensive agitation, it tended to lose itself in the political manipulations of the pressure groups. Military dictatorship makes it easier for political opposition to unite, but it masks the fundamental reality of capitalist society and therefore impedes the development of the full revolutionary dialectic, thus encouraging the development of liberal deviations. This liberal deviationism is one of the clearest dangers anarchist groups have to overcome. Only by means of action can anarchist ideals hope to be rejuvenated and the theoretical arguments necessary for contemporary anarchism be developed.

Certain aspects of the anarchist revolutionary model are being widely propagated: rejection of leadership and of legalitarian or parliamentary channels, the emphasis on direct action at the lowest level of management, and the need for non-reformist revolutionary and subversive political action. This tends to lead to a *rapprochement* with the Marxist Left on certain aspects of revolutionary praxis.

In this context, under the influence of what appears to be a new social situation, the *Grupos Anarquistas Revolucionarios* (GAR, Anarchist Revolutionary Groups) and the *Juventudes Anarquistas* ('Anarchist Youth') have been started up in Buenos Aires. There are also various groups linked to different faculties and secondary schools. At present they are at a stage where it is very difficult to predict future possibilities or the extent of the implicit ideological differences. There are also some groups in La Plata, Córdoba and Rosario, which can be classified along two general lines: those who operate within the *Federaciones Universitarias*, which are inclined more to liberalism, and those which are organized as independent groups and which in some places (La Plata, Córdoba) have formed direct-action groups together with revolutionary Marxists along the lines of the French 22nd of March Movement. These groups are reluctant to maintain formal contacts with the 'traditional' anarchist groups, and informal relations show certain generic lines of divergence.

The future, however, remains open, and, as Breton said, *'En matière de révolte nul n'a besoin d'ancêtres.'*

In Uruguay

As noted at the beginning of this article, Uruguay was known for its strong liberal political institutions, economic prosperity and almost uninterrupted internal peace since 1904; for its progressive increase on all the 'indices of social progress' (rising standards of living, stably functioning judicial institutions, etc.). This Uruguay, which was the haven of the persecuted in South America, no longer exists. It succumbed to the reality of colonialized Latin America.

The *Blanco* party won the 1958 elections; in 1966 the *Colorado* party returned to government. Both became increasingly authoritarian and a new constitution was promulgated which put an end to collegiate executive power and granted considerably increased powers to the presidency.[33] Martial law was imposed for limited periods which ran together so closely as to be almost permanent.

From the economic point of view Uruguay's commercial and

[33] Carlos M. Rama, *Uruguay en Crisis*, Ed. Siglo Ilustrado, Montevideo.

financial dependence has increased considerably over the last fifteen years. Capital is concentrated outside the productive sector. 'Industrial growth has been disproportionate to the agropecuarian base which provides foreign exchange. This has meant a growing deficit in foreign trade and in the balance of payments. It has increased the power of the cattle owners and the exporters who bring in most of the foreign capital. . . . ' Then came inflation: in 1951 the cost of living rose by 20·9 per cent and continued to soar. In the 1960s the increase in the cost of living reached an average annual 60 per cent and a record 136 per cent in 1967.[34] A wage freeze came into operation seven months later.

Meanwhile popular unrest increased, and big strikes took place leading in some cases to the militarization of the workers (as in the bank workers' strike). Street demonstrations were held and several people died in confrontations with the police. The country's only university became a centre of street activity and the government endeavoured to legislate to end its autonomy. Social conditions lent themselves to urban guerrilla warfare. Many political groups besides the anarchists distrusted parliamentary action and supported revolutionary action. The *Tupamaros* (Movement for National Liberation or MLN) have been in operation since 1962–3. They are named after the rebellious Inca Túpac Amaru who rocked the foundations of the Hispano-American colonial regime in 1780.[35] The *Tupamaros* began as an armed group formed of ex-members of the Socialist Party, the anarchists and the Marxist extreme Left who were disgusted with legalitarian politics. There seems to be a constant influx of activists of different origins into the MLN, which comprises various ideological trends, including a left-wing nationalist trend. Some of the first *Tupamaros* worked in the rural areas, for example with the Bella Unión cane-cutters. Their activity raised the question of whether to concentrate on urban or rural guerrilla warfare which was rapidly resolved in favour of the urban guerrilla, despite the weighty opinions of such experts as Che Guevara and Régis Debray. (Note that 80 per cent of the population of Uruguay lives in urban areas.) A document attributed to the *Tupamaros* states: 'Where more

[34] *La Crisis Económica*, Instituto de Economía, Montevideo, 1969, pp. 38, 46.
[35] Túpac Amaru was executed by quartering on 18 May 1781. He became the symbol of American rebellion towards the end of Spanish colonial rule. 'Around that time if a Spaniard wanted to insult an unruly or rebellious South American he would call him a *tupamaro*.' Boleslao Lewin, *La insurrección de Túpac Amaru*, Buenos Aires, 1963, p. 106.

than 50 per cent of a country's population lives in urban areas the revolutionary struggle should not take place in the fields or in the mountains but in the towns because the revolution is where the people are.'[36]

The *Tupamaros* operate frequently and keep the police in check in spite of their long run of operations and the inevitable losses this implies for this type of movement. Armed action focuses on the exposure of social reality. Banks are raided and stolen information exposing dubious dealings is passed on to the press for publication. People from government and financial circles are kidnapped, radio stations entered and broadcasts put out. The town of Pando was taken over and there were open battles with the police. Actions range from the procuring of arms and money to 'exemplary' activity.

Though of less importance, both numerically and organizationally, specifically anarchist and some other groups also practice this type of armed action. To an external observer their activity seems somewhat indiscriminate. Everything is blamed on the *Tupamaros* by the press and the general public.

In December 1967 a decree was passed ordering the dissolution of the *Federación Anarquista Uruguaya* and of the following left-wing movements: *Movimiento Revolucionario Oriental, Movimiento de Izquierda Revolucionaria, Movimiento de Acción Popular Uruguaya*, and the Socialist Party. All went underground. The Uruguayan Communist Party is still legal.

The *Federación Anarquista Uruguaya*, after the split in the early 1960s, has taken a coherent line which marks it out in Latin American anarchism. It is now a semi-clandestine organization based on workers' groups and with influence over several important unions within the CNT. Ideologically the FAU is anarcho-communist, taking its doctrine from classical Bakuninism. It regards *direct action* as fundamental for creating the conditions for revolution and as the organizational principle of the future society. Direct action, for the FAU as for all anarchists, is not only a tactic of confrontation with the capitalist structure but also the link between groups on different levels. Emphasis is laid on anti-reformism and the revolution. 'The revolutionary point of view, the belief that only by armed force can the system be overthrown, must condition *all* policies within a movement: its immediate objectives, its organization, its means of struggle and not just the final decisive stage of the struggle. No

[36] A. Mercader and J. de Vera, *Tupamaros, Estrategia y Acción*, Ed. Alfa, Montevideo, 1969, p. 15.

dialectic can move from reformist policies to revolutionary ends. To organize the present struggle within the framework of bourgeois "legality" is incompatible with the insurrectional illegality of tomorrow.'[37]

One can only move towards revolution by the radicalization of action and not by calling for democratic liberties. Liberalism – a trend within traditional anarchism that should not be underestimated – easily degenerates into reformism. In South America the frequent suspension of democratic constitutionalism by military *coups* leads to the illusion of reactionary solutions: in a bourgeois regime liberty at least exists in law if it never exists in practice.

But anarchism can never seriously advocate a return to parliamentarianism or the party game, even if some parties appear to be in favour of social revolution. 'All we want to say is that, though political parties may be verbally revolutionary, the praxis they offer does not lead to the destruction of bourgeois power but is merely a safety-valve for the system.'[38]

Thus the FAU, with its Malatestian revolutionary voluntaristic line, accepts organized terrorism in response to capitalist social violence but rejects individual violence. The organization of the revolutionary apparatus has brought to light disagreements between the FAU and the rest of the movement. The FAU affirms that, given a prolonged struggle (along the lines of Che Guevara's 'create many Vietnams'), spontaneity alone is not enough: 'It has to be channelled and directed. This necessarily implies an underground organization with subdivisions, security checks, and central leadership . . . '[39]

This brings us to the second important difference which arises over the seizure of power, the transition period. Traditional anarchism solves the problem by advocating the immediate destruction of all political power and declares that 'all organization of a supposedly provisional and revolutionary power designed to bring about this destruction cannot be other than a fraud and would be as detrimental to the proletariat as all present-day governments'.[40]

According to anarchist revolutionary theory, power should only be taken up at the level of the people's immediate organizations – in the factory, the district, the city and the street; the repressive system

[37] 'There are no two ways of going forward', in *Cartas* of the FAU, Montevideo, 4 November 1968.
[38] *Cartas*, 22 September 1969.
[39] *Ibid.*
[40] Congress of St. Imier, 1872.

should be dismantled and direct action undertaken by the community's organizations. But if no doubt remains on the errors of liberal deviationism, see for instance what García Oliver wrote on the Spanish revolution: 'The CNT and the FAI decided on collaboration and democracy and abandoned revolutionary totalitarianism which could only lead to the death of the revolution in an anarchist and confederal dictatorship.'[41] The FAU feels that anarchism has not developed an effective political strategy of insurrection: it declares that political power is not easily destroyed and therefore anarchists should not refuse to collaborate in the central power during the first stage after the revolution. It should also take the key political decision-making positions in order to avoid the danger of centralist groups moving in to fill the power vacuum and thus frustrating low-level self-management.

A FAU leaflet, *Recortes*, dealing with Bakunin, sums up with these words: 'Bakunin correctly foresaw the risks of state centralism, but he did not outline clearly any intermediate or genuinely transitory solution for the suppression of all power once the period of construction of socialism-communism was complete. His choice between the despotic state and spontaneous freedom has not provided a practicable model in concrete historical situations. The solution to the problem of power during the post-insurrectional period must be looked for in concrete historical events. The Cuban revolution, the first stages of the Russian revolution and Spain in 1936 can provide valuable information here.'

It is obvious from the above that within old-style anarcho-communism the FAU is moving towards Marxism. This is correct as far as the general theoretical framework of the revolutionary struggle goes, but needs to be discussed and refined in certain key aspects of theory and strategy. For instance, on the theoretical level the development of centralized organizations and involvement with political power results in structural modifications which invalidate the theoretical formulations and 'good intentions' of the militants; an alien factor has been brought in and praxis begins to stray from theory on a fundamental issue. On the strategic level, struggle for control of revolutionary decision-making centres involves a degree of 'organic' participation which would reintroduce the struggle for power into the revolutionary ranks themselves.

In spite of these differences within the anarchist movement, the

[41] Quoted by José Peirats in *La CNT en la Revolución Española*, Ed. CNT, Toulouse, 1951.

FAU defines itself as anarchist in the confrontation with oligarchy and imperialism in the Third World. It supports the peoples' liberation struggles from colonialism following the example of China, Algeria, Cuba and Vietnam. It actively defends the Cuban revolution, publishes Fidel Castro's speeches and Che Guevara's writings and reproduces articles from Castroist papers.

In terms of internal organization the FAU distinguishes between several areas of operation: the unions – to an anarchist no revolution is possible without mass participation: people must realize through action that it is up to them to make the revolution; ideological activity – general propaganda and the preparation of their own militants; armed struggle – this must be on a popular level or it becomes suicidal.

The *Comunidad del Sur* (the Commune of the South), founded in 1955, is very important for anarchism in Uruguay. It is an integrated commune; property, production and consumption are all communal. All members work in the commune's printing press which is one of the most important in Montevideo. Forty adults and children live together. All decisions are taken in common and there are no leading groups, only working ones which combine over the commune's multiple activities. Everyone has to take their turn in the kitchen, laundry, looking after the children, etc. When the children reach school age they no longer live with their parents but move in with their own age-group and share rooms, activities and decisions.

Ideologically the Commune of the South takes its own line. It sees the commune as the basic cell of socialist society and simultaneously as the instrument for immediate social change. It feels that the historical process of change calls for the creation of a movement which fights not only on the ideological and political levels but also at the production and working level. 'All social development basically takes place along a single chain of decisions. [. . .] The revolution is the inevitable result of the historical developments of the previous years. One link in the chain determines the nature of the next.'[42] Following G. Landauer's ideas, the commune hopes to create a new type of relationship between men and feels that this has to be put into practice now if it is to have any meaning in the future. 'Socialism is always possible if enough people want it', says Landauer.

[42] *La Comunidad*, a publication of the Commission for Ideological Promotion, Comunidad del Sur, Montevideo, 1969.

The following are extracts from a publication which illustrates some of the commune's basic viewpoints: 'The commune can continue to exist and evolve within the capitalist system because it is dedicated to the struggle and takes an everyday part in the vital confrontation of our generation, our country, Latin America and the whole world for revolutionary transformations of the economy, society and culture.' [. . .] 'No defensive walls separate the community from the outside world. It influences us in thousands of visible and invisible ways. Our fortress is both culturally and socially vulnerable. It is exposed to constant political aggression which tries to destroy it, devalue it and discredit its aims.' [. . .] 'Our productive relations with the outside world are capitalist and these perpetually threaten to move inside in the guise of wages or collective egoism and destroy us.' To overcome this the commune has to face the system combatively, 'directed by its pioneer libertarian socialist ideas in all aspects of life'. [. . .] 'The commune is not a prosperous commune within a world socialist system, but a fighting vanguard group which precedes the general process and prepares the way . . . as part of a fighting movement, under the banners of liberty and socialism.'[43] Having their own printing press predetermines most of the commune's activity. It publishes a bulletin called *Comunidad*, leaflets on ideological points and many pamphlets on topical issues.

It is too complex to go into all the different anarchist groups which do not belong to the FAU and do not have the consistency and stability of the Commune of the South or of the Medical or Fine Arts groups. Affinity groups may be vital and active during periods of popular unrest, but later they may decay or turn inwards, or dissolve themselves to reform in some other way. The influence of anarchism has also extended among intellectuals and artists. Some artists have formed groups which have obviously been influenced by anarchism.

Recently the question of the Bella Unión cane-cutters in the north has become very important.[44] The cane-workers' revolutionary and anti-parliamentarian union (UTAA) organized

---

[43] *Ibid.*

[44] Part of a manifesto of the cane-cutters (UTAA), *Unión de Trabajadores Azucareros de Artigas*) reads as follows:

BROTHER LABOURER:

We live your life, we come from the same class. We are cane-cutters from

marches on Montevideo. The workers' demands are centred on the *Movimiento por la Tierra* (Movement for Land) in which all the groups of the revolutionary Left, including the FAU and other anarchist groups, have taken part. They have begun to publish a paper, *Tierra y Libertad* ('Land and Liberty'), and to organize a peasant gathering in Bella Unión. In its first number *Tierra y Libertad* proclaims: 'The name of our paper takes up again the cry which America learnt in the Mexican revolution. On hearing it a whole people awoke. Today it sounds again, calling for a world where *land* and all sources of labour are held in common, without owners or managers. And where *liberty* reigns in all political and social organizations, without domination. Land and liberty for all!'

All this gives some idea of the multi-faceted, long-lived anarchist movement which is at present struggling in historical circumstances which suggest that there will be violent change. The anarchists have confidence in the clarity of their basic ideas and know that, as Malatesta said, it is not a question of achieving anarchism today or in a hundred years but of marching towards it today, tomorrow and always.

Bella Unión, a district of Artigas, in the corner where the Cuareim meets the Uruguay River.

When we cut cane, we live in huts, the earth floor is our bed, chair and table.

We exist on dishwater soup, noodles and salt, even though our hands make millions of pesos for the rich, the Yankees or the land-owners.

You can see, comrade, that our life is like yours, our clothes are like yours, our hands are like yours, our death in hospital or the street will be like yours, and our coffin, like yours, will be on the edge of the cemetery, just as our piece of land is on the poor side of the village [. . .].

For us, as for you, when we get paid we have to leave the money at the store where we buy food and clothes [. . .].

Besides all that they make us pay the firm's price for our dinners, sometimes they even pay us in vouchers [. . .].

We cane-cutters know that while the rich are in power elections won't achieve anything [. . .].

We want to take over 30,000 hectares of land to make a giant co-operative, to work all together, everything for everyone, where there are no exploiters and exploited [. . .].

If they beat us instead of giving us land, we want it known that sooner or later we shall also use violence to achieve bread, equality and justice.

James Joll

Anarchism – a Living Tradition

LIKE THE HISTORICAL ANARCHIST MOVEMENT THE NEW LEFT TODAY is an international phenomenon, and it is recognized as such both by the revolutionaries themselves and by the authorities, just as the revolutionary movement was a century ago. In June 1871, a few weeks after the suppression of the Paris commune, Jules Favre, the Foreign Minister in the provisional government, said 'Europe is faced by a work of destruction which is directed against all nations and directed against the principles upon which civilization rests.' And on 14 November 1968, a few months after the attempts at revolution in Paris in the spring, M. Raymond Marcellin, Minister of the Interior in the French government, said 'a study of the movement launched in the German Federal Republic in November 1967, in Britain from 1968, and the attempts observed in Holland at the same time disclosed the disturbing simultaneousness, a complete identity of methods of action and of intervention between communist and activist groups. We observe in the convergence of the phenomenon between Europe and the United States in the last few years the action of determined and militant minorities cultivating close contacts with each other across frontiers and living in a state of permanent conspiracy against society.'[1] This conception of an international permanent conspiracy against society is an essential element in the anarchist tradition as it was formulated in the 19th century, and it is this idea of permanent and total conspiracy against society that makes anarchism so attractive to a certain type of temperament in the 20th.

The rich and often contradictory variety of ideas in the anarchism of the past continue to be found in the revolutionary movements of the present. Many contemporary revolutionists deny that there is any direct influence; and Daniel Cohn-Bendit has emphasized the extremely eclectic nature of such intellectual forebears as there are: 'Some people have tried to force Marcuse on us as a mentor; that is

[1] *The Times*, 15 November 1968.

a joke. None of us have read Marcuse. Some have read Marx, of course, perhaps Bakunin, and of the moderns Althusser, Mao, Guevara, Lefebvre. Nearly all the militants . . . have read Sartre.'[2] Many of the guardians of traditional anarchist doctrines, as emerges from David Stafford's article and others, have been as anxious to dissociate themselves from contemporary revolutionary developments as the revolutionaries have been to deny links with them, and have shown themselves, as Antonio Gramsci remarked some fifty years ago, 'persuaded that they are the repositories of revealed revolutionary truth'.[3] Yet what emerges strongly from the studies we have collected in this volume is to what a large extent traditional anarchist ideas and attitudes, whether as the result of direct influences or of contemporary circumstances, can be found in the ideas and actions of the extreme left all over the world.

One can look at the anarchist tradition in three different ways – as a doctrine; that is to say, a set of ideas about social organization and about social relations; as a movement, that is to say as a technique of revolution; and as a certain type of temperament, based on a desire to push things to extremes, to carry ideas through to a logical practical end, to overthrow society from top to bottom, a temperament which in many cases enjoys or believes in the act of revolution for its own sake, without worrying about the consequence of the revolution later.

THE AMBIVALENT DOCTRINE

One of the attractions of anarchism has been the extent to which it has offered something for everybody. It has offered, that is to say, the hope of a rational peaceful society of gentle people co-operating with one another, while also offering the excitement of a total revolution with its concomitant violence and terror. The rationalist streak in anarchism is balanced all through the history of anarchism by an anti-rationalist one. The classical anarchist writings contain many rationalist theoretical accounts of what society would be like after the revolution. The most obvious case of rationalism, sometimes carried to an absurd extent, is in the writings of William Godwin.

[2] Hervé Bourges (ed.), *The Student Revolt – The Activists Speak*, English Edition, London, 1968, p. 78.

[3] Antonio Gramsci, 'Discorso agli Anarchici', *L'Ordine Nuovo 1919-1920*, (Opere di Antonio Gramsci, Vol. 9), Turin, 1954, p. 396.

This is a world in which all passions are subordinated to reason, and in which all problems are solved in a rational way. Men are naturally reasonable; it is only institutions which make them behave unreasonably, and with the abolition of the state, the innate human potentialities for justice and rational co-operation will assert themselves. Throughout the 19th century, anarchist thinkers vacillated between the two extremes of violence and reason. Proudhon made a real attempt to face the problem, though, as always in his writing, his inability to carry through a long piece of systematic thinking makes his solutions rather fragmentary and unsatisfactory. But he had a sense of the dark forces in man and of the necessity of a constant struggle if reason and justice are to prevail against them. For all the violence of his own feelings and prejudices – or perhaps because of them – he still kept a belief in rational argument and a reluctance to advocate violence for its own sake.

Kropotkin, writing in the full flood of post-Darwinian thinking about man and society, was very concerned to produce a rational scientific justification of co-operation, as against the view of life as a violent struggle for survival, in which the weak are exterminated by the strong. His interesting and somehow very touching book, *Mutual Aid*, sets out to refute this version of the Darwinian theory and to show that, on the contrary, evolution was the result of co-operation and mutual aid, and that those species and those primitive societies which have survived are those which have the best power of co-operation and are able to work together.

Yet, for many anarchists, the belief in education, co-operation and peaceful persuasion goes hand in hand with a belief in direct action and even with active involvement in schemes for assassination. The Spanish anarchist educationalist Francisco Ferrer, for example, is a man who is generally thought of as a pioneer of modern education, of a new type of school in which pupils would not be coerced or subjected to discipline but would run their own lessons for themselves, organize their own work and so on. Ferrer was arrested after the disturbances in Barcelona in 1909; and it was always thought that his subsequent execution was a monstrous miscarriage of justice and that he was sincere in his repudiation of violence. However, Joaquín Romero Maura has shown in a recent article that Ferrer had been at the centre of a plan to assassinate the king of Spain.[4] He provided the money with which the plan was made possible and

[4] J. Romero Maura, 'Terrorism in Barcelona 1904–1909', *Past and Present*, No. 41, December 1968.

he was one of the coolest and most calculating of people in his belief in the necessity of violence to achieve an immediate and, it was hoped, very sensational political end. He is an example of the curious co-existence in the anarchist tradition of enlightened reason and a belief in violence.

For many contemporary revolutionaries, the violent element in anarchist theory and practice is more important than the rational, utopian one. As Michael Lerner disturbingly shows, the acceptance of violence is characteristic of the 'counter-culture'; and there is no aspect of the revolutionary movement among the young which separates it more clearly from that of the liberal radicals of the previous generation. In philosophical terms, they are obsessed by what Herbert Marcuse calls 'the liberating function of negation'; and this is very easily transferred from the philosophical to the practical plane. This is perhaps why it is Bakunin among the classical anarchist thinkers who has most strongly captured the imagination of the contemporary revolutionaries. This is not however just because his love of practical revolution led him to participate personally in revolutionary outbreaks wherever he could find them, or even because his remarks about violence sometimes seemed to justify it as an emotional experience as well as a method of revolution. Even though recent research by Michael Confino suggests that the famous Revolutionary Catechism of 1869, which Bakunin was long believed to have written in collaboration with Nechayev, was the work of Nechayev alone, and that Bakunin dissociated himself from Nechayev's extreme praise of violence and cruelty, Bakunin's belief in direct action and in the effectiveness of the example of a revolutionary few to spark off the spontaneous revolt of the masses has much in common with the assumptions of the contemporary apostles of direct action. Bakunin summed up his programme to Nechayev as follows: 'Total destruction of the world of the legal state and of all the bourgeois so-called civilization, by means of a popular revolution, directed not by an official dictatorship, but by a collective, imperceptible and anonymous dictatorship of the partisans of the complete liberation of the people from all oppression, firmly united in a secret society and acting everywhere and always with the same goal and according to the same programme.'[5] It is a programme to which many of the groups discussed

[5] Bakunin to Nechayev, 2 January 1870, printed in Michael Confino, 'Bakunin et Necaev', *Cahiers du Monde Russe et Soviétique*, Vol. VII, No. 4, October–December 1966, pp. 629–30.

in this volume would be prepared to subscribe. Many of them, moreover, would go all the way with Nechayev, and, indeed, with Bakunin himself, who saw in the brigand in Russia the true and only revolutionary, just as Dave Harris finds 'no more honourable position in modern America than that of criminal'.[6] But there is another aspect which draws many contemporary revolutionaries to Bakunin; the fact that he insisted again and again that the form of the revolutionary movement itself must foreshadow the form of society after the revolution. In his arguments with Marx he was constantly asserting that if you have an authoritarian revolutionary movement of the kind Marx wanted, then you would have an authoritarian society after the revolution. The circular which Bakunin's supporters produced in the middle of his quarrel with Marx in 1871 said 'How can you expect an egalitarian and a free society to emerge from an authoritarian organization?'[7] And this is one of the points which is reiterated again by contemporary libertarian revolutionaries: 'L'organization révolutionnaire a du apprendre qu'elle ne peut plus combattre l'aliénation sous des formes aliénées.'[8] In his emphasis on the necessity of having the right kind of organization in order to produce the right kind of society after the revolution, Bakunin insisted that the movement must not rely on permanent leaders. At certain moments a militant elite, prepared to go the whole way in making the revolution, would be needed, but they must never be regarded as occupying permanent positions, and therefore developing into autocrats or people consumed with the desire for power. This belief that there should be no permanent and identifiable leadership has its practical aspect, of course, in that it makes identification and thus arrest and punishment harder, but it also represents a genuine ideal of co-operation which was of particular importance in the organization, or lack of it, in the Spanish anarchist movement.

THE FUTURE WHICH HAS BEGUN

Much of the utopian element in the contemporary revolutionary movement is to be found in its concept of what the movement itself

[6] See p. 47 above.

[7] The *Sonvillier Circular*, November 1871, quoted in J. Joll, *The Anarchists*, Paperback ed., London 1969, p. 105.

[8] *Adresse à tous les Travailleurs*, 30 May 1968, published by 'Comité Enragés – Internationale Situationniste'.

is. The feeling of liberation and excitement which participation in the revolts in Paris produced is documented in every report one reads and in every conversation with participants. For these young people, the revolutionary movement is not only the pattern of future society which Bakunin believed that it should be: it *is* future society. Their Utopia is realized here and now in the process of revolution itself. A typical example of this way of thinking is a remark of a Columbia student, printed in the Cox Commission's report: 'Always meetings and more meetings lasting long into the night. Participatory democracy. There was a real community spirit; everything belonged to everybody; the building was "liberated". Girls . . . were not expected to do the kitchen work alone for this was a "liberated" area, and boys had to help. Couples slept together in public view, nobody cared, we were "liberated": here was a single commune in which adult hypocrisies did not apply any longer, where people shared and shared alike, where democracy decided everything, where people were free of adult values and codes.'[9] As Richard Gombin points out, this aspect of the revolution has become of extreme importance in contemporary movements of revolt. In a sense very different from that intended by Eduard Bernstein in a famous phrase 'The goal is nothing, the movement is all'.

In addition to Bakunin's insistence on the relation between the revolutionary movement and post-revolutionary society, many contemporary revolutionaries share his belief that the revolution will be made possible by the action of a militant elite of people totally dedicated to the revolutionary cause. In adopting this attitude the revolutionary becomes an outlaw in practice as well as an outlaw emotionally. He identifies himself with the bandits, the robbers and the people who attacked bourgeois society directly by stealing or destroying other people's property.

For Bakunin, as perhaps for Che Guevara, the people who were going to make a revolution were the people with nothing to lose – the hopeless and helpless, the totally dispirited – the proletariat of the cities, as in Barcelona from 1902, with no hope of redress through orthodox trade union activities, the landless rural workers constantly threatened with famine and at the mercy of unscrupulous and often absent and remote landlords.

In the 1870s when Bakunin's ideas were receiving considerable

[9] *Crisis at Columbia:* Report of the Fact-Finding Commission, New York, 1969, p. 138.

currency, the anarchists linked them with another doctrine that has been revived by the contemporary revolutionaries, the doctrine of propaganda by the deed. In a bourgeois society the only way to get anybody to make a revolution is by showing them the way, by taking some extreme action which would show that revolution was possible, and which would encourage other people to follow the example. A famous example is that of Errico Malatesta in 1876, when he thought that he could start the revolution in Italy by getting the peasants in a very small area to revolt. He and two or three friends went into the mountains of the south of Italy, arrived at a small town or large village, proclaimed the revolution to the bewildered peasants, then led them to the Town Hall to destroy the files -- a great ritual gesture of anarchists -- the records of contracts, the records of property ownership, of births and marriages. They did this successfully in one village and then went on to the next, where the peasants were less enthusiastic. Then it started to rain, and the little band was quickly rounded up by the police. This belief that you can set off the revolution in a small area, that this would then have the effect of starting a conflagration and would consume the whole of society is something that has always a great appeal, because it appears to justify revolution in a situation where all the forces appear to be massed against you and where the odds appear not to be on your side at all. In discussing the events in Paris in 1968 several writers maintained that the students' role was that of a detonator. Once one section of society, even on a comparatively small scale, is in open revolt against the whole structure of the existing order, then the other oppressed classes, and the other members of similar groups in other parts of the country would follow the example.

The other aspect of propaganda by the deed was the most sensational form of anarchist activity, namely direct individual terrorism. It is the chapter of anarchism which has become most notorious, and also the anarchist technique which has been most widely imitated. Between 1880 and 1914 a whole series of anarchist outrages were directed against the symbols of power and corruption in existing society. Kings, prime ministers and members of imperial families were assassinated; bottles of vitriol were thrown into the Stock Exchange, a bomb dropped over the balcony of the chamber of deputies in Paris. Bombs were thrown into fashionable theatres and restaurants as a protest against bourgeois society. And in one famous case in Paris in the 1890s, a man threw a bomb into a very ordinary cafe where workers as well as members of the bourgeoisie were drinking, on the assumption that nobody is exempt from guilt and that in attacking society anywhere you are bound to hit some guilty men. This is certainly an argument used by some radicals today. Any section of existing society contains guilty people who are responsible for the whole, and therefore you may as well start your revolution right away and throw your bombs at whatever is the most immediate target that presents itself. The nuisance value of these tactics or of similar ones has been fully utilized by subsequent extremist movements both of the right and the left – the Young Bosnians who assassinated the Archduke Francis Ferdinand in 1914, the suffragettes in Britain before the first war, Arab terrorists, Jewish terrorists, French right-wing groups at the time of the Algerian war, were all inspired by the anarchist example.

The advantage of propaganda by the deed is that it can create a great stir. There is no doubt, for instance, that in the 1890s these terrorist activities worried the authorities and the police of Europe very much indeed. The police archives of this period in France and Spain give a very exaggerated picture of the strength of the anarchist movement, and give the false impression that there really was an enormously well-organized widespread mass movement which was almost certain to triumph unless massive measures were taken to repress it. In fact however, beyond winning notoriety, the anarchists did not achieve very much by these isolated actions, and consequently had to evolve another method of action that would be more effective than these terrorist gestures. It was this which led to the anarchist link with the syndicalist movement.

REVOLUTIONARY MYTHS

Proudhon had believed that the only effective way to get rid of the state and the whole range of abuses which the state machinery carried with it was through direct control of the means of production by the producers themselves, and through the establishment of a direct relationship between producers and consumers. This meant abolishing the whole structure of credit, finance and middlemen so as to get back to a very simple and very primitive economic state where the producers of one commodity would exchange their products directly with producers of another commodity, and where the people who had some services to offer would offer their skill in exchange for something produced by someone else. Above all this must be done in as direct a way as possible. This gave rise to a piece of anarchist romanticism which survives down to our own day: the belief that if only money were abolished then society would be purer and better and more efficient. And it is very revealing in this connection to see how Castro, at certain moments in his more utopian speculations, talks about the day when money will be completely abolished and when everybody will get what they need without the necessity of any medium of exchange.

Proudhon believed that workers must control their own means of production; the workers must control the workshop, the peasants must control the fields and all these producing communities must be decentralized politically as far as possible, independently of any central authority. In India these ideas have combined with traditional religious beliefs to produce a significant social movement. In Europe, Proudhon's doctrines have never been lost in the French working-class movement; and by the end of the 19th century the idea of workers' control in the factories was linked with the idea that it was only by direct control over production that a revolution could be made. Political changes of government meant nothing, it was alleged: politicians had all already sold out to the system. The way to make a revolution was to ignore elections and parliament and to concentrate on gaining workers' control in the factories and building up decentralized economic units on this basis. As for the method to be adopted, the correct procedure, it was argued by the militant syndicalists, was to use strikes, not as was advocated by the orthodox trade unionists and by the socialists to obtain piecemeal improvements, more wages, shorter hours and so on, but rather to immobilize the means of production preparatory to taking them over at the great moment of the general strike, when everything would come to a standstill and the workers be left in control.

The idea of workers' control has, of course, never wholly vanished from the international working-class movement. And, as is only to be expected, it figures largely in the ideals of the New Left. 'I am not a theoretician', Alain Geismar has said. 'For me, socialism can be defined negatively with respect to existing structures by a rejection of all bureaucracy, of all centralized direction, by granting power to the producers at their point of production.'[10] Indeed, one of the

[10] H. Bourges (ed.), *The Student Revolt: The Activists Speak*, p. 60.

great apparent successes of the French revolt of 1968 was not only the links – tenuous and precarious as it turned out, but more extensive than anywhere else – established between the students and the workers, but also the launching of the idea of 'participation', whatever that may mean, and of seeing it accepted in theory even by General de Gaulle himself. The older supporters of anarchist or near-anarchist ideas, such as Daniel Guérin, point eagerly to the experiments in workers' control in revolutionary states, at what is promised in Cuba and at what is being achieved in Yugoslavia. (It is, indeed, in the latter country that the most interesting experiments in this direction are being made, and we need to know a great deal more, especially in connection with our own discussions in Britain and Trades Union legislation, of how the Yugoslav Economic Reform of 1965 is working out in practice.) One can suggest, however, that even where a system of workers' control has been successful in overcoming a feeling of 'alienation' by giving workers a sense of participation in the running of their enterprise, there are still a number of unsolved problems: there are still strikes; and these have been resolved by the intervention of either the state or the party authorities and not within the factories themselves. There are still problems about determining the overall priorities in economic planning involving a large number of different industries, the need for investment from outside the concern and many others. Yugoslav communists have always accepted the orthodox doctrine of the withering away of the state – though the unfortunate Mr Djilas was sent to prison for asserting prematurely that something should now be done to put it into effect – but there is something paradoxical in the spectacle of a one-party revolutionary communist state that is trying to put into practice one of the basic anarchist doctrines.

In trying to assess which elements in the anarchist tradition are to be found in contemporary revolutionary movements, one is constantly struck by the fact that the thinker whose ideas come closest to those of the New Left is not strictly anarchist. This is, of course, Georges Sorel. His ideas have been so widely discussed and commented on in the last few years that there is no need to say much about them. However, his belief in violence, not only as a means, but as a valuable experience in itself, the role he allots to the professional revolutionary militants and the importance he attaches to direct workers' control are all commonplaces of the revolutionary movement today. But there are two other important aspects of Sorel's thought which go some way, alas, to justifying Daniel

Halévy's claim, made already nearly thirty years ago: 'Those who listened to him . . . owe it to him that they have not been surprised at the changes in the world.'[11] The first of these points is Sorel's anti-intellectualism. He insisted, as the leaders of the First International had done, that the revolution must be the work of the workers themselves, but combined this with a strong anti-intellectual streak. Sorel himself was characteristic of that type of revolutionary – and they are common today – who comes from the middle of the classes which they are actively concerned to attack. He was a member of the French bourgeoisie; he was a skilled professional engineer; and he was an intellectual, who used to take the tram into Paris from his suburban home to listen to Bergson's lectures once a week. His attack on intellectuals reads very similarly to the attacks on liberal hypocrisy and double-talk in such classics of contemporary revolutionary literature as the work of the late Franz Fanon, who indeed has recently been described by Professor E. Shils, in an article in *Encounter*, as 'only an eloquent Sorel'. Sorel maintained that it was the intellectuals who were corrupting society by suggesting that there were easy answers to social problems, whereas the truth was, Sorel believed, that political programmes rarely had any relevance to the problems which they attempted to solve. It was, on the contrary, just because there were no easy solutions and no piecemeal answers that revolution must be an act of all or nothing. And it was for the same reason that revolution must be the result of a passionate act of faith, of belief in the 'myth' which was to enable society to be changed at one blow. For Sorel, the most important myth was that of the general strike; and there are moments when he writes as if you might never actually need to have one, that bourgeois society would be so demoralized by the belief that the general strike was coming one day that it would fall to pieces of its own accord. The importance of Sorel's doctrine of the 'myth' is that it provides one explanation why people attempt revolutionary outbreaks at moments when they seem to have little chance of success. If you believe in something hard enough, if you create the impression that there is going to be a revolution, if you spread the conviction that society is rotten to the core and is about to collapse, then you are already taking a big step forward towards the collapse of society. Belief in the possibility of the impossible can sometimes be as important as action itself.

---

[11] D. Halévy, *Péguy et les Cahiers de la Quinzaine*, Paris, 1941, p. 108.

PERENNIAL ATTITUDES

So far I have been stressing what the New Left of today has in common with anarchist doctrines of the past; but there are obvious and important differences, if not in doctrine, at least in circumstance. Bakunin always maintained that revolutions are made by those with nothing to lose; and the success of anarchism in parts of Spain and Italy where it was a creed especially attractive to impoverished landless agricultural labourers may be said to bear this out. Anarchist ideas have also attracted support where there is a tradition of small enterprises and skilled workers – in parts of France or among the watch-makers of the Swiss Jura – or where a strong tradition of federalism and regional independence is accompanied by economic depression and by governmental repression, as in Catalonia.

Today, although some of the French revolutionaries of 1968 claimed that 'this is the first time that there has been a revolutionary struggle on this scale in an economically advanced country', much contemporary revolutionary activity exists in a kind of vacuum. In Europe, the revolution has so far been the work of students, and largely middle class ones at that; and even when their aims have been political – as in the case of some of the French groups or the *Ausserparlamentarische Opposition* in Germany – they have attracted little support from any other class than the *Freischwebende Intelligenz*. Their ideas of decentralization, workers' control, the abolition of money, all presuppose a society that is uncomplicated in structure, and comparatively easy to transform into the kind of basic federated communal system which the anarchists envisage. They are clearly not entirely appropriate to a highly centralized industrial society, even if they perhaps suggest ways of humanizing it and making it more tolerable.

The idea of workers' control and decentralization has played a big part in the history and in the mythology of the Left. The totally ineffective workers and soldiers councils in the German revolution in 1918–19 have become objects of a cult for the German student revolutionists today, who ignore the reasons for their failure and do not see that the Soviets were successful in 1917 in Russia because the framework of the state had collapsed, which it had not done in Germany in 1918, still less in Western Europe today. In France, and now of course in the student movement everywhere, the reaction against centralized bureaucracy has suggested its own revolutionary techniques, which are linked to the myth of workers' councils. It is because the trade unions themselves are suspected of being heartless bureaucratic organizations that workers have acted on their own, by spontaneous occupation of factories – as in the famous weeks in France in the summer of 1936 where the technique of the sit-in was first practised on a large scale in department stores and offices as well as in workshops, to the dismay, as in 1968, of the Communist Party as well as of the employers.

Are we to conclude, then, that the anarchist elements in contemporary revolutionary thought are as is often maintained, a spontaneous and inevitable reaction against bureaucracy, against the boredom of mass industrial production, against the hypocrisy and vulgarity of the mass media? Are the supporters of the New Left what Professor Scheuch has called 'The Anabaptists of the Affluent Society'?[12] This is certainly one reason for the attraction of anarchist ideas in the contemporary western world. But the reason why anarchism is still a living tradition lies not just in how far its doctrines are applicable or inapplicable to advanced industrial society, but rather in the fact that they offer something for everybody. If you are a peaceful person who wants a vegetarian life in a garden city, then anarchism has something to offer. If you are a man of violent temperament who thinks that only by direct action and by the purgative quality of violence itself will you be able to cleanse yourself and society of guilt and make an effective revolution, then there is a long line of anarchist thought and action to support your view.

What these strands of the anarchist tradition have in common is their belief in the possibility of total and instant transformation of society, their faith that anything can be achieved, even if it seems impossible. (This leads often to a denial of the value of history and historical evidence; it is interesting to see how often contemporary anarchists suggest that the Catalan anarchist movement has been a wholly successful one.) Every situation is a revolutionary situation, whatever the odds against success. There is however another sense in which the anarchist tradition comes close to that of a religious movement. This is in the sense in which the militant, whether violent or pacific, is thought of as a man with a mission. Gandhi, for example, describing the way in which he foresaw the transformation of Indian society, wrote 'For the creation of the ideal village,

---

[12] Erwin K. Scheuch (ed.), *Die Wiedertäufer der Wohlstandsgesellschaft*, Cologne, 1968.

no speech-making is necessary, nor is there any need of legislative councils or legislation. One thing only is essential, and that is a small number of selfless working-men and women. They can by their example and spirit of service get the requisite improvements made.'

I have been suggesting that, if there is a living anarchist tradition, it should be sought in psychological and temperamental attitudes to society as much as in a sociological analysis of the societies in which anarchism has flourished. This also accounts for the somewhat incoherent nature of anarchist philosophy and indeed the difficulty anyone who talks about anarchism has in defining just what it is he is talking about. Even Proudhon, perhaps the greatest anarchist thinker, is contradictory and unsystematic in his thinking, and Marx's criticism of the poverty of his philosophy has considerable justification. Nor has the present revival of interest in anarchism produced much in the way of serious political theory: the ideas, such as they are, of the New Left largely come from non-anarchist sources. It is significant that the most striking of the contemporary examples of anarchism in action described in this volume have come from rich and prosperous societies with a high degree of industrialization. Moreover, Joaquin Romero Maura has made the point that anarchism in Spain was more effective under a regime in which the forms at least of constitutional liberalism existed, than under the present authoritarian system. Anarchism owes more to conventional liberalism than some of its exponents are willing to admit. Contemporary anarchism is a product of the permissive society; and it is just because liberalism has lost its effective political content that the critics of existing social arrangements have felt obliged, in order to give their personal protests a social meaning, to use the opportunities provided by the permissive society in order to attack its fundamental values and the presuppositions on which its structure is based. Whether, in the long historical run, this is going to be a significant social movement, it is too soon to say. But, certainly in the United States, and perhaps in France, it has already provided a severe shock to existing society. At least, as the essays in this volume clearly show, the international experience of the past few years has proved that, in one form or another, anarchism is, in the second half of the 20th century, still very much a living tradition.

Contributors

David E. Apter *is Professor of Political Science in Yale University, New Haven, Conn.*

Richard Gombin *is Attaché de Recherches au Centre National de la Recherche Scientifique, Paris*

Michael Lerner *is Research Assistant at Yale University, New Haven, Conn.*

J. Romero Maura *is Research Fellow at Nuffield College, Oxford*

David Stafford *is Assistant Professor of History in the University of Victoria, British Columbia*

Chushichi Tsuzuki *is Professor of Social Thought in Hitotsubashi University, Tokyo*

Nicolas Walter *is a member of the Editorial Staff of the Times Literary Supplement*

Geoffrey Ostergaard *is Senior Lecturer in Political Science in the University of Birmingham*

Rudolf de Jong *is a member of the staff of the International Institute of the Institute of Social History, Amsterdam*

Eduardo Colombo *was formerly Professor of Social Psychology in the National University, Buenos Aires*

James Joll *is Stevenson Professor of International History in the London School of Economics and Political Science*

Index

INDEX